P9-DND-993

A Handbook of
Chakra
Healing

Spiritual Practice for Health,

Harmony, and Inner Peace

K A L A S H A T R A   G O V I N D A

KONECKY&KONECKY

Contents

1 The Meaning of Chakra Work

Although knowledge about the chakras has its origin in ancient India, similar teachings are found in many different cultures.

The teaching concerning the chakras, centers of energy and awareness within each person, is thousands of years old. It originated with the *rishis*, holy men and seers of ancient India. They were deeply interested in the hidden energies residing in human beings. With extraordinary sensitivity, they directed their attention to the hidden power within, and through the practice of meditation they moved beyond the world of outward appearances. Through their efforts, a comprehensive body of knowledge concerning the chakras developed over the course of generations.

Holistic Healing

Until recently, even the word *chakra* was practically unknown in Western culture. Today, however, there has been an upsurge of interest. Many people have a nodding familiarity with the concept, and some have explored the subject more thoroughly. The awareness and work with chakras has come to play a role not only in yoga but in aromatherapy, healing practices that employ gemstones, psychotherapy, and a wide range of alternative healing methods.

The awakening interest in the study of chakras can best be explained by its practical application to many of the problems that currently confront us. Working with chakras quickly leads to positive change. Anyone can feel its beneficial effects on mind and body. At the same time, the growing interest in holistic healing methods has highlighted the importance of the chakras in furthering physical and psychic healing. We have come to recognize that healing should provide more than symptomatic relief; the more subtle and encompassing the method, the more effective it will be.

Applied to psychological disorders, the teaching regarding the chakras goes beyond the mental causes of problems to their very root. You can start on this simple practice right away, no matter what your age, sex, or religious belief. The only requirements are time to establish a regular practice, a place where you can work without interruption, an openness to new ideas, and a willingness to experiment. Through this practice, you will make your life better. Every improvement in the state of your inner energy system will have far-reaching beneficial effects on your health and well-being. Here is a way you can feel better with each passing day.

How to Use This Book

The heart of this book consists of practical techniques. You will learn the underlying principles of chakra work and how they can be applied within the context of contemporary culture. We will then provide detailed information concerning the chakras and the subtle energies at work within your body. Theoretical knowledge will help you understand chakra work and how to apply it to your own life:

- The underlying principles of chakra work provide an entryway to actual practice.
- Classification of colors, smells, planets, mantras, and symbolic animals will lead to a deepening understanding of the chakras.
- Numerous exercises will demonstrate which of your chakras are highly activated and which need special attention.
- You will learn the essential features of a chakra-based psychological approach: how it provides a deeper self-understanding and solutions to particular psychological problems.
- The program of harmonizing the chakras will help you balance the flow of inner energy through gentle healing practices and improve your health and sense of well-being.
- You will discover the nature of the subtle energies to which chakra work directs itself and learn about such concepts as the astral body, the aura, prana, and kundalini through direct experience.
- To begin with, a program of chakra yoga will be presented through which you can activate your chakras.
- You will learn to stimulate the chakras of your hands and feet. You will learn to activate your sexual energy and develop the erotic aspects of your being together with your partner.

All of the practices presented in this book are gentle, flowing and harmonious, so that you can awaken and connect with the hidden energy in your body without strain or stress.

All of the prescribed methods are gentle and safe. Spiritual practice has the effect of stimulating one's energy, and this leads to harmony within the body. The activation of the chakras is a simple and effective method of healing body, mind, and spirit.

All you have to do is take the first step.

2 Learning About the Chakras

Chakra work is one of the subtlest methods of healing. The chakras are important energy centers in the body that can be activated and harmonized using certain techniques. This will lead to marked improvements in physical and mental health, psychological stability, and inner peace.

In this book, you will find many ways to connect with your chakras and their subtle energy. You can pick one particular method or try several at once—whatever brings the best results. You can use the methods and programs described here as a guide to your own personal practice. Always follow your intuition in chakra practice and listen carefully to your inner voice.

The Basis of the Teachings on the Chakras

The knowledge and teachings on the chakras come from yoga—the oldest system addressing the development of the whole person. Yoga is a philosophical system and meditative practice directed toward the mastery of one's body and mind. It is at least five thousand years old.

The goal of yoga is liberation from suffering and union with one's divine self. Many yogis (masculine) and yoginis (feminine) who have devoted themselves to this practice for many years develop extraordinary power. But the ultimate significance of the physical and spiritual practice of yoga lies in the recognition of one's higher self.

Although we have the yoga tradition to thank for transmitting the teachings on the chakras, the phenomenon of the chakras has been recognized in many other cultures as well. The first reference to chakras is found in the Vedas, the most ancient religious texts of India, which date from around 1500 B.C.E. In the Upanishads, which comprise the esoteric parts of the Vedas, specific mention is made of techniques for activating the chakras. This can be found in the *Shandilya Upanishad* and the *Cudamini Upanishad*.

Down through the ages people have gathered information and experiences about the healing nature of chakra work.

The Chakras: An Overview

Through deep meditation yogis and illuminated beings have acquired knowledge about centers of subtle energy.

Chakras are centers of awareness in the human body. These energy centers are neither physical nor anatomical. They are found in the subtle energy system, although their radiant energy does correspond to positions within the body.

The chakras influence cells, organs, and the entire hormone system and affect one's thoughts and feelings. They are also centers of psychic energy.

The term *chakra* comes from Sanskrit, the sacred language of ancient India. It literally means "wheel" or "turning." In fact, the chakras revolve continuously. Through their rotation, they absorb energies from without and convert them into the subtle material of the astral body—about which we will speak later. Through the chakras, we take in energy from our surroundings.

The seven principle chakras form an axis of radiating energy that extends from the coccyx to the top of the head.

How Seers Have Envisioned the Chakras

Yogis have described chakras as funnel-shaped, much like a calyx. From that perception, chakras came to be pictured in ancient India as lotus blossoms. But not all sensitive people see the chakras as open flowers; some have described them as miniature suns whose light radiates through the body.

Both descriptions point to important functions of the chakras. The chakras take energy from the environment, from the natural world of plants, animals, and other people, as well as from the sun, moon, and planets and the entire cosmos. As such, they can be likened to funnel-shaped flowers. At the same time, the chakras allow cosmic energy (*prana* in Sanskrit) to radiate from within the person and so act as miniature suns.

Each chakra forms a focal point for thousands of rays of subtle energy (*nadis* in Sanskrit), which are then directed outward. Thus the chakras serve as a kind of way station in which energy is collected, transmitted, and made available for the ongoing processes of an individual's physical, mental, and spiritual life. One can thereby make a positive impression in the world and influence one's surroundings for the better. The chakras also promote harmony between one's inner and outer worlds.

The Primary and Secondary Chakras in the Body

Eastern philosophy considers seven to be a sacred number; it is not surprising that one speaks of seven chakras.

In traditional writings, we read that there are up to 88,000 chakras. For the purposes of this book, we will concern ourselves with the seven principal chakras. Some schools speak of five, some count nine, and other numbers have been mentioned, but seven is the count most widely accepted, and that conforms with the traditional teaching on the subject. These seven chakras are aligned on the spinal column.

One exception concerns the secondary chakras residing in the hands and feet; these are discussed in chapter 9. The thousands of minor chakras that are found throughout the body have in themselves no great influence on the body, and through the activation of the primary chakras, their functioning is automatically enhanced.

According to the esoteric tradition, chakras are associated with particular colors, symbols, mantras, elements, and deities, which correspond to their vibratory frequencies (see tables on pages 298ff.).

The vibratory frequency of each chakra is expressed by the number of petals in the flower that acts as its symbol. The lowest chakra (the root chakra) has only four petals; the highest (the crown chakra) has one thousand. These petals represent different levels of human awareness, and chakra work is directed toward its development.

By connecting with the centers of awareness and opening ourselves to positive energy, we can treat ourselves and the world around us in a loving fashion.

In chapter 3, you will find an introductory discussion of each chakra. Working with the related colors, mantras, flowers and other symbols, elements, and so on helps to awaken the unconscious to an intuitive grasp of their hidden meaning.

What Is Chakra Work?

Chakra work is the term used to describe the gamut of techniques that are directed toward the chakras and the circulation of their energies. Classical chakra yoga practices belong under this heading as well as approaches using sound, color, aromatherapy, and naturopathic practices that seek to harmonize the energies of the chakras and promote well-being.

Chakra work serves to activate the body's seven primary chakras. A number of practices and techniques are of central importance. Despite the use of the word *work*, the recommended techniques are not taxing: None of the practices explained in this book requires advance preparation. They are gentle and safe.

Chakra work has a spiritual dimension as well. One needs to set time aside on a regular basis, and it calls for a collected and concentrated attitude.

You should embark on the practice with a sense of calm and inner quiet. You will obtain the best effects for body, mind, and spirit when you engage in the practice in a meditative state. This is not a product of willpower or intentional effort. It requires the right mixture of wakefulness and relaxation.

The lotus blossom symbolizes the passage from darkness into light and is a fitting symbol for the chakras.

Chakra Work and Other Methods

Many individuals who practice traditional forms of yoga find it difficult to get comfortable with other esoteric approaches and connect them with work on the chakras. Experience shows, however, that these different approaches work quite well together. Ancient cultures recognized the healing power of precious stones, colors, and scents. They all form parts of traditional healing practices. Only their use in combination with chakra work is new.

You can activate your chakras through breathing techniques and asanas (yoga positions) as well as with the help of aromatherapy and precious stones. The most important thing is to take a concentrated and sensitive approach to chakra work.

It is up to you to choose how to activate the chakra energy. Many people use visualization practices. Others subscribe to chakra yoga practices and put little faith in the use of scents or precious stones. Look for the methods described here that correspond best to your inner nature and that you feel most comfortable with. This book presents a number of different alternatives. The more approaches you have to contact your chakras, the better the results will be.

Chakra work is multifaceted. This book will acquaint you with practices drawn from aromatherapy, vocalization, chakra massage, and the use of gemstones and Bach flower remedies as well as the teachings of chakra yoga.

The Beneficial Effects of Chakra Work

Chakra work is an energy therapy that improves the condition of your energy system. Through simple exercises, you can raise your level of energy and strengthen your powers of intuition. You will learn to recognize sickness and problems that arise from energy blockages and find ways to dissolve these blockages. Activation of the chakras is a simple and effective method for healing body, mind, and spirit.

Through chakra work one learns how to approach one's body more lovingly and how to free oneself from unhealthy habits such as smoking and the abuse of alcohol.

Beneficial Effects for the Body

Work on the chakras will improve your physical health. Its positive effects include stimulation of the metabolism, detoxification, and strengthening of the immune system by infusing cells and organs with healing energy. By working with the energy of the chakras, you can expect to do the following:

Peace, contentment, and a sense of physical well-being result from chakra work.

- Strengthen the body's defenses
- Harmonize the cardiovascular system
- Detoxify and improve the functioning of internal organs
- Heal circulatory problems
- Correct orthopedic problems
- Strengthen the metabolism
- Increase retention of oxygen
- Retard the aging process

Beneficial Effects for the Mind

Chakras are not just energy centers; they are centers of awareness as well. Over time, chakra work can help resolve psychological afflictions such as anxiety, stress, and depression. You can look forward to experiencing serenity, happiness, and inner peace within a short period:

- Anxieties diminish.
- Mood swings become less intense.
- Mental fatigue and depression disappear.
- Relaxation and inner peace are experienced.
- Sleep becomes deep and restful.
- Addictions are more easily overcome.

Chakra work can expand one's awareness and correct character defects.

Beneficial Effects on Spiritual Life

Chakra work leads to spiritual harmony as well. With steady practice negative attitudes toward life are replaced by positive thinking. That brings marked changes in behavior and can be seen in the following:

- Improved powers of concentration
- Sharper memory
- Elimination of the grounds for negative thinking
- Disappearance of boasting and self-pity
- Clarity of mind and spirit
- Recognition of one's true purpose in life
- Seeing what is really important

Chakra Work Leads to Greater Energy

There are rewards to chakra work that go beyond general considerations of health. The seven chakras symbolize different stages of human development. By involving yourself in these different levels of being, you can actualize your full potential, the totality of possibilities open to you. The practices that you will learn in this book can serve to open the doors to many dimensions. You will discover how you can recharge yourself with new energy and feel more vital and refreshed with each passing day. You will be able to transform your aura, which will lead to easier and more productive communication with others. Your relationships with loved ones, friends, and your surroundings will all change for the better.

Not least important, work with the chakras will promote spiritual development. Inner growth is a natural result of the unfolding of the chakras. And conversely, the conscious focus on the subtle levels of the body's energy centers creates conditions that will accelerate one's spiritual development.

The chakras reveal our true potential, the possibilities that we can realize, and the way to self-development.

Open yourself to new dimensions by working on your chakras.

Awakening the Chakras

At each level of awareness corresponding to one of the seven chakras, you trigger a learning process through the spiritual practice of chakra work that will lead to greater intensity and awareness:

- Through the unfolding of the first chakra, you will learn to say yes to life and discover the source of life energy.
- When you awaken the second chakra, you will be able to affirm your sexuality and sensual nature and feel at home in your own body.
- Developing the third chakra allows you to say yes to yourself and find the inner strength to reach your goals.
- By activating the fourth chakra, you will come to say yes to love and develop compassion.
- With the unfolding of the fifth chakra, you will say yes to your creative potential and perfect your communication with others.
- Developing the sixth chakra brings contact with your higher self and sparks the power of intuition.
- Through the unfolding of the seventh chakra, you begin to approach the Divine and realize the true source of all being.

Today, health practitioners and therapists often make use of the teachings on chakras to loosen blockages and bring buried problems to light.

As already mentioned, chakra work is a holistic method. When with the help of this work you begin to activate and open these energy centers, you will experience positive changes in all aspects of your life. By awakening and strengthening your chakras, you will enhance your physical well-being and raise your spiritual awareness.

Chakra work leads to improved relationships with your partner, friends, colleagues, and the other people around you. It will help you to dissolve sexual and emotional blocks that lead to anxiety and depression.

Finally, you will gain a better understanding of the work you were meant to do and the goals you ought to pursue. You will realize the sense of assuredness that derives from intuitively knowing what direction you want to take in life.

3 The Seven Chakras and Their Meanings

The following overview provides descriptions of the seven chakras and the most important symbols associated with them. It also discusses the planets, sounds, senses, and elements in nature that correspond to each chakra and the particular areas of the body and aspects of the mind that they govern. These themes will be discussed more thoroughly in later chapters. At the end of the book you will find tables that summarize this information.

The Root Chakra (Muladhara Chakra)

- **Central theme:** stability, the will to live, self-preservation, sense of trust and security, groundedness
- **Number of petals:** four
- **Color:** red
- **Mantra:** LAM
- **Element:** earth
- **Basic symbol:** square
- **Planet:** Mercury
- **Sensory function:** smell

Description, Arrangement, and Symbolism

The root chakra is the lowest chakra and as such is the foundation of all of the other chakras. Its Sanskrit name is *muladhara*: *mula* meaning "root" and *adhara* meaning "support." This chakra is also referred to as the base center, the tail chakra, the root center, or the first chakra. Ancient Hindu depictions portray the root chakra as a four-petaled flower. The four petals correspond to four Sanskrit syllables: *vam, am, sham,* and *sam.* The primary mantra that is used to activate this chakra is LAM (pronounced LANG). The root chakra is associated with the Hindu deities Brahma and Dakini. The red color of the root chakra represents life energy, passion, and strength, which this chakra is responsible for. In addition to the four-petaled flower, the square is used to symbolize this chakra. In many representations of the root chakra, one sees symbolic animals such as elephants, bulls, or oxen—all of which remind us of the stability and strength related to this energy center. The root chakra is also associated with the element lead, the vowel sound *u,* and the planet Mercury. The energy of the muladhara chakra is also related to the times of sunrise and sunset, red earth, and fire. The chakra is most fully activated during the phase of the full moon.

Work on the root chakra stimulates and strengthens all of the chakras.

Position and Influences on the Body

The root chakra is the lowest chakra. It lies in the region of the coccyx.

The root chakra lies in the area of the coccyx between the anus and the perineum. It corresponds to the base of the spinal column. It supplies the pelvic regions (pelvic girdle) and the large and small intestines with energy. It also governs the skeleton, which gives us stability, and the legs and feet, which bind us to the earth.

The teeth and nails, blood formation, the digestion, and the sciatic nerve are all influenced by the root chakra. There is also a close connection between this chakra and the functioning of the adrenal and suprarenal glands.

Central Theme

It is through the root chakra that our energy is connected to that of the earth. Through no other chakra do we draw as much energy from the earth as through the root chakra. For this reason, the root chakra is considered the source of our life energy. Kundalini energy, the power of creativity, resides in the root chakra. When the kundalini is awakened, it animates all of the other chakras in turn. More will be said about this later.

The strength for living and the feeling of trust and security are the central themes of the root chakra. It represents the will to live and the sense of self-preservation. When energy flows freely through this chakra, it is easy to be secure in your existence in the world. You are steady on your feet and not easily thrown by circumstances around you.

With a strong foundation, you feel secure and protected. A sense of rootedness is the best starting point for a successful life. It is not surprising that Ganesha, a Hindu deity in the form of an elephant, is a symbol for the root chakra. Ganesha is the god of prosperity, abundance, and satisfaction.

A powerful will to live, inner strength, passion, and a sense of trust and security are signs of a well-developed root chakra.

People with strongly developed muladhara chakras have enormous amounts of energy at their disposal and an especially strong will to live. They are known for their stamina and ability to see things through to the end.

Blockages in the first chakra account for ruptures in one's harmonious relationship with Mother Earth. A lack of this chakra's energy is evidenced by lassitude, apathy, and lack of trust in life. In such cases the muladhara energy needs to be aroused and cultivated through the recommended exercises. In time they will lead to stability, confidence, and serenity.

Alternative Methods of Harmonizing the Root Chakra

There are a number of different approaches from the field of alternative medicine that one can take to activate the energies of the root chakra:

- Gemstones: ruby, hematite, garnet
- Aromatic oils: cloves, rosemary, cypress, cedar
- Bach flowers: Clematis, Rock Rose, Sweet Chestnut
- Spice: ginger, sweet flag
- Medicinal plants: valerian, lime blossom, elder blossom

The Sacral Chakra (Svadhisthana Chakra)

- **Central theme:** sexuality, sensuality, fertility, creative life energy
- **Number of petals:** six
- **Color:** orange
- **Mantra:** VAM
- **Element:** water
- **Basic symbol:** crescent moon
- **Planet:** Venus
- **Sensory function:** taste

Description, Arrangement, and Symbolism

A natural, uninhibited sexuality and a caring acceptance of one's own body come from a strong sacral chakra.

The sacral chakra is the center of sensuality and sexuality. The Sanskrit word *svadhisthana* means "sweetness" or "loveliness." It can also be translated as "one's home base."

The sacral chakra is also called the sexual chakra or simply the second chakra.

Most depictions of the sacral chakra show a flower with six petals. Six Sanskrit syllables correspond to the petals: *bam, bham, mam, yam, ram,* and *lam.* The principal mantra used in chakra yoga to activate its energies is VAM (pronounced VANG).

The Hindu religion associates the second chakra with the deities Vishnu and Rakini. Its symbolic animals include different kinds of fish, marine creatures, and the crocodile. All of them are closely related to water, which is the symbolic element of the second chakra. The liveliness of free-flowing water as well as its purifying and transforming powers point to important aspects of the energies of the sacral chakra.

The crescent moon—the symbol, along with the water element, most closely associated with this chakra—expresses its close association with the feminine aspect. Through the activation of this chakra, we can come into contact with the feminine side of our nature and be more open to the wisdom that resides in the unconscious mind.

The metal iron is associated with this chakra, and its corresponding planet is Venus. The vowel sound that best activates it is *o*. The power of the sacral chakra can be seen in nature in flowing water and the gentle light of the moon. The chakra becomes most active during the waxing phase of the moon.

The sacral chakra is the gateway to a more intense love of life, creative energy, enjoyment, and sensuality.

Position and Influences on the Body

The sacral chakra lies a little above the sacrum and the sexual organs, a finger's width below the navel. It governs the sexual organs and reproductive system, the kidneys, and the bladder.

The working of the second chakra affects the entire sacral and pelvic area. Its energy also directs the circulatory and lymphatic systems, the flow of semen and urine, and the urinary tract, which flushes poisons from the system. It also regulates the glandular functions of the ovaries and testicles.

Central Theme

The sacral chakra is the center of human sexuality and feminine energy.

Sexuality serves for constant renewal, the continuation and propagation of the species. The sacral chakra stands primarily for sexuality, creative energy, sensuality, and joy in living. By activating the sacral chakra, we can come into contact with the wellsprings of our passion for living. The free flow of energy through this chakra sharpens all of the senses and increases the pleasure we take in life. The creative energy and sensuous

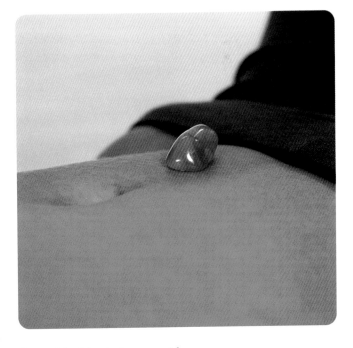

appreciation that come from the connection with this chakra provide the foundations for new beginnings and the richness and fertility expressed and symbolized in the union of the sexes. The proper

The sacral chakra is situated a little below the navel.

relationship with the sacral chakra makes it possible to say yes to one's sexuality and sensuality and fully accept one's body and physical being. This is of great importance for erotic fulfillment and a true and enriching partnership with another person.

People who have strongly developed the energy of the sacral chakra display great vitality and emanate what is best expressed by the French phrase *joie de vivre*. The power of the sacral chakra leads to increased self-esteem and a positive self-awareness. Through their infectious capacity for enthusiasm, such people can have a pronounced effect on those around them. And even someone who is not considered physically attractive according to conventional standards can generate strong interest on the part of the opposite sex.

Too little or too much energy in the sacral chakra can lead to a host of problems. Characteristic symptoms include jealousy, persistent anxiety, and diminished sexual desire. Other possible consequences are sexual ambivalence, addiction, feelings of guilt, and aggression.

When the sacral chakra is activated and harmonized through chakra work, we learn to enjoy life and develop a healthy relation to the sensual and sexual sides of our nature. As Western psychology has made clear, this is necessary for a balanced, healthy emotional life.

A strong sacral chakra is the best preparation for a well-balanced emotional life.

Alternative Methods of Harmonizing the Sacral Chakra

To gently stimulate and strengthen the sacral chakra, one can make use of a number of methods drawn from the different fields of alternative medicine:

- Gemstones: gold topaz, aventurine, coral, fire opal
- Aromatic oils: sandalwood, myrrh, bitter orange, pepper, vanilla
- Bach flowers: Oak, Olive, Pine
- Spice: vanilla, pepper
- Medicinal plants: nettle, yarrow, parsley

The Navel Chakra (Manipura Chakra)

- **Central themes:** willpower, self-confidence, personality, self-development, self-control, feelings, sensitivity, power, forcefulness
- **Number of petals:** ten
- **Color:** yellow, yellow-gold, gold
- **Mantra:** RAM
- **Element:** fire
- **Basic symbol:** triangle
- **Planet:** Mars
- **Sensory function:** sight

Description, Arrangement, and Symbolism

In Sanskrit, the navel chakra is called the *manipura* chakra. *Manipura* means "shining jewel" or "place of jewels." According to traditional teaching, the manipura chakra is considered to be particularly rich in energy. As a shining sun, this chakra sheds its radiance through the entire body, animating it with *prana*, the universal life energy. This chakra is also called the solar plexus chakra or simply the third chakra.

The manipura chakra is symbolically portrayed as a flower with ten petals. The corresponding ten Sanskrit syllables are *da, dha, na, ta, tha, da, dha, na, pa,* and *pha.* The principal mantra, which when repeated will bring the navel chakra to life, is RAM (pronounced RANG).

Lakini, Rudra, and especially Agni, the fire god, are the principal deities associated with this chakra. Traditionally, this chakra is depicted in gold and yellow-gold colors. It corresponds to the element of fire. This symbolizes the fiery, vital energy that emanates from this center.

The navel chakra is represented by the triangle. The ram is its symbolic animal. Known for its fiery strength, the ram is portrayed in Hindu painting as the steed of Agni, the fire god.

Fire is the primary element of the navel chakra, expressed in high levels of energy and animation.

Volatile quicksilver, which in nature comes from the quicksilver mineral cinnabar, is the metallic and chemical equivalent for the navel chakra. Its corresponding planet is Mars, the red planet, commonly associated with the element of fire. The vowel sound that most effectively stimulates this chakra is a short *o* (as in *cork*).

In nature, one finds echoes of this chakra in bright sunlight, fields of yellow grain, yellow flowers, and lava, which is a kind of liquid fire. During the moon's waxing stage, the activity of this center is particularly marked.

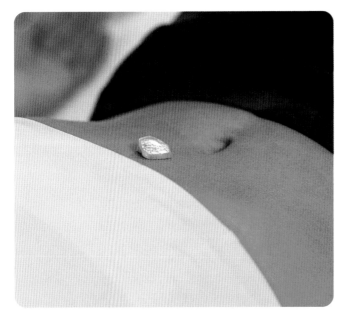

The navel chakra lies just above the navel in the solar plexus region.

Position and Influences on the Body

Although referred to as the navel chakra, the manipura chakra does not lie right at the navel, but rather a bit above it in the stomach area between the loins and breastbone. Since so much energy is stored in this chakra, it is of the greatest significance for the entire organism. Its energy is especially directed to the stomach, small intestine, and liver. It also governs the spleen and gallbladder. As is to be expected, it regulates the digestive system and the autonomic nervous system as well. It also plays an important role in the proper functioning of the pancreas and in the production of digestive enzymes and insulin.

Central Theme

The navel chakra provides the energy upon which the formation of a healthy personality depends. It gives one the ability to see things through to their conclusion. Strength of feeling arises from the navel chakra. People with a well-developed navel chakra are sure of themselves and their abilities. The fire element maintains their high energy level and zest for life. This energy is indispensable for developing self-awareness, achieving one's goals, and actively engaging with one's surroundings.

With energy flowing freely through the navel chakra, it becomes easy to pursue one's destiny forcefully. It is the basis for people with strong personalities, but it is a strength that does not degenerate into mere force. Rather, it is tempered by sensitivity and sympathy for others.

We recognize people who have strongly developed the navel chakra by their spontaneity. They follow their gut instincts and usually hit the bull's-eye. They don't hold back emotionally. They enjoy merriment and laughter, but they may just as easily express their sorrow and let their tears flow. If you tease them or treat them unfairly, their anger will clearly let you know that you've crossed a line.

A superabundance of energy or a blockage in the navel chakra brings a number of serious problems. One may, for example, suffer from apathy, insecurity, a lack of feeling, or a diminished sense of self. But too much or too little energy can have a contrary effect as well and lead to arrogance, an obsession with power, and a need to control, as well as thoughtlessness and fits of rage.

The exercises that are directed toward harmonizing and caring for the energies of the navel chakra provide the foundations for an active and successful life. A well-developed navel chakra makes it possible for one to strike a balance between the many shades of one's emotional world and necessary objectivity and self-control.

A harmonized navel chakra leads to the right balance between emotion and self-control.

Alternative Methods of Harmonizing the Navel Chakra

Using gentle methods, one can activate and strengthen the navel chakra. You will find the best ways to promote its harmonious unfolding in the following list:

- Gemstones: citrine, chrysoberyl, amber, tigereye, yellow jasper
- Aromatic oils: lavender, chamomile, lemon, anise
- Bach flowers: Impatiens, Scleranthus, Hornbeam
- Spice: cardamom, anise
- Medicinal plants: fennel, chamomile, juniper berries

The Heart Chakra
(Anahata Chakra)

- **Central theme:** love, compassion, humanity, empathy, tolerance, openness, warm-heartedness
- **Number of petals:** twelve
- **Color:** green
- **Mantra:** YAM
- **Element:** air
- **Basic symbol:** hexagon
- **Planet:** Jupiter
- **Sensory function:** touch

Description, Arrangement, and Symbolism

The heart chakra lies at the center of the chakra system. In nearly every culture, the heart is linked to the power of love. The heart chakra forms the center of one's humanity and feelings for others.

The heart chakra links the three lower chakras with the three higher centers of awareness.

In Sanskrit, the heart chakra is called the *anahata* chakra. *Anahata* means "whole" or "unbroken." This tells us that we are free and protected from fault in our spiritual heart center. Whatever happens to us in life, we will always be able to return to the fundamental power of love and find comfort and strength.

The heart chakra is also called the chest chakra or heart center. It is most commonly pictured as a flower with twelve petals. The petals correspond to twelve Sanskrit syllables: *kam, kham, gam, gham, ngam, cham, chham, jam, jham, nyam, tam,* and *than.*

The mantra that most effectively awakens and opens the heart chakra is YAM (pronounced YANG).

Isa and Kakini are the two Hindu deities most closely associated with the heart chakra. Even though this chakra is associated with the power of love, its corresponding color is not red but green.

The love of the spiritual heart is not the passion-filled, physical love that the Western tradition often seems to confuse with true love. The love of the heart chakra is a kind of awareness. It does not express itself in the pursuit of one's own interest or the satisfaction of instinctual drives but rather serves as the foundation for selflessness and compassion. For this reason, it is seen as green rather than red, since green represents harmony and balance.

The heart is the symbol of love. People with well-developed heart chakras exhibit tolerance and openness.

The symbol of the heart chakra is the six-pointed star—a harmonious juxtaposition of two triangles, one above, one below—also a symbol of harmony and balance.

In traditional representations of the heart chakra, one finds the antelope as a symbolic animal. But more commonly the chakra is associated with birds of all kinds and the dove in particular, which in Eastern and Western cultures is considered the symbol of peace.

The metal associated with the heart chakra is copper; its corresponding planet is Jupiter. The vowel that works most strongly upon it is *a*.

The energy of the heart chakra finds its equivalents in nature in woods, green fields, and peaceful, unspoiled landscapes.

The heart chakra is most active during the phases of the new moon and the full moon.

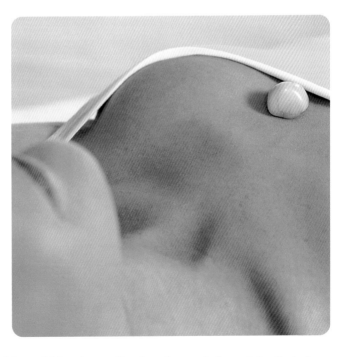

Position and Influences on the Body

The heart chakra lies at the level of the heart, not on the left side but in the center of the chest. Its energy works within the rib cage, governing heart, lungs, and the circulation of energy throughout the body. It also affects the skin and blood as well as hands, arms, and upper back. The glandular functions of the thymus, which plays an important role in the maintenance of a healthy immune system, also depend upon the activity of this chakra.

The heart chakra lies in the middle of the chest at the center of the chakra system.

Central Theme

In the teachings concerning the chakras, the heart chakra is spoken of as the center of universal, transpersonal love. It radiates the power that binds people together. True compassion, the willingness to put others before oneself, and the ability to gain a deep understanding of another person are all emotional capacities that show that one has reached a high level of consciousness.

The heart chakra stands for brotherly love, devotion, and humility.

People with highly developed heart chakras go beyond selfish interests and can transcend their own limitations. In contrast to love that is directed to one's own partner or a narrow circle of family and friends, the love generated by the heart chakra extends to all people. From this open posture comes tolerance. This tolerance—for other people, ideas, and cultures—is the basis of a sense of the human brother- and sisterhood, which is encouraged by every religion. When the heart chakra is strong, it becomes easy to take responsibility for others. And it also promotes loving acceptance of oneself, despite one's weaknesses and failings.

When the heart chakra is blocked, a person can become heartless and bitter. Loneliness and difficulty connecting are the chief consequences. This leads to feelings of isolation and separateness from others. Conversely, disturbances in the heart chakra can cause one to feel easily overwhelmed by others to the degree that one can even lose a sense of one's own identity.

There are diverse methods to activate and harmonize the energy of the heart chakra. They will lead to openness and warm-heartedness and enrich our relationships with other people.

Alternative Methods of Harmonizing the Heart Chakra

Here is a list of therapeutic means drawn from the different fields of alternative medicine:

- Gemstones: emerald, chrysoprase, jade, rose quartz
- Aromatic oils: cloves, rose, jasmine, tarragon
- Bach flowers: Red Chestnut, Willow, Chicory
- Spice: saffron
- Medicinal plants: whitehorn, thyme, melissa

The Throat Chakra
(Vishuddha Chakra)

- **Central theme:** Communication, verbal ability, inspiration, truthfulness, intelligence, synthesis, creativity, musical talent
- **Number of petals:** sixteen
- **Color:** sky blue
- **Mantra:** HAM
- **Element:** ether
- **Basic symbol:** circle
- **Planet:** Saturn
- **Sensory function:** hearing

Description, Arrangement, and Symbolism

The throat chakra in Sanskrit is called the *vishuddha* chakra. *Vishuddhi* means "pure." Consciousness of language and truth belong to this level. Its role is to purify awareness and provide inner clarity. The vishuddha chakra is also called the neck chakra, the communication chakra, or simply the fifth chakra.

The throat chakra is depicted as a flower with sixteen petals. Its color is sky blue (or sometimes a shimmering silver). Just as the color blue recalls the expanse of heaven, so its corresponding element, ether, brings space and purity to mind. In yoga philosophy, sound is transmitted through the ether. Thus ether is considered to be the basic medium of communication.

The throat chakra lies near the larynx and leads the way to the highest chakras.

The mantra that is used to awaken the energy of the fifth chakra is HAM (pronounced HANG). Its symbol is the circle, which stands for the place of emptiness. Only those who penetrate this circle can acquire the deepest understanding.

The symbolic animal of the fifth chakra is the white elephant, the mount of Indra, the mightiest of the Vedic gods. Indra is called "the Powerful." He is the god of thunder and fertility. He summons the rain that renews the parched earth. Two other Hindu deities, Sakina and Sadashiva, are also associated with this chakra. Its corresponding metal is silver.

The vowel sound that is linked to this chakra is *a* (as in *maid*). Its planet is Saturn. Natural phenomena that correspond to the energy of the throat chakra include the blue of the cloudless sky and the open sea. The throat chakra is particularly active during the phase of the waning moon.

Position and Influences on the Body

A strong throat chakra provides a harmonious balance between thought and feeling and enhances one's ability to communicate with others.

The throat chakra lies in the area of the cervical vertebrae, near the larynx. Its energy influences the neck, jaw, larynx, esophagus, and windpipe. The breath and voice also depend upon this chakra. It energizes the neck and shoulders; the thyroid and parathyroid glands can function harmoniously only when energy flows freely through this chakra.

Central Theme

According to the teachings about the chakras, the vishuddha chakra is the center of sound. It is responsible for speech and communication. The conscious use of language, the desire to speak the truth in all circumstances, and the ability to express oneself are all dependent upon the energy that arises from this chakra.

The throat chakra also plays an important intermediary role, since it connects the heart and forehead chakras and is thus responsible for balancing the worlds of feeling and thought.

People who have developed the throat chakra are gifted with great verbal ability. They know how to use their voice and how to get their message across to others. Speech is not only a vehicle that conveys information. It also expresses feelings. Orators and actors are well aware of how the voice can move the minds of their listeners when they succeed in infusing their words with feeling.

The throat chakra represents the sense of hearing. It offers us the key to the powerful world of sound. Sound can change a person's mood in an instant. A well-developed throat chakra accompanies musical talent. Not of least importance, the throat chakra has a great influence on our thought processes. A great part of thinking has to do with words. What we say to others, and above all what we say to ourselves, influences our mental world and our feelings about life.

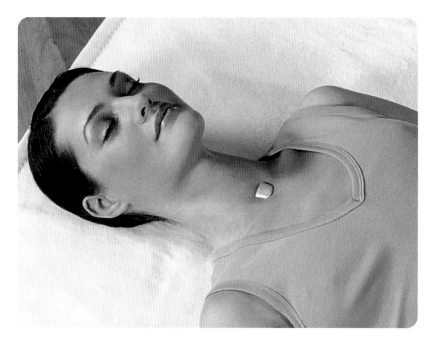

The throat chakra, which lies at the level of the larynx, connects the heart and forehead chakras.

Disturbances in the throat chakra are often accompanied by speech disturbances such as stuttering and stammering as well as difficulties in expressing oneself. Conversely, they can lead to a distorted thirst for fame, the desire to manipulate others, and a tendency to gossip.

The throat chakra forms the center of sound and language in the human body.

Alternative Methods of Harmonizing the Throat Chakra

By using the following methods, you can stimulate the throat chakra and awaken its energies:

- Gemstones: lapis lazuli, aquamarine, topaz
- Aromatic oils: eucalyptus, peppermint, camphor
- Bach flowers: Mimulus, Agrimony, Cerato
- Spice: star anise, cloves
- Medicinal plants: peppermint, sage, coltsfoot

The Forehead Chakra (Ajna Chakra)

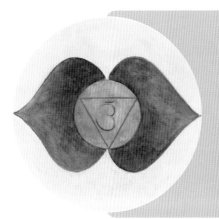

- **Central theme:** intuition, wisdom, realization, awareness, fantasy, power of the imagination, self-knowledge
- **Number of petals:** two
- **Color:** dark blue, violet blue
- **Mantra:** KSHAM or OM
- **Element:** none
- **Basic symbol:** winged circle
- **Planet:** Uranus
- **Sensory function:** sixth sense, transcendental awareness

Description, Arrangement, and Symbolism

The two principle energy channels, ida and pingala meet at the forehead chakra. Their union corresponds to the transcendence of duality, a state that can be reached during meditation.

The forehead chakra is the spiritual center of awareness and intuition. In Sanskrit, it is called the *ajna* chakra. *Ajna* means "to know or perceive." Higher knowledge can be obtained only by stepping beyond duality. The two most important energy pathways, *pingala* and *ida*, end in the ajna chakra. These two currents of energy represent duality—sun and moon, masculine and feminine—and they meet in this chakra. By meditating upon it, one can attain freedom from dualistic thinking.

The forehead chakra is often referred to as the third eye, the forehead center, the center of wisdom, or simply the sixth chakra. It is depicted as a flower with two petals facing each other, which represents the harmony and union of the two poles, yin and yang.

Corresponding to one of the petals is the holy Sanskrit syllable *ham*, and the syllable *kham* corresponds to the other petal. The syllables have been identified as the primordial sounds of Shakti, creative life power, and Shiva, cosmic awareness. When the powers of Shiva and Shakti are united in the forehead chakra, one attains the experience of enlightenment.

The principal mantra that is used to awaken the forehead chakra is KSHAM (pronounced KSHANG). The universal mantra OM also works upon the energy of this chakra.

The deities Parmashiva and Shakti Hakini are closely associated with the forehead chakra. Shakti Hakini is an androgynous deity, standing for both masculine and feminine aspects, and is thus a symbol for the dissolution of duality.

The forehead chakra is normally depicted as dark blue. The precious metal platinum and the vowel sound *i* correspond to it, as does the planet Uranus. In nature, the energy of the third eye is reflected in the night sky and the light of the stars. It strongest vibrations are felt during the phase of the waning moon.

The forehead chakra provides us with our connection to the spiritual world. This is the center of consciousness and awareness.

Position and Influences on the Body

The third eye lies in the middle of the forehead, between the eyebrows, a little above the top of the nose. On a physical level, its influence extends to the cerebellum and the organs of the senses: sight, hearing, and smell. It also governs the face and sinuses and the hormonal and nervous systems. The proper functioning of the pituitary gland is dependent upon this chakra.

Central Theme

The third eye is the portal through which one gains entrance to the spiritual world. It provides the means of establishing contact with one's intuition and helps us gain awareness of higher realities and go beyond our limited consciousness. Extrasensory perception such as clairvoyance and telepathy are possible only when the third eye is awakened.

The search for self-knowledge is closely bound up with the awakening of the third eye. This leads to knowledge of the higher self that is not to be identified with the constricted world of the ego. Meditation techniques that concentrate on the third eye can lead to illumination. This experience indicates that the inner fire of one's awareness has been ignited.

The forehead chakra lies right in the middle of the forehead.

As a result, one can look at one's problems from a higher vantage point and thereby become free of them. People with highly developed forehead chakras have enhanced powers of visualization. Imagination and fantasy life are sharpened. Such people even experience visions that reveal the future, or at least they have a feeling for what lies in store for them, the so-called sixth sense.

When the energy of the ajna chakra flows unhindered, mental clarity ensues. One sees clearly with the help of a higher awareness and is no longer the victim of illusion or self-delusion.

A blockage or an excess of energy in the forehead chakra can bring on serious spiritual afflictions. Weakened concentration and attention-deficit disorders indicate disturbances of the forehead chakra. Forgetfulness, spiritual confusion, and the tendency toward superstition are also signs of problems in this chakra.

Selfishness, greed, and the lust for power are all consequences of the energy of the third eye directed toward egotistical ends. Through chakra work comes the strength to develop its energy in a harmonious fashion. And so over time it becomes easier to make contact with one's intuitive sense and inner wisdom.

A strong forehead chakra leads to intuition and contact with inner wisdom.

Alternative Methods of Harmonizing the Forehead Chakra

One can use the following methods to gently arouse and strengthen the energy of the forehead chakra:

- Gemstones: blue sapphire, opal, blue tourmaline
- Aromatic oils: lemongrass, violet
- Bach flowers: Crab Apple, Vine, Walnut
- Spice: bay leaf
- Medicinal plants: Saint-John's-wort, spruce

The Crown Chakra
(Sahasrara Chakra)

- **Central theme:** Spirituality, experience of higher planes, knowledge of God, enlightenment, self-realization, cosmic consciousness, religiosity
- **Number of petals:** one thousand
- **Color:** violet, white, gold
- **Mantra:** OM
- **Basic symbol:** lotus blossom
- **Planet:** Neptune
- **Sensory function:** cosmic awareness

Description, Arrangement, and Symbolism

The Sanskrit name for the crown chakra is the *sahasrara* chakra. *Sahasrara* means "thousand" or "thousandfold." The symbol for this chakra is a lotus with a thousand petals. The number one thousand serves to represent the highest fulfillment and perfection.

The crown chakra is also known as the thousand-petaled lotus or simply the seventh chakra. The most important path of energy is called *sushumna*. It runs from the root chakra at the base of the spine up through the crown chakra. Through this channel arises the serpent power, kundalini, which stands for the arousing of human potential. Through one's journey of spiritual development, the Shakti power, which resides within the root chakra, is awakened. It rises upward, animating all of the other chakras through which it flows, and then finally merges with universal consciousness in the crown chakra, which is represented by Shiva. The crown chakra serves as the residence of Shiva.

The ascent from lower to higher planes of awareness and the union of the individual with the Divine Self is the goal of the spiritual quest. This journey from darkness into light is beautifully symbolized by the lotus. The lotus grows out of mud and darkness and finally unfolds into a pure, radiant flower. This is the template for the development of

The crown chakra is the center of spirituality and enlightenment—the highest level of consciousness that one can attain.

human awareness, which starting with the unawakened state of animal awareness reaches upward and realizes the soul's light. The mantra that is used in meditation to enliven the crown chakra is the universal mantra OM.

Many pictures paint the sahasrara chakra in violet and white tones. These colors symbolize purity and light, as does gold, which is also often seen in representations of this chakra.

The god Shiva rules the seventh chakra, and its symbolic animal is the rising serpent, the kundalini power. The metal gold and the planet Neptune correspond to this chakra.

The energy of the crown chakra evokes feelings of great harmony and peace.

The exalted quality of the crown chakra is mirrored in nature by lofty mountaintops. It is most active during the phase of the new moon. There are no elements or vowels that correspond to this chakra.

Position and Influences on the Body

The crown chakra lies at the top of the head. In fact, as the highest chakra, its energy transcends human boundaries and rises directly into the aura. For this reason, some teachers are of the opinion that this chakra lies wholly outside the body.

In any case, the activity of the crown chakra influences the cerebrum and the entire organism. It has an especially close connection to the functioning of the pineal gland.

Central Theme

The central themes of this chakra are spirituality, self-realization, and enlightenment. Once we reach the stage of development represented by the crown chakra, we attain consciousness of our divine nature and the deepest sense of peace.

By coming into awareness of the crown chakra's qualities, one reaches a sense of the sacred unity of the cosmos. The development of this center leads the personality to the highest level and results in a profound transformation. One becomes a great soul (*mahatma*).

The crown chakra ought not be awakened unless the energy of all the other chakras has been awakened and can form a firm foundation for it. The practices offered in this book are designed to stimulate the seventh chakra very gently without disturbing its subtle circulation of energy. For intensive work with the crown chakra, one must have the help of an experienced teacher. Disproportionate concentration on the crown chakra can lead to a flight from the world and reality, as well as depression and deep confusion. Within the normal course of development, the last step to which our inner guide leads us is the awakening of the energy of the crown chakra, the highest stage of awareness. This awakening is almost always accompanied by a wonderful condition of awareness. Unshakable serenity, the deepest peace, and connectedness to the universe are signs that the highest goal has been reached. The yogis call this state *samadhi* —the state of perfect union and bliss.

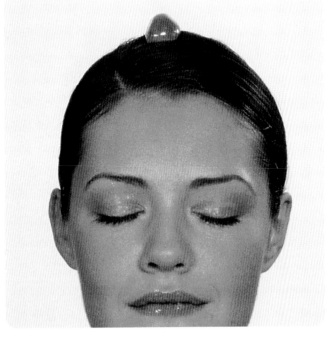

The highest chakra, the crown chakra, lies at the top of the head.

Alternative Methods of Harmonizing the Crown Chakra

To stimulate the crown chakra, you can resort to the following methods drawn from the different fields of alternative medicine:

- Gemstones: diamond, rock crystal, amethyst
- Aromatic oils: rosewood
- Bach flowers: Wild Rose, White Chestnut

When the crown chakra is opened one touches the transcendent reality that can bring about the transformation of the human being into a *mahatma*, a great soul.

4 Chakras and Personality

The teaching regarding the chakras is a powerful therapeutic approach to spiritual psychology. Our chakras mirror the actual condition of our souls and reveal our physical, mental, and spiritual development. In this chapter and the next, you will discover the following:

- Which basic personality type corresponds to the dominance of each of the chakras
- What strengths you have and what developmental work remains to be done based upon the condition of each of these energy centers
- What psychological problems accompany weakly developed or blocked chakras
- How the chakras relate to the various stages of life
- The great importance that knowledge of the chakras has for child rearing and the development of the unborn child
- How the chakras influence human interactions
- How you can make use of this knowledge to enjoy satisfying and fulfilling relationships

The psychology of the chakras gives us a better sense of the possibilities open to us and deepens our understanding of others.

Chakra Tests: Which Chakra Type Are You?

To learn which chakras are especially well developed, which chakra is dominant, and which chakras may have blockages, you can choose from the following methods:

Chakra personality test
Chakra pendulum
Kinesiological muscle test

The Chakra Personality Test

The statements listed below should help you find out which chakras are currently dominant and which are blocked. Respond to these statements with yes or no. Don't think about them too much. Your answers should be intuitive and spontaneous.

On page 43 is a chart of the chakras. Each chakra has four fields, and each field contains a number that corresponds to one of the statements below. For each statement to which you answer yes, fill in the corresponding field on the chart.

	No	Yes
1. I generally feel in harmony with the universe.	☐	☐
2. My intuition is quite well-developed.	☐	☐
3. I express myself well in words.	☐	☐
4. I feel emotionally connected with other people.	☐	☐
5. I follow my gut instincts.	☐	☐
6. I am full of vitality and joie de vivre.	☐	☐
7. I love to be in movement and feel my own body.	☐	☐
8. It is easy for me to meditate and find inner peace.	☐	☐
9. I have good concentration.	☐	☐
10. I feel socially confident.	☐	☐
11. I am deeply afraid of loneliness.	☐	☐
12. Eating is one of the great pleasures of life.	☐	☐
13. I know how to enjoy life.	☐	☐
14. I almost never worry.	☐	☐
15. I find it difficult to take the world seriously.	☐	☐
16. I often think about the world and life.	☐	☐
17. I can easily put my thoughts into words.	☐	☐
18. Love is the most important thing in the world.	☐	☐
19. I am at peace within myself and not easily thrown off center.	☐	☐
20. I am a very passionate person.	☐	☐
21. I feel a deep connection with nature.	☐	☐
22. My soul's home does not lie in this world.	☐	☐
23. I have intense, color-filled dreams.	☐	☐
24. I have many different interests.	☐	☐
25. I have the desire to express myself artistically.	☐	☐
26. I experience feelings mostly in my body.	☐	☐
27. Sex is very important to me.	☐	☐
28. I have a lot of confidence in life and the future.	☐	☐

Evaluating the Chakra Test

Once you have indicated the various fields that correspond to the statements that apply to you, you have a good picture of the condition of your seven chakras.

Based on the number and the distribution of the fields you have marked, you can clearly recognize which chakras currently have the greatest influence in your life and which are underdeveloped (the blank fields) and hinder the unfolding of your full potential.

To obtain an even better picture go back over these statements once again. For those to which you answered no, mark the fields in the chakra chart with a black circle.

You will find that just because you did not say yes to some statements does not mean that you have to say no them. Those questions to which you can unequivocally answer no indicate energy blockages in the corresponding chakra.

Repeat this chakra test in a few weeks. This will let you establish which chakras have changed over time, which are stable, and where possible blockages have been dissolved.

Use a colored pencil matching the color corresponding to each chakra to fill in each field.

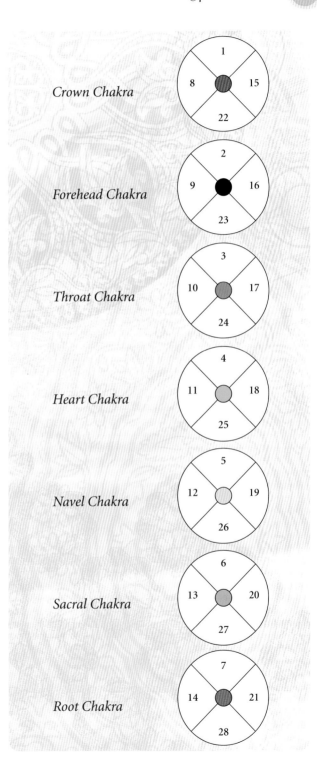

Crown Chakra

Forehead Chakra

Throat Chakra

Heart Chakra

Navel Chakra

Sacral Chakra

Root Chakra

Example 1

All chakras are equally developed and unblocked.

Example 2

The throat and heart chakras are dominant. The forehead chakra is weak and there is a blockage in the navel chakra.

Example 3

Though the heart chakra is dominant, it is also blocked, and there is a blockage at the root chakra.

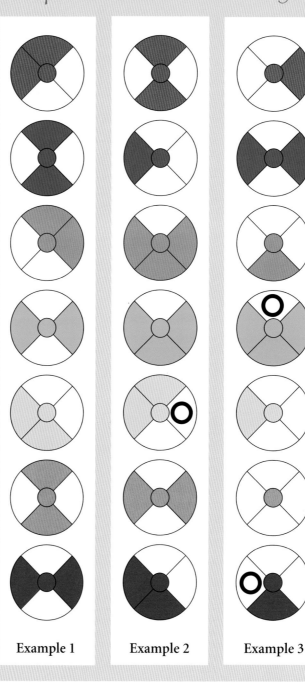

Example of Chakra Personality Portraits

Crown Chakra

Forehead Chakra

Throat Chakra

Heart Chakra

Navel Chakra

Sacral Chakra

Root Chakra

Example 1   Example 2   Example 3

The chakra pendulum will give you insight into the strengths and weaknesses in your chakras.

The Chakra Pendulum

Another way to test your chakras is to use a pendulum. By harnessing your intuitive powers, the pendulum helps you identify which chakras are well developed and which need work.

All that is needed is a pendulum and a correctly drawn pendulum chart: a circle divided into segments in which pairs of facing segments each correspond to a particular chakra (see page 47).

When the pendulum swings on a particular line, it provides a clear answer. The procedure is quite simple: Hold the pendulum over the center point of the diagram and repeat to yourself the question that you want to have answered. For example, Which of my chakras is the most active? Which chakra is the weakest? On which chakra should I begin to work?

Hold the pendulum loosely and try to repeat your question while in a relaxed frame of mind. You will discover that after a while the pendulum will begin to swing on its own. Then you can see from the diagram the answer to your question.

The movement of the pendulum is caused by small unconscious muscular movements. The pendulum itself does nothing.

The Orange Segments

The pendulum diagram contains an extra pair of segments. These are indicated by an orange circle. When the pendulum swings between these two fields, it indicates that the answer to your question is not just one chakra but a number of chakras or even all of them. You might obtain this answer when all of your chakras are equally well -developed or when two chakras are blocked and your unconscious cannot decide which to begin work on.

How Many Chakras Are in Question?

When the pendulum oscillates between the orange segments, then no clear answer has been given, and you must inquire further. You might ask the following question: How many chakras are affected? The segments between which the pendulum swings will give you that number. If, for example, the pendulum swings over the sacral chakra, then you will know that two chakras are affected.

Once you know how many chakras are affected, then you can ask which is the first (or second, or third) you should turn your attention to.

The unconscious mind with its hidden wisdom uses the pendulum to express itself.

The Pendulum Swings in a Circle

Finally, there is the possibility that the pendulum will swing in a circle. This means that your unconscious cannot or will not answer the question. In this case, you should revise your question and try again.

Yes/No Answers

You can also ask the pendulum to answer yes or no to your question. For this you do not need a pendulum diagram. If the pendulum circles clockwise, the answer is yes. If it circles counterclockwise, it is no. If the pendulum swings in a straight line, that means that your unconscious cannot or will not give a yes-or-no answer to the question.

Of course, when you work without a pendulum diagram, you have to phrase your question so that it can be answered yes or no. You might ask: Is my heart chakra the dominant center?

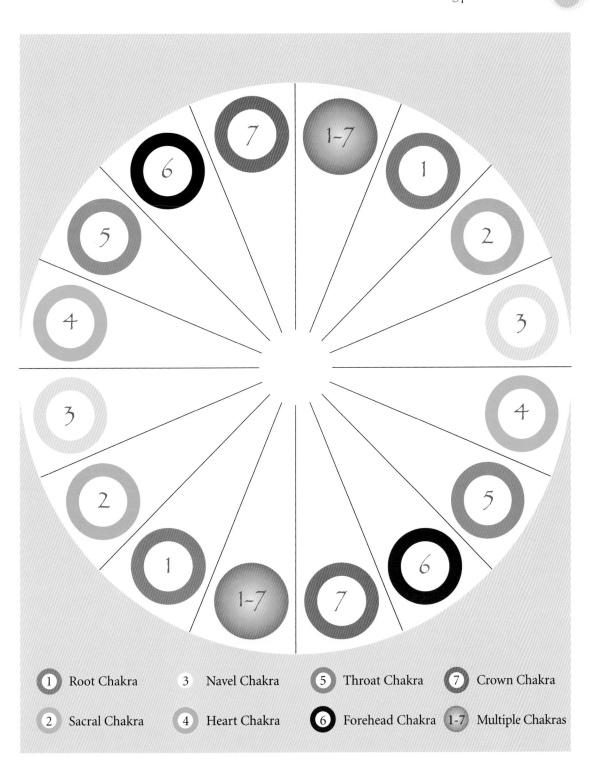

1 Root Chakra	3 Navel Chakra	5 Throat Chakra	7 Crown Chakra
2 Sacral Chakra	4 Heart Chakra	6 Forehead Chakra	1-7 Multiple Chakras

The Kinesiological Chakra Test

With the chakra personality test, you obtain answers from a mental and emotional level. The unconscious provides the answers when you use a pendulum. Through the kinesiological test, you will receive an answer from the body's intuitive wisdom. You can test your chakras either with a partner (the standard kinesiological test) or by yourself.

The Standard Kinesiological Test

For the standard kinesiological test, you need a partner, who will conduct the test. Your partner will ask you to extend your left arm so that the palm faces downward and to think of a very pleasant, enjoyable experience.

With the standard kinesiological test partners can gauge each other's chakras.

Then your partner lightly presses down on your outstretched arm and registers the muscular resistance. Recalling a pleasant experience will strengthen your muscles so that they resist the pressure from above.

Next, your partner will ask you to think of an unpleasant or unhappy experience and repeat the muscle test. The muscular resistance should be much weaker, since negative thoughts weaken the musculature.

This is the first phase of the chakra test. It serves as a kind of calibration, since you will be measuring relative rather than absolute muscle strength. What may be a relatively strong resistance for an elderly woman will certainly have to be considered weak for an athlete in peak physical condition. The results of this first test can serve as a baseline for the next phase of tests.

The second phase is directly concerned with the chakras. Once again, stretch out your left arm and place your right hand on one of your chakras. Your partner then follows the procedure described above. The stronger the muscular resistance, the stronger the chakra. Weakened resistance indicates weakness in the chakra. If your partner can push down your outstretched arm with little or no resistance, then you likely have a blockage in that chakra.

There are two phases to the standard kinesiological test. To do this test, you need to work with a partner.

Testing Yourself

Self-testing using kinesiology differs little from the standard test, but it has one disadvantage: It is easy to fool yourself or misread the results, so you have to be very attentive during the test. Place your left hand a hand's breadth away from the center you wish to test, with your palm facing your body. Concentrate on the chakra you are testing, and, using your right hand, press your left hand toward your body. You will feel stronger or weaker resistance depending upon the strength of the corresponding chakra. Thus you can obtain a good idea of the energy level of the different chakras. The easier it is to press your left hand against the chakra, the weaker the activity of that chakra.

You need to be attentive when testing yourself; it is easy to misinterpret your own reactions.

You can measure the strength of your chakras without a partner using the kinesiological test on yourself.

Evaluating the Tests

By using these tests, you should be able to tell which chakras are dominant, which are weak, and which have blockages.

In the following pages, you will find a description of each of the basic chakra personality types that correspond to the dominance of one of the seven chakras, and the respective character traits. Through this classification, you can determine where your strengths lie and what areas you need to work on.

We need to know who we are in order to know who we can be.

It is quite possible that more than one chakra is highly developed. You should read the descriptions of all the types, since some features of each may apply to you.

By considering all of the seven chakra personalities, you will also discover what problems arise from chakras that are blocked or poorly developed. Later chapters will concentrate on how you can remedy weaknesses and dissolve blockages, thereby overcoming personal difficulties and problems.

Complementary Chakras

Each chakra has a special relationship with one other chakra, its so-called complementary chakra. Their energies stand in the strongest opposition but also work to complete each other. This complementarity is of particular importance in solving the problems that arise from the dominance of one chakra. As a general rule, where one chakra is dominant, it is especially important to pay attention to the development of its complementary chakra.

The one exception here is the heart chakra, which does not have a complementary chakra. Standing as it does at the center of the chakra system, it has no opposite pole.

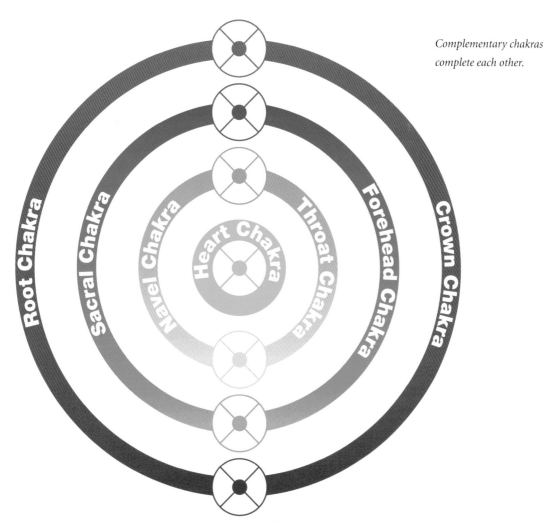

Complementary chakras complete each other.

Root Chakra

Sacral Chakra

Navel Chakra

Heart Chakra

Throat Chakra

Forehead Chakra

Crown Chakra

Chakra Personality Types

The seven principal chakras correspond to fundamentally different psychological constitutions. The harmonizing of all these energy centers is the goal of human development. A state in which the energies of all the chakras are balanced and integrated is an ideal state that only very few attain. Those who approach this state of being are regarded as saints or enlightened ones. They are a step ahead of other people; one might say that "they have started on the path before the rest of us." Most people are dominated by one chakra to a greater or lesser extent, and that is evidenced in their psychological makeup.

The seven chakras correspond to seven basic personality types. Of course, every person is a unique, irreplaceable being, whose individuality depends upon more factors than just the dominance of one chakra or another. Every soul is a reflection of the constant exchange of energies between all of the chakras. (If we were to suppose that there were ten different states for each chakra, then that would give rise to ten million different combinations. And in truth there are many more than that.)

The tests just described show which of our chakras are strong and which we need to work on.

By studying the psychological picture that is revealed by the dominance of one particular chakra, we can gain valuable insight into ourselves, our strengths and weaknesses, and our purpose and path in life. In the process, we will also develop greater understanding of other people, especially when we can view them in the context of their own chakra development.

The Root-Chakra Type

The first chakra connects us to the earth. This chakra is the source of our will to live, and from it arises our life force. It is, as it were, the glue that binds humans as physical, mental, and spiritual beings to the life of the planet. The root chakra is responsible for the material bases of our being, our instinct for self-preservation. It ensures our physical survival.

Character

For root-chakra personalities, the keystone is survival and material security. Their need for stability and security ensures that they do not lose themselves in ethereal dreaming. They are rooted in the earth and the natural world. They feel themselves to be a part of nature, and it is there that they find their true home. They have no need of verbal explanations or theories; they are secure in the underlying confidence that the energy of the root chakra provides.

The well-grounded root-chakra person accepts as a matter of course that he is part of the natural world.

People in whom the root chakra is dominant want to be as secure as possible. They are devoted to personal well-being, a comforting home environment, a stable family life, and a secure career. Accordingly, root-chakra personalities are naturally conservative. They concern themselves with the essentials: nature and good health.

The professions that are most suitable for this personality type are those that require practicality and a connection to nature. Thus such people will have good success as gardeners, builders, and craftspeople. They might also excel in sports or find sculpture or landscape architecture to be vehicles for self-expression. Root-chakra personalities are especially gifted at relating to animals. They are also capable of making a lot of money, although their relationship to wealth does not always bring out the best side of their characters.

The earthy root-chakra type needs to be open to spiritual discovery.

Strengths

The root-chakra person has a powerful will to live and a reservoir of life energy, resulting in great stamina and the ability to see things through to their conclusion. Such people can accomplish much and, using their strong life energy, reach whatever goals they set for themselves.

Their feeling for the value of life and nature, combined with their deep connection with the earth and its rhythms, makes them ideally suited to defend the environment and champion the benefits of healthy, natural lifestyles. Unlike other people, they don't get caught up in ideological battles. Their two feet are always firmly planted on the ground.

Root-chakra people often devote themselves to the protection and welfare of the environment and animals. They generally lead healthy lives.

A well-developed root chakra is the best starting point for the full unfolding of one's life energy. When these seeds are planted in the fertile ground of the harmonious development of the entire chakra system, then the root-chakra personality with its strength of purpose and stamina is well on the way to making a mark on the world.

Challenges

The strength of the root-chakra personality can also lead to danger when it is not harnessed in the proper direction. The greatest dangers such personalities face are egotism and lack of self-control.

Self-centeredness is a great hindrance along the spiritual path. If we only look after our own interests, we will find it difficult to recognize that ultimately all beings are one. By fixating on the tiny part of the world that is the personal self, we lose a sense of the richness of possibilities that surrounds us.

The root-chakra personality is subject to powerful physical urges when its energy is not mitigated by the influence of other chakras. These urges can lead to an unhealthy relationship with the basic necessities of life, especially food. From a spiritual vantage point, this is not as negative as the problem of egotism. But when the two are combined, it can lead to very unfortunate consequences. The aggressive assertion of one's own interests can lead to an impasse that is extremely difficult to surmount. To take and not give back reinforces an ever-deepening character imbalance.

The feeling for the natural rhythms of nature is axiomatic for root-chakra personalities.

Each chakra personality type is prey to a particular kind of fear. For those with root-chakra personalities, it is the basic fear for survival. This can be quickly triggered when material needs and desires, which are so important to them, remain unfulfilled. Self-centeredness and lack of self-control simply aggravate the problem.

Negative characteristics will manifest themselves more intensely when the root chakra alone is strongly developed and the other centers have blockages or are weakened. The best way to avoid this pitfall is to pay greater attention to the other chakras.

Most effective for root-chakra personalities is to strengthen and care for the complementary chakra, the crown chakra. However, this is no easy task. No other pair of chakras differ so greatly, while complementing each other so completely.

The greatest assets for root-chakra personalities are their persistence, energy, and self-confidence. These make it possible for such people to overcome daunting obstacles. The most important prerequisite is to recognize that spiritual matters are worth pursuing and that they represent the fulfillment, not the negation, of earthly life.

Because of their deep-seated needs for security, root-chakra types often devote themselves to the pursuit of material well-being.

The Sacral-Chakra Type

The second chakra corresponds to the element water—the element most closely connected with life-giving, creative power. The sacral chakra is the basis and the source for human creativity. It is responsible for the propagation of the species as well as the spread of ideas. It also governs our sexuality.

Character

The principal characteristics of sacral-chakra personalities are connected to the power of creativity. The joy they take in living places sensuality, sexuality, and creative activity in the foreground. Such people have a deep need to express themselves, to take what is inside them and bring it to life and share it with the world. They are driven by the imperative of self-unfolding.

Their creative momentum is very true to life. To bear children or to care for them provides these people with a deep sense of fulfillment. In the realm of creative endeavors, they are almost always involved with the visual arts. Within that area, their aesthetic approach will be connected to the work of their hands. Their art will be immediate and intelligible rather than abstract. A strong sacral chakra is an asset to sculptors, architects, and painters as well as carpenters, potters, and metal workers. On the other hand, sacral-chakra personalities rarely stand out as philosophers, writers, or composers. In addition to the fields of arts and crafts, the helping professions will benefit from the unique gifts of the sacral personality type. Because of the joy they take in life, their sensuality, their self-confidence, and their remarkable creativity, people in whom the sacral chakra is strongly developed attract other people and are naturally sympathetic to them.

Form and image are dominant themes for the sacral-chakra personality.

Strengths

People with the sacral-chakra personality type have many strengths that afford them many ways of developing their full potential. Their special talents direct them in the search for new experiences. They are always in movement and never fall into unproductive stagnation. Their creative powers, enthusiasm, and vitality complement each other and help them along their path. Women who have strongly developed sacral chakras often find their fulfillment in motherhood. With their creativity, their healing energy, and the joy they take in life, they are ideally suited to bring out the best in their children and help the full unfolding of their characters.

Men who belong to this personality type have a special advantage. The creative feminine energy that the second chakra emits results in an inner harmony between their masculine and feminine sides. At the same time, men suffer more from the problems that the dominant sacral chakra can bring.

Sacral-chakra women run the risk of losing themselves in motherhood and neglecting their own spiritual development.

The combination of a positive awareness of one's physical being, joie de vivre, and healing energy, all of which spring from the second chakra, give this type of person a great advantage—not only because these qualities are ideal conditions for stability, health, and long life. They enable one to reach beyond the physical to a higher level, for example, through yoga and other spiritual disciplines.

Furthermore, sensuality and free-flowing sexual energy are positive factors as long as they are not aimed in harmful directions due to unfortunate circumstances. Many psychological problems have their roots in blocked sexuality. People with dominant sacral chakras have the opportunity to use this energy to reach higher levels of being.

Passionate creativity is the mark of the sacral-chakra personality.

Bearing and rearing children is a very important theme for people with dominant sacral chakras.

Challenges

The strengths of the sacral-chakra personality type—their vital creative energy—can also be the source of the greatest danger. When this energy is devoted exclusively to sex, it can lead (especially in men) to an obsessive pursuit of pleasure and sexual satisfaction. And if such men's sexual needs are frustrated, they can become aggressive and destructive. This type of person can unleash powerful energies and use them to harm others, thereby blocking his own development.

The sacral-chakra personality's choice of partner is of primary importance, more so than for any other chakra type.

The particular fear that the sacral-chakra personality has to face is the fear of loss and abandonment by one's partner. This often leads to uncontrolled jealousy.

The best way for the sacral personality type to avoid these dangers is to pay particular attention to the development of the complementary chakra—the forehead chakra, which confers wisdom, intuition, and fantasy. Sacral-chakra types need to develop these powers to reach their full potential. They have a very good chance of finding fulfillment if they remain aware of their creative joyfulness and their healing power and use these gifts in everyday life. Then not only will they enjoy a particularly happy and fulfilled life, but they can have a positive influence on the world around them.

The Navel-Chakra Type

The navel chakra is associated with the element fire. From this chakra arises the most powerful energy. The proper development of this chakra is a prerequisite for the full unfolding of one's potential. Not only is it the most important reservoir of energy, it is the center from which *prana*, the life force, emanates. The chakra controls this energy and determines its circulation throughout the body.

Healthy self-awareness and positive self-esteem have their foundation in the strength of the navel chakra. Navel-chakra personalities act from their gut, their vital human center. At the same time, the fire of the third chakra is seen in sensitivity toward others. Serious problems often result if this energy center is blocked.

Character

The primary characteristics of the navel-chakra personality are willpower and self-control. The pursuit of their goals and control of their thought processes has absolute priority for these individuals. No wonder that the navel-chakra personality is the prototype for all successful people.

Will power, perseverance, and self-control make navel-chakra people most likely to succeed.

These personalities exercise great influence on the people with whom they come in contact and the world around them. They are the ones who set things in motion and bring them to their conclusion. Whatever profession they choose, they will almost certainly make a go of it. But they are leaders, not followers, and do not thrive in subordinate positions. They need to bear in mind that the drive to succeed carries certain responsibilities.

Strengths

The greatest strength of navel-chakra personalities is their extraordinary willpower. The abundant positive energy that is governed by the third chakra will in most cases ensure that their power and influence is used for good purposes. By combining their great willpower with their natural empathy, sensitivity, and ardent pursuit of higher levels of

Their extraordinary will power ensures that navel-chakra types will attain whatever goals they set for themselves.

being, they will find the proper path to follow. The important thing for them is to make sure that the goals they set out to achieve are of benefit to their environment and their fellows.

People with highly developed navel chakras often channel their will along the path of self-development and concentrate on realizing all of their capabilities. For that reason, they can succeed in the harmonious development of all of their energy centers. Many of the great enlightened souls, when young, showed the qualities associated with a dominant navel chakra.

Many great enlightened souls can be seen to have been dominated by the navel chakra in their youth.

It is of utmost importance that energy circulate properly throughout the body. The navel-chakra personality abides in the center of strength. It is easy for him or her to exercise control over the flow of energy. In this way, sickness and hesitation are easily avoided. Manifold possibilities lie open to those individuals if they can guard against the dangers that the strength of the third chakra calls forth.

Challenges

The great power of the navel chakra can bring about correspondingly great dangers if it is not properly directed. They can be particularly exacerbated by the extreme competitiveness of modern industrial society.

When the desirable qualities of strength and willpower become disconnected from the source of positive energy, people can use them only to attain their own ends. This will impede their spiritual development and can cause great pain to others.

As said before, the great abilities of the navel-chakra personality call for great responsibility in their use. When these energies are inharmoniously developed, their great positive strength can turn into its opposite. Then one seeks power for its own sake and becomes so obsessed with personal success that all other considerations are forgotten. Other people and their concerns are dismissed as unimportant or simply disregarded. Politicians hungry for power and unscrupulous businesspeople are often of this type.

Men are more at risk than women from dangers of these kinds, since their latent aggressive masculine energy will intensify the masculine energy of the chakra. Women are less easily caught up in these snares. Men are normally more ruthless and power-hungry than women.

Navel-chakra personalities are rarely dominated by fear. If they are afraid of anything, it is loss of control. The defects that we have spoken of will appear only if the many positive energies that issue from this chakra are suppressed. As a general rule, navel-chakra people have the natural and fortunate ability to develop their personalities in a harmonious and moral fashion. It is especially important for them to concentrate on two other chakras: the complementary chakra (the throat chakra), which stands for communication, inspiration, and truth; and the heart chakra as well. The heart's energy will suffuse the strength of the navel chakra with its healing power.

Finally, navel-chakra types need to learn the art of relaxation. It will help them find the peace and contentment that they may otherwise lack and that can prevent them from losing their way.

Lack of scruples and the desire for or misuse of power can result from one-sided development of the navel chakra.

The Heart-Chakra Type

The heart chakra corresponds to the element air. Its energy bestows peace. The fourth chakra lies at the center of the chakra system and is thus closely connected to all of the other chakras.

From this center flows energy that can penetrate all things and turn them to the good, that affects the highest and the lowest, the power of love.

Character

Love and compassion are the main characteristics of the heart chakra. The more strongly this center is developed, the more one is moved by the selfless love that has the power to conquer all things.

The heart-chakra person is distinguished by warmth, lovingkindness, tolerance, and compassion for his or her neighbors. And this warmth of feeling is not limited to those in one's immediate circle. It spills over to all living beings.

The heart chakra is the basis for harmonious relationships with other people.

Heart-chakra personalities are well aware that there is pain and suffering in the world, but this does not make them despair. They know (sometimes perhaps at an unconscious level) that all sorrow can be redeemed by love's power. They bring love into the world and thereby help to ease its suffering.

This loving attitude is also directed toward themselves. They know how to treat themselves with care and respect, accepting their weaknesses as part of their humanity.

Those who do what they do with love can be happy and do good work in almost any profession. But they can make particularly valuable contributions to the helping professions, where their healing energy and their wise counsel are put to their best use.

It is not unusual to find great artists who belong to this personality type, since only those works that are fashioned and suffused with love have the power to deeply move and comfort others.

Strengths

The strong points of the heart-chakra personality can take many forms, but all spring from the underlying force of love. People who have opened their heart chakra have the possibility of making the world a better place. And this does not have to mean that they need to occupy a grand role on the world's stage (although they are capable of doing so). The energy they bring to every encounter can make a positive difference.

The compassion and tolerance that result from the development of the heart chakra lead to an all-embracing love that is not limited by personal concerns.

By their simple presence, such people exercise a positive influence on their neighbors and their environment. The peace that is in their hearts and their capacity for self-acceptance radiate a harmony that has a calming and comforting effect on others.

The openness and tolerance with which heart-chakra personality types meet the world are especially pronounced. Here it is important to note that this tolerance is not at all the same thing as indifference, although the two are often confused.

Their thoughts and ideas can have a far-reaching influence, but they do not hold themselves apart from problematic situations or unpleasant people. Their hearts and hands are open to all. They are accepting of others but not thrown off course by them. Despite their openness, they remain true to themselves.

Whatever heart-chakra personalities do is done with lovingkindness.

It is easy for heart-chakra people to see that behind apparent differences and distinctions, all being comes from the same source, a source that is not separate from their own being. Through their caring natures, they have a transforming effect on everything around them.

Such people are bound to succeed in anything that has to do with spiritual growth and transformation. That may be because they realize that it is not willpower that will bring them to their goal. As counselors, doctors, or therapists, but also as mothers and fathers, people with dominant heart chakras will find deep fulfillment and satisfaction.

Challenges

There is one particular danger that heart-chakra types face: that they will show even greater tolerance and consideration to themselves than to others and not pay sufficient attention to the challenges of personal growth. In extreme cases, this can lead to complacency and even stagnation. That is a great pity, since the proper development of this chakra opens the door to higher dimensions, in which the power of love can make itself felt.

When their higher chakras are blocked, heart-chakra personalities can love indiscriminately and lose themselves in love. Although love can never be seen as a negative quality, incorrectly channeled it can prevent one from taking responsibility for oneself and impede self-development. This inappropriate, overpowering love can deprive others of the opportunity to develop the initiative and sense of responsibility that they need to travel their own path in life.

When the heart chakra is strong, it is light work to care for one's partner, children, friends, and neighbors.

The most important task for those whose heart chakra is dominant is to become aware that all levels of being need to be attended to and developed. Unlike the other chakras, the heart chakra has no complement—there is no need for a counterbalance for love. It is at rest in the center.

Thus it is advisable that heart-chakra personalities work on the development and harmonization of all their chakras. Such work can have wonderful results. The power of love can, for example, lead to the highest artistic expression.

The Throat-Chakra Type

The throat chakra is the lowest of the three higher chakras, which are connected with the higher mental and spiritual aspects of the personality. It lies between the heart chakra and the third eye, and thus it plays an intermediary role between thought and feeling and points the way toward overcoming duality.

The element with which this chakra is associated, ether or space, reinforces this intermediary function, as it is the link between the material and immaterial worlds.

Character

The principal theme of this chakra is communication. It is imperative for those in whom the throat chakra is dominant to share their ideas with others and clearly express their thoughts. They set great store by rational explanation. But this does not mean that they are devoid of feeling; on the contrary, they are gifted with emotional intelligence. Drained of emotion, thought by itself is irrational and unreasonable.

This need to communicate is by no means exclusively directed toward the outer world. It embraces inner communication as well: the exploration of the unconscious mind, one's inner language that brings clarity and fullness to thought.

Those in whom the throat chakra is dominant clarify things for themselves before explaining them to others. In so doing, they find the courage to stand by their opinions and give truth expression.

Throat-chakra people make good teachers and mediators. They have the greatest verbal abilities. They can also realize their gifts through the arts, as artistic expression is one of the highest forms of communication.

They are likely to be gifted with musical talent and are particularly drawn to singing. They also make fine actors. The greatest writers and poets belong to this type. In short, they will excel at any endeavor that is primarily directed at communicating with other people. They are especially adept at explicating complex ideas in such areas as academia and the sciences.

The need that throat-chakra types have to communicate and express themselves leads them into careers that put a premium on communication skills.

Strengths

The ability to communicate and verbal facility are the great strengths of the throat-chakra personality.

The strengths of throat-chakra personalities are many-faceted, and this is in itself a strength. Their lively interest in a great number of different subjects makes it easy for them to learn new things, make connections, and expand their horizons.

With the help of their highly developed intellects, they have the ability to synthesize, to see the patterns underlying disparate events and ideas. This is a prerequisite for clear thinking and the basis of true creativity, which results from bringing together common things in new and unexpected ways.

Clarity of thought has its natural milieu in a world of symbols, particularly the world of language, our most fundamental symbolic structure. Those who have a throat-chakra personality are the masters of this world. Not only are they possessed of great verbal ability, but they have the gift of clearly expressing their thoughts and making their ideas comprehensible to others. That is their greatest strength—the ability to communicate.

But people don't only use words to understand others and make themselves understood. Feelings, intuitions, and spiritual insights cannot always be translated into words. Here other kinds of communication become important: gesture, vocal intonation that conveys

Throat-chakra types can achieve great success as singers or actors.

emotion, or the expressive powers of art and music. Though their greatest strength lies in the spoken word, throat-chakra types are versed in all of these different modalities of communication and, as was mentioned before, often blessed with great musical talent. Music perhaps offers the richest opportunity to integrate the material and spiritual levels and thus to transcend dualistic thinking.

For such people, the truth is the highest goal. This is the organizing principle behind all of their striving and activity. They put their great power to communicate in the service of the truth. This struggle for the truth and the power to express it are the distinguishing features of the throat-chakra personality.

Challenges

This commitment to the truth is the greatest strength of the throat-chakra personality, but it can also become the greatest problem. These individuals are compelled to speak the truth, but they can only express the truth as it appears to them. Everyone is stamped by his or her own experience and sees the world through that lens. For this reason, truth is always subjective and relative.

Unfortunately, those with dominant throat chakras sometimes equate their perceptions with absolute truth, commiting the error of spending all their strength announcing a truth that is merely relative and does not hold for everyone. They have a hard time recognizing and accepting that other people see things differently and that differing points of view are legitimate.

Throat-chakra personality types sometimes consider their subjective truth to be absolute.

If these errors are aggravated, such people, through their considerable powers of speech, may manipulate others who are not as adept and become self-aggrandizing and grandiose. They often insist on having others see things their way, and this can easily lead to disharmony and bruised feelings.

These snares can be easily avoided if one pays attention to the complementary chakra, the navel chakra. The development of the heart-chakra qualities of warmth and tolerance are also of tremendous importance.

The one lesson that the throat-chakra personality needs to learn is that the truth is not just one thing and that to honestly strive for it one must begin by saying, "It seems to me . . ."

The Forehead-Chakra Type

The sixth chakra is the source of intuition, fantasy, and pure perception. It does not correspond to any element, since it is concerned with stepping beyond materiality and the connection to the world of the mind and spirit. The forehead chakra makes it possible to attain intuitive awareness and direct experience of that which lies outside the realm of the senses. These experiences include what we refer to as extrasensory perception. By binding humans to the spiritual world, this chakra transforms ordinary dualistic thinking and leads to a sense of inner peace.

Character

Forehead-chakra personalities can envision abstract goals and realize them.

The central themes of the forehead chakra are wisdom and self-awareness. This type of person strives for the full unfolding of his or her higher self. The means used is the search for self-awareness, and the goal is the wisdom that lies beyond the world of thought and duality.

People for whom the forehead chakra is dominant can penetrate to the heart of matters and see things that remain hidden to others. Their power of fantasy contributes to this. It is the source of their creativity, their gift for bringing new ideas into being. Such people can find the greatest fulfillment as teachers, psychologists, and artists. As artists they are often pioneers; they don't depend on the opinion of others and can be said to be proponents of "art for art's sake." As healers they can greatly benefit anyone with whom they come into contact.

Strengths

The greatest strength of forehead-chakra types lies not in what they are but in what they are striving to become. Their quest for knowledge of the world that lies behind the world of appearances will make them complete people. They find it easy to fulfill their potential, provided that their development is not obstructed by blockages in the other chakras.

Those with highly developed forehead chakras will see farther and deeper. They can create a picture for themselves of what is to come and are thereby in an ideal position to realize their vision of the future. This holds for their own personal growth as well as for the amelioration of suffering in the world.

By and large, the acute perceptions of forehead-chakra personalities are not projected upon the outside world; rather, they serve to cultivate and shape their inner life. Every step on the path of self-awareness will take them closer to their final goal, true wisdom.

Their visionary power lets forehead-chakra types be shaped not by what is but by what might be.

Such people have an innate ability to recognize falsehood and delusions and avoid their snares. From this stems the inner peace they experience and the positive energy they radiate. This increases as they make their way along the path of spiritual development.

One distinctive characteristic of forehead-chakra types is intense creativity. This often goes unrecognized even by them. For these individuals, creative ferment is a natural element; it is as if there were nothing special about it. This creative energy often assumes forms of expression that are hard for others to fully comprehend. They are pioneers. Those who do recognize their gifts respond enthusiastically as if to an entirely new way of looking at things.

The forehead-chakra personality is a natural healer.

Forehead-chakra personalities have another gift as well. They allow their ideas to ripen within themselves. They attain what Patanjali, author of the Yoga Sutras, describes as the goal of yoga: "Bringing peace to the constant movement of the mind." Once this still point is reached, one transcends duality; male/female, right brain/left brain, intellect/emotion, intuition/perception are all united in the abiding awareness of oneness and peace.

In their search for higher realities forehead-chakra types need to avoid losing their connection to the material world.

Challenges

The great abilities of forehead-chakra personalities can lead to equally great dangers. By seeing through appearances, they can lose contact with the material world in which people have their being, and thereby distance themselves from their fellows. Their insight and independence enable them to go it alone, but true spiritual development requires deepening involvement with others.

Loss of contact with the material world can lead to isolation and depression when the forehead-chakra person has not progressed very far in his or her inner development.

If one develops this chakra at the expense of all the others, and if blockages in other chakras are not dealt with, acute powers of perception can work to one's disadvantage and even lead to grave mental and emotional problems including psychosis and schizophrenia. These are, unfortunately, ailments to which forehead-chakra types are particularly prone.

But these problems will occur only when there is an unbalanced development of this center and the other chakras are blocked or extremely weak.

The most important task for forehead-chakra personalities is to work on the harmonious development of the entire chakra system as an integral component of their search for wisdom. It is especially necessary to cultivate the energies of the sacral chakra to serve as a complement to their highly refined sensibility.

Crown-chakra personalities strive for the highest levels of being and self-transcendence.

The Crown-Chakra Type

The crown chakra connects humanity to the oneness of being. Here rests pure awareness untainted by any duality: cosmic consciousness. The full unfolding of this chakra signifies the state known as enlightenment.

The crown chakra does not have a corresponding element, since its energy lies wholly outside of the material world. Its activation will open one's perception of that which lies beyond the grasp of the senses. All religious and spiritual experiences are mediated by the crown chakra.

By fully developing one's crown chakra one attains enlightenment.

Character

The central theme of the crown chakra is enlightenment and self-realization. Crown-chakra personalities seek liberation, directing their faith, spirituality, and striving toward the highest level of self-realization, where the self itself is transcended. This goal gives meaning to their lives. Sometimes such people seem not to be of this world.

Crown-chakra people are drawn to self-renunciation and self-abnegation.

Religion is important to people with dominant crown chakras. They may become monks, pastors, or spiritual teachers.

But that is a serious misconception. In fact, they live fully as a part of this world but remain untouched by the illusions and delusions that most people confuse with reality.

The crown-chakra personality is not easy to comprehend; it can take many forms. Crown-chakra personalities are affected by all the other chakras, more so than any of the other types.

This may explain why crown-chakra types are easily misunderstood by other people. It is not that they seek to shroud themselves in mystery. Rather, their experiences and perceptions are so different from ordinary people's that they may seem incomprehensible.

Crown-chakra personalities can succeed in any position, situation, or profession. They are not dependent upon circumstance.

However, they are often engaged in areas having to do with religion or spirituality. They may serve as lowly monks or potent religious dignitaries. Some can be seen actively engaged in society, others found in remote hermitages. Crown-chakra people are often spiritual teachers.

Strengths

The primary strength of the crown-chakra type is unconditional striving for perfection. These individuals will let nothing stand in the way of their goal and will stretch beyond the limitations of material being to get there. The well-developed crown chakra furnishes powers that others may look upon as supernatural. But for crown-chakra personalities, they are natural by-products of their approach to their true nature.

The one who has reached the highest level of self-realization can become a source of strength and inspiration for others.

Crown-chakra people radiate energy that effects positive transformation. Their goodness and peace make themselves felt, and they give strength to other people.

Often crown-chakra people will serve as catalysts: They inspire people to turn their attention toward spirituality and self-realization. Often they accomplish these positive effects quite without meaning to. Such benefits seem to flow naturally from their being.

It should not be surprising that the well-developed crown chakra personality shares many of the strengths associated with the other chakras. The crown chakra elevates the energies of all the other chakras.

Challenges

It is somewhat misleading to speak of dangers insofar as crown-chakra personalities are concerned. Circumstances that may endanger other people do not really pose a threat to them. But there are less advantageous roads they can travel. They may, for example, completely withdraw from the world and practice extreme self-denial. This can retard their development and diminish the positive influence they have on others.

Where the crown chakra is developed and the other chakras are ignored or blocked, a person can be prone to superstition, drawn to black magic, or subject to spiritual sicknesses.

So it is vital that crown-chakra types pay due consideration to the development of the other chakras, particularly the root chakra. The energy of this chakra provides the connection to the earth, while the crown chakra draws them heavenward. The activation of the root chakra will provide a powerful impulse in the process of spiritual growth.

5 The Psychology of the Chakras

The dominance of any of the chakras produces certain psychic effects and gives rise to certain qualities: blocked or weak chakras also leave their mark on the mind and spirit. This chapter deals primarily with psychological problems that may arise and presents some possible ways of remedying them.

Later chapters will explore methods that address other kinds of problems and suggest, for example, ways to purify and elevate the energy of particular chakras.

Fundamentally we will be treating blocked and weakened chakras in much the same fashion. A blockage is more narrowly limited, even though it can weaken a well-developed chakra. When we speak of a weak chakra, we are normally referring to the chakra in its entirety. The difference between the two is most clearly seen when it is a question of a strong chakra that nonetheless is blocked.

The effects of a weak or blocked chakra on the soul can manifest themselves in psychological problems.

When Energy Doesn't Circulate

The underlying causes of blockages and weaknesses are similar. Blockages prevent energy that is present from flowing. In weak chakras, there is not enough energy to ensure its circulation. The difference is important only insofar as blockages need to be removed, whereas weak chakras need to be infused with energy. The psychological effects are not really all that different.

Once you have completed the chakra personality tests and checked the results, you will be in a position to judge the health of your chakras. You will have filled in the fields that indicate weak chakras and marked with black circles those chakras where blockages may exist.

Turn now in the following pages to the section for each chakra that needs work in one or both of these areas.

Blockages in the Root Chakra

When the root chakra is weak, a person is not well grounded. Serious blockages or weaknesses are obstacles to human development. Just as the overall growth of a tree is dependent upon the health of its root system, so the functioning of all the other chakras depends upon the proper development of the base chakra.

Children who are rejected by their parents often develop disturbances in the root chakra.

At a psychological level, one encounters the problem of a basic lack of trust; this is then expressed on all other levels. The initial causes of this misfortune usually lie in early childhood. People who were unwanted as children, neglected or abandoned, or, worse, treated cruelly or abused have a hard time learning to trust in others, in themselves, or in life in general. A deep, abiding suspiciousness cautions them to always keep their guard up. Often they project their fear onto concrete things and develop phobic reactions to such things as spiders or dogs.

Lack of Trust: Anxiety and Depression

Because of their fear, people so affected can become overly dependent on others, who seem to provide a sense of security. Ideally, they can then be helped to strengthen the root chakra and become more self-reliant. But dependency can often lead to catastrophe: The already inadequate root-chakra energy can become more attenuated or blockages more entrenched. A poorly developed root chakra also manifests itself as indecisiveness, the sense of being easily overwhelmed by difficulties and going from one crisis to the next.

To direct one's attention toward spirituality in the hope of finding a secure resting place won't produce good results in these cases. That would be going about things the wrong way. The premature development of the higher energy centers will only further weaken the root chakra. A well-grounded spirituality that will advance one to higher levels of being must be built upon solid ground. Otherwise there is the very real danger of self-delusion and unfounded negative imaginings.

Such people must turn their attention to the earth. They need to learn to develop trust in being, become aware of their own physicality, and forge deepening connections to the natural world.

Blockages in the Sacral Chakra

Blockages in the sacral chakra disturb one's connection with the world of the senses and diminish one's sensuality. They keep one from taking pleasure in life. Without a sense of joy, one can neither attend to nor fully respect the process of one's own unfolding.

The basis for these blockages frequently extends back into childhood, to the early stages of sexual development. Adults who consider sexuality to be somewhat taboo dam the flow of energy from their sacral chakra. This can hinder the healthy development of their own children. Symptoms such as impotence, frigidity, or diminished sexual appetite are often common in such people. It should be noted that the root of such problems cannot always be traced back to childhood. They can also arise from later experiences. But they almost always indicate a weakness in the sacral chakra. People with poorly developed or blocked sacral chakras will feel themselves to be without the power or the motivation to set something new into motion. They can't see how their efforts will be rewarded. From this stem depression and creative blocks.

The Lack of Sensuality

For creative people, blocks are warning signs that are not easily ignored. These people have the advantage that the weakness in the sacral chakra usually does not have its roots in early childhood; it is rather a result of failure at a later stage of development and will resolve itself once the chakra is reactivated.

The lack of sensual pleasure leads in many cases to paradoxical reactions. Many so affected become prey to addictions. This arises from an unconscious urge to heighten all sensual experience. This need is answered by intoxication. And although intoxication can for a time loosen blocks and inhibitions, the end result is a numbing of the senses and disturbances in the flow of energy.

When the sacral chakra is weakened or blocked, one should pay attention to one's senses. Joy and desire for life can emerge only when a sensuous appreciation of the world is coupled with a loving acceptance of one's own body.

If parents who are repressed or afraid of their own sexuality transmit these traits to their children, they in turn will suffer from problems related to the thwarted development of the sacral chakra.

Blockages in the Navel Chakra

The navel chakra serves as the body's most important reservoir of energy and the central distribution point for that energy, which is also known as prana. Weakness in no other chakra has as detrimental an effect: A weak navel chakra will hinder the development of all the other chakras.

People in whom the third chakra is weak suffer above all from a lack of life energy. This has serious consequences, since all the other chakras are also affected by this lack of energy. On a psychological level, such people are prey to feelings of insecurity. They also find it very difficult to see things through to their conclusion. Often they are too easily swayed by authority figures, even when they recognize at some level that this is not in their own best interests. Or they can react in an opposite fashion. Feeling that they are overly susceptible to authority, they may become defiant and develop an allergy to authority of any kind. The result is doubt and mistrust in people, even those who might be able to help them.

Lack of Self-Esteem

Eating disorders like anorexia can be traced to disturbances in the navel chakra.

This insecurity and thoughtless adherence to or defiance of authority is related to another problem that comes from a weak navel chakra: lack of self-esteem. People who do not pay attention to or care for themselves will have little luck in unfolding their full potential. On the contrary, they believe that they have nothing and are worth nothing.

A blockage in the navel chakra can lead to psychological problems such as eating disorders, especially anorexia. (These problems may not arise when the chakra is just weak but not blocked.) Often they are indicative of a blocked sacral chakra as well.

Also common are insomnia and nightmares with themes such as being chased or killed, being sick, or being unable to move. The sudden transition from deep sleep to anxious awakening is also a sign of problems with this chakra. Those affected wake from sleep unrefreshed, feeling tired and worn out.

Serious weaknesses or blockages in the navel chakra are always the first problem to be addressed when one begins chakra work. Solving these problems often results in a sudden burst of energy that spontaneously resolves problems in other chakras as well.

Blockages in the Heart Chakra

The heart chakra is the seat of love and compassion. People with poorly developed or blocked heart chakras are faced with problems that have to do with loving relationships and the proper balance between giving and taking. They often complain of loneliness and feelings of isolation. They have a hard time connecting with others or enjoying satisfying emotional relationships. They can't easily open themselves to other people or share their thoughts and feelings. They can't give love or receive it.

When one's heart chakra is disturbed it becomes difficult to give or receive love.

To other people they appear cold. This is only true in part: A weakened or blocked heart chakra prevents one's inner feelings from unfolding. Such people can't seem to find a way of expressing what they feel, and the world around them often takes this as a sign of hostility and responds accordingly.

Impersonal Friendliness

People in whom the heart chakra is weak but not fully blocked understand that they have a problem and take it seriously. They try to be friendly, helpful, and tolerant. But despite their best efforts, their relationships remain somehow impersonal, in a way that is hard to describe.

Sometimes when people with weakly developed heart chakras open themselves, they do so in an indiscriminate or inappropriate manner. They lack proper boundaries and tend to make excessive demands on others to compensate for the lack of love they feel.

A blocked or weak heart chakra stems from earlier experiences that have impressed one with the lesson that opening oneself up is fraught with danger. Children from broken homes often suffer from blockages in the heart chakra.

When the heart chakra needs more energy, the first thing you need to recognize is that you are not satisfying your emotional needs. Then you can begin to work on the problem. It is not enough to simply give free rein to your emotions. You have to really experience the power of love. This means, for example, that you shouldn't take for granted the little things that other people do without expecting anything in return.

Blockages in the Throat Chakra

The throat chakra is above all the center of the powers of communication. Most of the difficulties that accompany a weakly developed throat chakra have to do with interchanges between people. Those affected have a hard time expressing themselves. In extreme cases this can manifest itself in speech impediments such as stuttering. Speech defects almost always indicate that work needs to be done on the throat chakra.

But not all problems troubling people who suffer from a weakened throat chakra are so easy to spot. Such people may find it difficult to find the right words, to express their thoughts and feelings, or to strike the right note in their communications with others. All of these are symptomatic of weakness in the throat chakra.

Shyness and the Fear of Expressing One's Opinion

Even less obvious are other difficulties, as for example the fear of asserting or maintaining controversial opinions. Often those who have this problem are unaware of it or unaware that a problem exists. They feel shy about sharing their thoughts and feelings but don't recognize that this is a product of fear. Inhibitions and timidity often are caused by difficulties in communicating, and these point to weakness in the throat chakra.

A speech defect is a clear sign that one needs to work on the throat chakra.

A weakly developed throat chakra also causes problems in communicating with oneself, that is, keeping a channel open to one's unconscious. This leads to a sense of confusion in which it is difficult to get in touch with one's own needs and feelings. This is not a sign of mental illness. Those with weak or blocked chakras are not confused about the reality of their situation, their place in space and time. They are not irrational. Rather, it is hard for them to decide and to express what it is they really want; the communication with deeper levels of their being is compromised.

People who encounter these problems are well advised to turn their attention to music. Even if they believe that they aren't musical, they can benefit from music's healing power, which can help them to develop their powers of self-expression.

Blockages in the Forehead Chakra

The higher functions of mind and soul are centered in the forehead chakra. When it is blocked or weakened, the capacity for clear thought, insight, and fantasy is diminished. That does not mean that those affected are stupid. Someone with a strong forehead chakra can make full use of his or her intelligence. People of high intelligence who have a weak forehead chakra do not become less intelligent; they simply have a hard time translating their intelligence and imagination into action.

Learning disabilities and lack of concentration are also signs of weakness in the sixth chakra. Smart, imaginative people can suffer a great deal from such problems, especially since they have the feeling that there are latent or dormant powers within themselves that they can't make use of.

Disturbances in the forehead chakra make it difficult to concentrate or organize one's thoughts.

Improving Concentration

Attention-deficit disorders are also symptoms of a weak forehead chakra. The energy level of this chakra is insufficient to let one gather one's thoughts. Thinking is scattered, skipping from one subject to another. This is not only reflected on the level of ratiocination but in one's fantasy life as well. Here it is perhaps harder to observe, since creative imagination is often confused with ungoverned thinking and arbitrary associations. Taken to an extreme, these thinking disorders can manifest as mental illnesses such as schizophrenia, which is a direct product of a blockage in the forehead chakra. Blockages also lie behind such problems as free-floating anxiety, delusion, superstition, or mental confusion. People with underdeveloped forehead chakras often complain that life seems purposeless or devoid of meaning.

If your forehead chakra is weak or blocked, you should not start meditation right away. Success will be hard to attain, since the scattered nature of your thinking will prevent you from stilling the mind or concentrating it on a fixed point. Free meditation, letting your thoughts run freely, will only aggravate the problem. To build the necessary foundation for further progress, the powers of concentration must be gradually improved. Learning to read music or embarking on a serious course of study is a good place to start.

Blockages in the Crown Chakra

The crown chakra is the transmitter of pure being, spiritual completion, and the highest level of awareness that transcends duality. People in whom the crown chakra is only weakly developed (strictly speaking, there is no such thing as a blocked crown chakra) feel trapped in the material world and have a sense of emptiness that they can't fully understand or describe.

When depression arises for no apparent reason, it may be a signal of a disturbance in the crown chakra.

General discontent is a clear sign of problems in the crown chakra. Even when everything seems to be going fine, there remains a persistent sense of dissatisfaction, a feeling that something is missing. One feels unhappy without knowing why.

In extreme cases, people can fall into deep depressions and be overcome by a sense of the world's pain or existential angst.

Difficulty Deciding and Discontent

In lieu of depression, people can experience emotional numbness and exhaustion, a kind of anomie in which it becomes difficult to get interested in anything—especially spiritual disciplines. They believe that their emptiness stems from a lack of material goods or ill health. But even when these problems are dealt with, the feeling of discontent does not go away.

People in whom the crown chakra is weak also have a hard time making decisions. They lack a worthy goal for which to strive. This condition can give rise to confusion: They feel that there is an emptiness inside them, but they don't where it is. There is a blind spot in their awareness.

When the crown chakra is weak, the imprint of the other chakras on the personality is more distinct, and consequently this weakness manifests in different ways. A root-chakra personality with a weak crown chakra will have difficulty restraining and controlling his or her instinctual drives; a heart-chakra personality will be less negatively influenced by a weak crown chakra and can more easily make up for this defect.

Anyone whose crown chakra is weakened must learn the way to stillness. In the experience of conscious stillness, the highest chakra will open itself to the energy of the universe.

The Chakras and Human Development

Everything in the universe is in the process of change. Nothing stays the same. The universe is developing; the galaxies, stars, planets, and all living things are always changing. To stop changing is to die—and even death is just the beginning of a new phase of development.

Human beings are no exceptions to this universal rule. On a physical level, this is obvious, but our minds and souls are also involved in this same process of development. We are not the same people we were a year ago, a month ago, a second ago.

Human development is closely connected with the energy flow within the chakras. This insight can help us to attune ourselves with natural rhythms and identify the needs and demands of each phase of life. In the next section, you will learn the following:

- How developmental phases follows a septenary (seven-stage) rhythm
- How the chakras of the unborn child develop in the mother's womb
- The child's developmental phases
- The steps to take to fulfill each stage of life
- That even the highest levels of awareness are not immune to change

The Cycles of the Seven Chakras

Human life unfolds in a rhythmic fashion and is characterized by changing needs and demands. This rhythm is bound up with the chakras and corresponds to the energy that is continuously rising and falling through the chakra system. But there isn't just one rhythm; the rhythms are many and varied.

Human life is subject to rhythmical patterns, in which the chakras play an important part.

One of the most basic rhythms is the heartbeat. With each beat of the heart, one of the seven chakras receives an energy impulse. Every second that impulse changes and another level becomes affected. Encompassing this rhythm is that of the breath. At every breath, the energy rises to a higher chakra until, reaching the crown chakra, it returns once again to the root chakra, and the cycle is renewed. This

Knowledge about the role cycles of energy play in human development can help you get in sync with life's natural rhythms.

The seven-month cycle is the general rule. But its exact length will depend upon the individual.

rhythm influences our mood and state of mind. Life, of course, has broader rhythms than these. The rhythmic cycle of the waxing and waning moon is of the greatest importance for prenatal development. By being aware of this, the mother-to-be can have a positive influence on her unborn child's growth and prepare it for its first steps into the world.

Ideally, at birth the child's development is subject to a seven-month rhythm. In actuality, the rhythmic period can last longer than seven months. For most people, it is closer to a year, and a child's growth is usually measured in years. It is important nonetheless to be aware of intervals of seven (lunar) months.

The first septenary cycle of the child is thus completed somewhere between seven times seven months (about four years) and seven years. This corresponds to what trained practitioners have actually observed.

The seven-month developmental cycle guides us through our entire lives, but is overlaid with a longer, seven-year cycle. This is comparable to the seven-times-seven-month cycle, though it is a bit longer.

This encompassing rhythm is even more elastic than the foregoing one. It is best to regard each phase as lasting somewhere between five and seven years.

For convenience, we will refer in the following discussion to the period of the rhythmic cycle as seven years. This is in fact the duration for many people and is a useful generality as long it is not taken to be a hard-and-fast rule for everyone.

The great cycle of life's development can then be seen as seven times seven years (forty-nine years) or in the ideal case seven times seven times seven months (twenty-nine years). The Buddha came close to this ideal. He achieved enlightenment at the age of thirty-four.

We will now focus on the three most important of these septenary cycles:

Parents can influence the prenatal development of their children and shape their future for the better.

- The seven-month cycle that the unborn child undergoes in the mother's womb
- The seven-times-seven-month cycle that encompasses the first stage of the child's development (which can last up to seven years)
- The great cycle of development that will last between twenty-nine and forty-nine years and defines our lives.

The Development of the Unborn Child

While the embryo is in the womb, its chakras are developing and shaping its future life. If its parents are aware of this process, they can help get their child off to the best start. Thus, for each stage of prenatal development, they can take into consideration the chakra that corresponds to that stage and support its healthy unfolding.

The Seven-Month Birth Cycle

Chakra	All	7	6	5	4	3	2	1
Month	1–2	3	4	5	6	7	8	9

First and Second Months

In the first two months after the fertilization of the egg, the embryo is perceptible only through a microscope and is hard to recognize as human. It begins to develop arms and legs, a spinal column, a face, eyes, and a heart. After two months, the embryo is visible to the naked eye and is just over an inch long.

From the primordial condition of oneness with the universe to enlightenment is a long tortuous journey for the human being.

In this phase, the child-to-be is still at one with the universe. The chakras are not differentiated but rather, as in the higher stages of enlightenment, unified in one energy field. The embryo dwells in a condition that the adult will strive to attain. In this phase, the only thing necessary for the fetus's development is the unconditional love and happiness of its mother.

Third Month

The fetus develops from the embryo. The main organs of the body become differentiated and connect with one another. After blood cells begin to form, the little person can begin to develop. The production of hormones begins.

Now the differentiation of the chakras also begins. The first active chakra is the crown chakra. The developing child approaches the material world, although it is still immersed in the world of spirit.

The mother can support the development of her child with practices that awaken the activity of the crown chakra, for example, meditation. The energies that are awakened through the human power of stillness can to a large extent be transmitted to the fetus. The foundations of one's spiritual life are established in this phase.

Fourth Month

In the fourth month, the child's face begins to take shape. The fetus is now six inches long. Eyelids, nose, and lips are recognizable. The fetus becomes more animated and makes grasping motions with its hands. Beginning in the fourth month, it can perceive smells. In this phase, the forehead chakra is active. This means that, among other things, prepa-

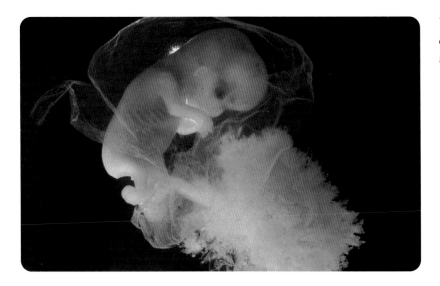

The chakras begin to develop while the child is still in the womb.

rations begin for the higher mental functions. Now the development of the growing child approaches the world of the mind, which it will enter at birth. The fetus is becoming human. During this time, the mother has many opportunities to foster the energies associated with the forehead chakra. In this way, she promotes the future unfolding of the mental capacities of her child. She ought to read a lot, occupy herself with a world of ideas—and speak to her child in her thoughts. This will greatly help the child, who will perceive and respond to her.

Fifth Month

In the fifth month, there are no radical changes in the child's body. Nonetheless, this is an important phase. The fetus grows; its organs assume the form required for their future functioning. The inner structure of the body is better defined. The child begins to distinguish between smells and to perceive light through the mother's belly.

The throat chakra develops in the fifth month, and with it the ability to communicate at all levels. The mother now becomes aware of her child's movements. The sensory organs necessary for communication emerge: the child can see, hear, and sense the world outside.

In the fourth month of life the embryo is governed by the forehead chakra. In the fifth month the energy of the throat chakra asserts itself.

During this time, the mother has many possibilities to actively support the development of her child. She can increase the flow of energy to its throat chakra, which is now in the process of unfolding. Mother— and father—can now speak and sing to their child, play music, and use light to stimulate its awareness. The child begins to be able to distinguish its parents' voices from those of others. Gently speaking to the child will have a calming effect as the sense of hearing sharpens. Music is very important during this phase. And the kind of music played will make a big difference. It should be complex, rich in overtones, but at the same time harmonic and peaceful. Best is classical music, especially Vivaldi, Handel, Bach, and Mozart. Classical Indian music is also highly recommended.

In its fifth month the fetus can distinguish voices and react to them.

Sixth Month

In the sixth month, the child is more constricted by its mother's body. It is now about sixteen inches long and has to assume the typical fetal position. Its physical development proceeds. In the sixth month, in fact, the child's viability outside of the mother's body is theoretically possible. This is the optimal time for the unfolding of the heart chakra. Now

By the fifth month of pregnancy the unborn child has acquired a sense of smell and can recognize its parents' voices.

the feeling of love begins to reside in the human heart. The growing child not only communicates on a mental level with its environment but begins to feel its connection to the world outside. The earliest recollections that a person can possess date from the sixth month (although most people never become aware of them). The brain is not yet sufficiently developed to grasp logical information, but feeling leaves an imprint on it. The sixth month is very important for later relationships and for developing the power of love. The mother needs to communicate her love to her child and provide it with a deep sense of security. The two parents should grow closer together. The child perceives every loving impulse and thereby takes nourishment.

Other possibilities for strengthening the heart chakra are readily available. Meet with good friends. Loving people support the harmonious relationship between the mother and her unborn child. Music is also very important. It should be calming, and its rhythm should correspond with the mother's heartbeat.

Seventh Month

In the seventh month, life gets stronger. The child has a growth spurt. The mother's belly is now markedly swollen. Children who come into the world at this stage will, as a general rule, survive. During this phase, the navel chakra develops. The child has now stepped fully into the physical world. The foundations of its sense of self, its own strength, and its emotions are set down. The child develops the capacity to access and control its life energy. This is evidenced by the fact that the child now becomes very active, and its movements affect the mother as well as itself. This phase is of the utmost importance for the development of self-confidence and will influence the child's chance for success in the world.

The mother should now make a focused effort to respond to her child. She should show that she understands it, that its needs are heard, and that it has an effect on her. She can, for example react to the movements of her child, perhaps sing or speak to it, or gently rub her belly. There are many other ways in which she can actively support the developing energies of the navel chakra. Practices that involve prana are now particularly advantageous for the child, since the navel chakra is vital for storing and controlling prana.

The heart chakra and the navel chakra begin to develop in the sixth and seventh months. The foundations of one's ability to love and relate to others are established at this time.

Eighth Month

There is noticeable growth in the eighth month. The sexual organs are now fully developed. The mother is now very pregnant.

The energetic development corresponds to the unfolding of the sacral chakra. This phase is of great significance for the child's later sexuality, which is mirrored in its physical development. Other areas related to generation in a metaphoric way also come into play: above all, the impulses toward creative and artistic expression and also the ability to transmit healing energy.

This phase of development has a determinative effect on a healthy bodily awareness and the ability to enjoy life.

The mother can help ensure that her child will be able to take pleasure in later life and that his or her artistic abilities will flourish. She should engage in creative activities herself during this period, such as writing, painting, and playing music. The results are not important; what counts is the creative impulse. Even the passive engagement with art and beauty (above all, that found in nature) will be of benefit. Not least, the mother should make use of her own sacral-chakra energy.

In the eighth month of prenatal development the ground is prepared for healthy sexuality, positive body awareness, and the ability to take pleasure in life.

Ninth Month

In the ninth month, the child is ready to emerge from the protective embrace of the mother's body into the world. It still has a bit more growing to do, but in this stage it primarily develops a layer of fat and puts on weight. (Most newborns are heavier than they will be at the age of one month.) The child now prepares itself for the birthing process. Its position changes, with the head down in the birth canal.

This is the time for the development of the root chakra. On an energetic level, the child is now at a crossroads. It has to get ready for life in the material world. Sometimes when its preparations are not complete, the child fights against the birth process. This incomplete development must then be compensated for after birth.

On an energetic level, the fetus is now completely ready to begin life in the world outside of its mother's womb. In the last month of pregnancy, the child is occupied with tasks that will assume new meaning once it is born.

The first year of life is also concerned with the development of the root chakra. The theme of this chakra corresponds to the child's basic survival needs: the will to live and basic sense of trust.

Children who receive enough root-chakra energy will be less prone to illness. Their chances for survival are greater.

In this phase, the mother should make a special effort to radiate a sense of security. Anxiety and depression weaken the root chakra and with it the will to live.

If the mother is happy and secure during this period, the child will find its way more easily. In order to avoid unnecessary anxiety and not become overwhelmed by the birth process, the mother needs to prepare for labor and the birth of her child. Above all, she should strive to focus on the beauty of, and the positive things that will result from the birth of her child. Her child will feel and understand all of this. The many opportunities available for strengthening the root chakra will help not only the child but the mother as well.

A mother can strengthen her unborn child's will to survive and sense of trust if she looks forward to the birth with confidence and joy.

The sense of being lovingly welcomed makes the child's first steps into the world much easier.

Development of the Child

At birth, the child begins an entirely new phase of life. The energetic cycle turns in the opposite direction. Each phase lasts for about a year, although the optimal natural rhythm lasts for seven months. The development of the chakras begins where prenatal life left off, with the development of the root chakra.

After the child's birth the development of the root chakra continues. The more loving acceptance the parents can display during this phase, the more secure their child will be in later life.

Prenatal development lays the child's energetic foundation. In the first seven years of life this foundation will be built upon and patterns become engrained. This is why the first seven years are so decisive for later life. At the end of this cycle, the child emerges as a specific chakra personality type, though this can later change.

As psychology has long recognized, the patterns that are adopted in childhood can be changed later in life only through conscious effort. For this reason, early upbringing is extremely important. If parents are informed about the individual stages of chakra development, they will not only better understand their child but also ensure that his or her physical, mental, and spiritual development proceeds unhindered. Through the stimulation of the chakra energies that are important for each phase, the healthy influence of a positive upbringing can be reinforced.

Year One

In the first year of life, just as in the last month of pregnancy, the root chakra is particularly active. Important themes are the basic sense of trust, stability, stamina, the will to live, the connection with earth and nature, and the feeling for the natural rhythms of life. Indeed, the first year of life is the most important of all. All cycles meet at this point in time. The prenatal cycle ends with the unfolding of the root chakra, the seven-year cycle begins, and the great seven-times-seven-year cycle of human life is established upon the energy of the root chakra. The first year of life is entirely bound up with the activity of the root chakra and its basic theme: the sense of trust. False steps at this point can later lead to self-seeking, lethargy, compulsiveness, and existential anxiety. Of greatest concern is the possible emergence of a basic lack of trust in life. This can be overcome later on only with the greatest difficulty.

The most important thing at this point is that the child feel unconditionally accepted by its parents. The mother, in particular, has to devote herself entirely to the child so that it doesn't become fearful and can develop a healthy sense of trust. When a baby cries, this indicates that it is in need. It is a mistake to think that letting a child cry will make it stronger. Rather, it will learn that it cannot rely upon protection and care, and this will only make it more afraid.

During this period, the child should be with its mother as much as possible; she should often hold it in her arms. A child who feels loved, cared for, and protected by its parents will develop a healthy sense of trust that will last for life.

Year Two

In the second year, the sacral chakra, with its themes of sensuality and emotional expression, becomes particularly important. Now the child needs more than the closeness of the mother. Children require sensory stimulation, to be touched and caressed. Lacking this will make it difficult for them to develop a good relationship with their own bodies and with the sensual world around them.

In the second year of life the sacral chakra becomes dominant. Now the child needs to be held, touched, and caressed.

Parents should let their child express emotions freely without imposing the grown-up point of view. The child needs to explore, experience, and consciously express his or her emotions. Feelings that are considered negative at a later stage in life, such as rage or aggression, are not signs of a failing of development in a two-year-old. Rather, this is the first stage of development. The expression of feelings in this phase is entirely normal and of the utmost importance to a child.

If parents don't accept this and only give the child their affection when it is good, then blockages in the sacral chakra can follow. Such children learn to suppress parts of their personality and will have difficulty expressing and understanding emotions as an adult. They will only be able to respond to strong emotional stimuli and will tend to take emotional advantage of others. A lack of sensitivity and feeling are signs of obstructions in the development of the sacral chakra.

A child who is free to explore the full repertoire of his or her emotions will outgrow anger and aggression and accept that not everyone will respond to temper tantrums. The important thing is that children know that despite their behavior, they are loved and cared for, and their parents need to show this to them. A little child who throws a tantrum should still be accepted with open arms.

Year Three

In this phase, the energy of the navel chakra takes center stage. The principal theme is power. If you have children, you know that this is the time for power struggles between parent and child. Children are exploring their own personalities and their ability to influence the world around them.

In the third year the child will test boundaries. If the parent's discipline is too harsh, the child will have trouble with authority figures later on in life.

Parents now have an important task. They have to take their children's personalities seriously and accept them as their own person. Children now learn to control their inner and outer worlds and perceive other people as independent personalities. Parents who seek to constrict the unfolding of their children with narrowly defined rules will contribute to the development of blockages in the navel chakra. These energetic restrictions can lead children to become overly compliant and compulsive or tyrannical and obsessed with power later in life.

It is especially important in this phase of life that children try to overstep their boundaries in order to garner different (sometimes painful) experiences. It is good for their development at this point that they gain a sense of achievement relatively easily. They shouldn't have to throw a fit or placate their parents in order to get what they want. They should learn that they don't have to be aggressive to get attention and that they can accomplish things when they sets their mind to it, and also that it is not necessary for them to repress their own strength or to subordinate or disguise their desires in order to be successful.

Year Four

As the heart chakra develops, themes of empathy, tolerance, love for oneself, and artistic expression emerge. At this age, children begin to learn how to understand others. Parents need to set an example of tolerance and empathy. Children of this age need a lot of love. They learn the nature of exchange, of giving and receiving. These experiences will shape their behavior toward others. If their need for love is not ful-

One should treasure every picture a child creates as it is an expression of the soul.

filled, children will react later in life with overdependency and jealousy. They will gain the impression that dependency is the same thing as love, and for that reason they will find it difficult to give and receive real love.

This phase is decisive for the feeling of self-worth and for artistic expression. These two are interconnected. Creative expression is deeply personal; it has to come from the heart. Any attack on their creative expressions will deeply wound those who are not firmly established in themselves.

Children of this age like to paint, sing, dance, or make up stories. Their parents shouldn't laugh at them, criticize them, seek to improve them, or react indifferently. Every artistic creation of a child is a piece of that child's soul, offered freely. It deserves special recognition, support, and effort in understanding.

The fourth year is devoted to the development of the heart chakra. Now the parents should help their child learn tolerance and empathy.

Year Five

At this age, the throat chakra becomes particularly active. Children develop the capacity to communicate with their inner and outer worlds. Language acquisition forms the bridge between the worlds of childhood and adulthood. Grammatical structure and the basis for speech are now well established and they will not change much later in life. Only a

Communication, language, curiosity, and the desire to learn characterize the time just before the child begins school.

child's vocabulary will continue to grow. Parents can support the unfolding of the communication chakra by engaging their children in discussions, telling them stories, and encouraging them to make up their own stories. Oftentimes children at this stage express the desire to read. Parents should encourage this. The child also develops repertoires of body language, intonational expressions, and the language of the unconscious. Now is the best time to learn a musical instrument.

Year Six

In this phase, the energy of the forehead chakra broadens. Children take their first steps into the world of ideas. Now they display a natural pleasure in discovering connections and acquiring new knowledge. Children of this age are sent to school, where often their thirst for knowledge is stifled and they learn, among other things, to associate learning with unpleasantness, such as having to sit still and be inactive. This is sometimes even reinforced by punishment. Parents should try to combat these forces and encourage the child's curiosity and hunger for knowledge.

Year Seven

In the last phase of the cycle of early childhood, the crown chakra plays a central role. Now the foundations of one's spirituality is laid down Children begin to become interested in questions of God, death, and the meaning of life. Parents should take seriously their child's thoughts, feelings, and questions about such topics. This is the right time to introduce a child to religion and meditation. Naturally, the question of your own spiritual orientation arises. This will determine whether you bring your child to church, introduce him or her to simple yoga practices, or wander together in nature to listen to the wind and the birds.

The Great Developmental Cycle

With birth begins not only the seven-year cycle of early childhood but also the encompassing great cycle of seven times seven years. Each seven-year cycle has a particular theme, task, and chakra to which it is related.

The same pattern that is established in the first seven-year cycle repeats itself in each of the following cycles. The basic theme of a seven-year period runs through all of the chakras and all of the aspects of which the life of the soul is composed.

Life Phases

The great cycle comprises the following seven shorter cycles: early childhood up to the seventh year; later childhood to age fourteen; adolescence, which begins with puberty and lasts until the twenty-first year; early adulthood from twenty-two to twenty-eight; mature adulthood from twenty-nine to thirty-five; the period of knowledge from thirty-six to forty-two; and the completion of the great cycle from forty-three to forty-nine.

Even people who are unfamiliar with the system of the chakras will intuitively sense the importance of these life phases.

Information about the various life cycles will enlighten us as to our developmental needs and the tasks that face us. If we know when certain capacities have to be developed, we can avoid disappointment despite not having fully completed the tasks of each stage of life.

At birth, the child enters into an entirely new phase of life. The energetic cycle spins in the opposite direction. Now each phase lasts longer, on average for about one year, although in optimal conditions the natural rhythm is a cycle of seven month's duration.

The development of the chakras after birth takes up where the prenatal development left off, with the expansion of the energies of the root chakra.

In the seventh year a child begins to become interested in questions about religion, God, death, and the meaning of life.

The First Seven Years of Life

Patterns set down in childhood shape one's adult life and are very difficult to break out of.

Prenatal development provides the energetic foundation. In the first seven years of life, this foundation is built upon and stabilized. That is why these seven years are so decisive for later life. At the end of this cycle, the individual belongs to a specific chakra personality type—even though this can change later in life. The patterns with which the child is stamped can be set aside in later life only through conscious effort. That is why the way we bring up our children is so important. If parents understand the stages of chakra development, they not only can better understand their children, but they can also contribute to their children's physical, mental, and spiritual development. The healthy influence of a positive upbringing can be reinforced by concentrating on the chakra that corresponds to each phase of development.

The Great Development Cycle

| Age | 1 to 7 | 8 to 14 | 15 to 21 | 22 to 28 | 29 to 35 | 36 to 42 | 43 to 49 |
Chakra	Root	Sacral	Navel	Heart	Throat	Forehead	Crown
1. Chakra	1	8	15	22	29	36	43
2. Chakra	2	9	16	23	30	37	44
3. Chakra	3	10	17	24	31	38	45
4. Chakra	4	11	18	25	32	39	46
5. Chakra	5	12	19	26	33	40	47
6. Chakra	6	13	20	27	34	41	48
7. Chakra	7	14	21	28	35	42	49

The years overlaid with color are particularly significant. At these times the energies of the greater and the smaller cycles overlap.

The table on page 98 shows how the chakras develop and how the smaller cycles repeat themselves within the greater cycles. You will see that in each seven-year period, there is a crucial year in which the energies of the great cycle and the smaller cycle overlap. This year offers a great opportunity for the development of the corresponding chakra, but it can also give rise to personal crises:

In the great cycle of human life, years in which smaller cycles overlap are extremely significant.

- The crisis of the infant who will decide whether or not to take up the challenge of life
- The crisis of the child who is exploring his or her senses
- The crisis of the adolescent who in the heat of puberty has to learn self-control
- The crisis of the young adult who is confronting decisions about career and family
- The crisis of the adult at the peak of power in the material world, facing the need to confront the truth about his or her own existence
- The crisis of mature adulthood and the need to decide between the demands of the material and the spiritual worlds
- The crisis of the person who has the chance for fulfillment but may instead be caught in a midlife crisis

Early Childhood (Ages One to Seven)

In the first phase of life, early childhood, the theme of basic trust is dominant. Each of these early years will witness the strengthening or weakening of trust. The first year is the most important. At this point, all cycles intersect. The prenatal period ends with the unfolding of the root chakra. The first seven-year cycle begins, and so does the seven-times-seven-year cycle, which has its foundation in the energies of the root chakra.

The first seven-year phase begins with a strong impulse of energy from the root chakra. Building trust is the dominant theme. The foundation is laid for trust in life, in the sensory world, in one's personality, in love and the underlying connection between people, in the world of thought and communication, in knowledge and understanding, and ultimately in the world of the spirit.

Youth (Ages Eight to Fourteen)

This is the second phase in the great cycle of human development. Each of the following years has a relationship to a particular chakra, beginning with the root chakra, but the overarching theme is no longer trust but sensuality.

Gradually children begin to experience the sensual world in regard to material things, in the control and influence they have on their environment and themselves, in the pleasure they take from their senses, in love and fellowship, in communication, in the capacity for insight, and in spirituality.

Children's senses are very active; they experience the world through sight, hearing, and touch. This is not, however, given enough attention in their everyday experience. In school they are forced to sit still and learn. They acquire knowledge, but their senses are given short shrift. Many teachers recognize this problem but think that if children don't learn now, they won't be able to master complex thoughts and ideas later in life.

Chakra learning teaches just the opposite, that sensory experience is the basis for constructive thinking. If the sensual energies of the sacral chakra are not allowed free play, the energies of the higher chakras will be constricted. Children who have not learned to grasp the world with their senses will have difficulty later in life organizing and processing their impressions.

Children need sensory as well as intellectual stimulation in order to enjoy life when they grow up.

Parents therefore should take care that children of this age can sharpen all of their senses and that they spend a lot of time in nature, playing outside, climbing trees, and even rolling around in the dirt. When children in this phase are given the opportunity to expand their senses, they learn how to enjoy themselves and acquire the ability to take pleasure in what life has to offer.

Adolescence (Ages Fifteen to Twenty-one)

This is a tempestuous time. Now the developmental task encompasses everything that relates to the themes of the navel chakra: sense of self, control, and power.

While they traverses the seven chakras, adolescents learn to control the various energies that correspond to each of the chakras and to solidify all aspects of their personality.

Their peer group, parents, and school often stand in the way of important developmental steps. In this phase, young people need to learn to take life into their own hands in order to gain a sense of control. It's only natural for them to engage in experimentation with sexuality and love and to open themselves up to other possibilities, radical thinking, and spiritual experiences. They try to break through the limitations of tradition and hard-and-fast rules. If, because of their passion for experimentation, they meet with punishment or neglect, the energy of the navel chakra will become blocked or weakened. They may then become doormats or, alternatively, defiant rebels who challenge everything and everyone in order to force their way through obstructions that they feel, if only on an unconscious level.

After the stormy period of adolescence young adults can focus their energies and work wholeheartedly on life goals.

Young people need room to expand and experience their powers of imagination. If they are given this room, later on they will become valued members of society and their own persons.

Young Adulthood (Ages Twenty-two to Twenty-eight)

In early adulthood, the challenges one faces change, and the chakra energies unfold under a new aspect. Now the themes of the heart chakra, which is particularly active, come to the fore: love, warmth of feeling, empathy, and devotion. People are now ready to share and become involved in family, career, and society. This phase is often the most productive period of life, since everything one does during this time is done wholeheartedly with the greatest enthusiasm. Those who master the challenges of this stage will possess the strength to act from their heart for their entire lives. The challenge is to recognize that everyone deserves love and that even the smallest things are meaningful. Depending upon which chakra is active, the focus of one's love will be directed accordingly—from a narrow focus on material well-being to the aspiration for the Divine. For most people, their development brings them somewhere in between the two extremes, but nonetheless one should take the challenge to heart and make every effort not to imprison one's love in too narrow a channel.

Full Adulthood (Ages Twenty-nine to Thirty-five)

Toward the end of one's third decade, the underlying theme changes once again. Over the next seven years, the throat chakra will play a dominant role and the theme of communication will become of key importance. The way this theme manifests itself will accord with the rhythm of the seven-year cycle.

By the time they reach mature adulthood, most people have made important career decisions. Now they can turn to new challenges.

The primary task that the individual faces now is to draw the right lessons from one's experiences in the material world thus far. The energy of communication that works through the throat chakra also entails better communication with oneself. People of this age are prepared to look within and come to terms with who they really are. Most people learn to reach an accommodation between what they imagined they would become and what their limitations are. Now is the time to open up a channel of communication between the conscious and unconscious, to establish a new, mature sense of self, and to rationally evaluate one's possibilities for further development. Often people make definitive decisions regarding their career path. The power of communicating with oneself and others can guide one to the best results.

Time of Realization (Ages Thirty-six to Forty-two)

Now the forehead chakra with its themes of realization and insight becomes the motivating force. At this time of life, people often discover new areas of interest. The various qualities of the forehead chakra allow them to look more deeply into the different aspects of their being. The new directions one takes will in large part be determined by the earlier development of the chakras.

Many people look only to improve their material conditions. They are concerned with buying a house, investing money, and the security of their family. Their attention is focused on matters connected to the root chakra. Others look to their senses and give up their earlier life to find new partners and rediscover their own sensuality (activities that correspond to the sacral chakra). Some strive to have more influence on the world around them—here the energy of the navel chakra reasserts itself. Those for whom the heart chakra is particularly active deepen their relationships and warmth toward others.

The burgeoning awareness that steers people toward the involvement with the energies of the higher chakras is particularly valuable. Throat-chakra personalities hone their communication skills and use them to uphold the truth. For forehead-chakra types, now is a time for realization and the creative ideas that follow. And finally, those people in whom the crown chakra is highly activated will be confirmed upon their spiritual path and may even develop extraordinary powers.

Completion of the Great Cycle (Ages Forty-three to Forty-nine)

Now the great cycle of seven times seven years comes to an end. The highest chakra, the crown chakra, with its themes of spirituality, illumination, and mental power, penetrates one's awareness. How strongly it affects a given individual will depend on the earlier stages of his or her development.

At this point, it should be easier to find a vantage point from which to view the totality of one's existence—one's physical, emotional, mental, and spiritual needs and abilities. In this period, one prepares the ground for spiritual enlightenment.

That is not to say that the fulfillment of the great cycle is an enriching experience for everyone. It can plunge some people into doubt and perplexity. They look back over their entire lives, see chances missed and abilities that remained dormant, and mourn for what might have been. For such people, now is a time of midlife crisis.

With the ending of the great cycle, a new cycle begins. It is hoped that with the benefit of maturity and greater experience, one can start on a higher level. Now is the time for second chances. With the advances in medicine and the spread of information about healthy living, many people are now living longer and remaining more active and engaged. This affords us the opportunity to concentrate on the essential things in life. It would be a pity not to take advantage of it.

This is the time of the midlife crisis. A person looks back at the passing years with disappointment at the goals not reached. But with the end of the cycle comes a second chance.

6 Chakras and Health

Chakra work comprises many methods, but all have the same goal: the improvement of the energy functions of the chakras and the harmonization of the flow of energy between them. This is of the utmost importance. When the circulation of energy is unbalanced or impeded, countless problems can arise. We have examined how chakras affect our personalities and give rise to various psychological conditions. This chapter will consider the ways in which they affect the body.

Chakra therapy is the art of healing with energy. Its goal is to bring about balance on an energetic level.

Health and Well-Being Through Chakra Therapy

The state of the chakras influences all of our organs, the skeleton, and the hormonal, digestive, circulatory, and nervous systems—in short, the entire organism. Chakra teaching asserts that behind every ailment lies a problem with the level or flow of energy and that this leads to a disturbance in the body's natural equilibrium. This insight is the point of departure for many traditional healing practices, including Chinese medicine, Ayurveda, and Tibetan and shamanic healing practices.

Total Healing

Holistic healing approaches such as chakra-oriented therapy are not directed toward relieving illness—although that may be the initial reason we turn to them. For true healing to take place, the deeper reasons for sickness must be addressed. The healing process entails not only the alleviation of symptoms but an inner freeing, a maturation, that reestablishes a healthy equilibrium. As we know from the study of psychosomatic disorders, such complaints as stomach troubles, asthma, and high blood pressure are often connected to emotional conflicts.

When one's chakras unfold as they should, the way is paved for physical, mental, and spiritual health.

The source of many of our problems lies in the energy centers and the circulation of energy through the subtle body.

Everybody experiences this at one time or another. We are more susceptible to colds when we are stressed, and anyone who is prone to allergies knows that they become aggravated when we are tense or irritable. Chakra teaching takes this a step further and points out that many other sicknesses have their roots in deeper levels of our being. Emotional sicknesses have causes that are related to a lack of serenity, inner strength, and peace. When our spiritual growth is hindered and the energy transmitted by the chakras does not flow freely, it burdens our spirits, our minds, and ultimately our bodies.

Stomach disorders, for example, often develop from spiritual and mental problems that stem from trying to suppress irritation and a tendency to anger. The basic problem is that energy is not circulating as it should be, and as a result the relationship with our higher self is lost. Chakra therapy aims at healing these energetic disorders. It works to bring order to the various levels of energy. At the same time, it can expand our awareness and lead us to deeper levels of integration and understanding.

To arrive at the true causes of our physical complaints, it is helpful to consider the different areas of the body that are governed by each of the chakras. By considering why you suffer from a particular illness, you can gain valuable insights. The concern with deeper causes of ill health always leads to increased self-awareness.

The Root Chakra and Good Health

The root chakra lies at the bottom of the spinal column. The activity of this chakra affects the entire pelvic region and, to a large degree, the large intestine. This chakra also governs the skeleton and the lower part of the body, including the legs and feet.

A person with a healthy root chakra stands with both feet firmly on the ground.

The Healthy Root Chakra

When the root chakra is strong, so are the body's structural elements. Bones, teeth, and nails are in good condition. When the large intestine and the body's processes of elimination are working smoothly, this is a good indication of the health of the root chakra.

The root chakra is the energy center that connects people to the earth. It takes care of the legs and feet, which provide our physical contact with the ground. It also protects the sciatic nerve and affects the quality of the blood. Allergic reactions are also connected to the activity of the root chakra.

Influence on Hormones

The proper functioning of the suprarenal gland depends upon the root chakra. It is in charge of the body's production of cortisone, adrenaline, and noradrenaline. These hormones govern basic life functions and are especially important in dealing with stress.

Through hormone production, the root chakra has an indirect effect on our survival mechanisms and on the body's ability to relieve physical tension.

This corresponds to the theme that we have already explored in connection with this chakra: the sense of basic trust and the struggle for survival.

Lower back pain, throwing one's back out and sciatica are all indications of a weak root chakra.

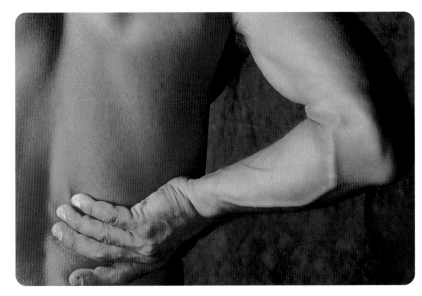

Ailments Related to Blockages in the Root Chakra

When we begin to gently regulate the energy of the root chakra and remove blockages, we find that many different complaints are alleviated. Chakra work supports the body's own healing power when its natural balance has been lost. The following health problems are associated with energetic disturbances in the root chakra:

Blockages in the root chakra cause a number of ailments, mostly to do with the lower half of the body.

- Digestive disorders
- Hemorrhoids
- Constipation
- Lower back pain
- Sciatica
- Skeletal problems
- Osteoporosis
- Pain in the legs and feet
- Varicose veins
- Anemia and other blood disorders
- Stress-induced ailments
- Allergic reactions

The Sacral Chakra and Good Health

The sacral chakra is situated a few finger widths below the navel. It is also known as the sexual center, since it is primarily responsible for the sexual organs and reproductive system. Its energy radiates throughout the pelvic area and influences the kidneys, bladder, and uterus. The hip joints and the lower vertebrae also lie within its purview. The sacral chakra is associated with the element water and governs the flow of bodily fluids. Thus it affects the blood, the lymphatic system, urine, and the production of sperm. Problems in these areas often come about because those affected resist the flow of change. (A particularly clear example is the presence of kidney stones.)

A strong sacral chakra helps in detoxifying the body, strengthens the immune system, and results in the health of the reproductive system and sexual organs.

The Healthy Sacral Chakra

A well-developed sacral chakra ensures the health of the testicles and prostate in men and the ovaries and uterus in women. It also prevents impotence and reduces menstrual pain.

Influence on Hormones

On a hormonal level, the sacral chakra is related to the gonads and the production of sexual hormones. Potency, procreation, fertility, orgasm, and reproductive success all depend upon a healthy sacral chakra. According to Eastern philosophies, sexual energy is very important for one's health and vitality.

The production of sexual hormones has a major effect on one's feelings and moods. Severe mood swings, for example, can result from disorders in the sacral chakra. Not least important is its influence on the defense mechanisms of the immune system, which depend on the sacral chakra for their smooth functioning.

The sacral chakra governs the fluids in the body. It is responsible for vitality and the enjoyment of life.

Ailments Related to Blockages in the Sacral Chakra

Using the techniques of chakra work, you can activate the sacral chakra and dissolve blockages. This will increase your sexual energy, your appetite for life, and your vitality. The following problems arise from a weak or a blocked sacral chakra:

Problems with sexual organs as well as bladder and kidney ailments result from disturbances in the sacral chakra.

- Menstrual pain
- Uterine ailments
- Inflammation of the ovaries
- Cysts
- Prostate problems
- Impotence
- Testicular ailments
- Fungus infections in the sexual organs
- Sexual ailments
- Kidney problems, including kidney stones
- Weak bladder
- Bladder and urinary infections
- Lower back pain
- Pain in the hip joints
- Skin problems due to toxins in the body

The Navel Chakra and Good Health

The navel chakra is also known as the solar plexus chakra. Strictly speaking, from an anatomical perspective, this chakra is not located right at the navel but a finger's width above it in the area between the pit of the stomach and the solar plexus. The navel chakra affects all of the digestive organs. In its sphere of influence are the stomach, gallbladder, liver, small intestine, spleen, and the entire stomach cavity.

The digestive system and the regulation of body temperature are dependent upon the navel chakra.

The Healthy Navel Chakra

People with strong navel chakras have good appetites and make optimum use of the nourishment they take in. They seldom complain of problems with the stomach, liver, or any of the digestive organs. Since the navel chakra also affects the autonomic nervous system, such people will as a rule have steady nerves, sleep deeply, and deal well with stress. On a psychic level, the navel chakra is linked to one's emotions. It is well known that emotional problems often manifest themselves as psychosomatic symptoms in the stomach region, as evidenced by the expression "having a nervous stomach." Eating disorders also are attributable to psychic problems that center around the navel chakra. The struggle against obesity on the one hand or therapy for anorexia on the other can also work to harmonize this chakra.

Influence on Hormones

On a hormonal level, the navel chakra is related to the pancreas. It supplies digestive enzymes; regulates the metabolism of carbohydrates, digestion, and the conversion of food into energy; and neutralizes stomach acids. It also is connected to the islet of Langerhans, the glands that produce insulin. If the body's cells do not receive enough insulin, diabetes is the result.

A good appetite and the enjoyment of food are signs of a healthy navel chakra.

Ailments Related to Blockages in the Navel Chakra

Chakra work will gently regulate the energy flow in the navel chakra and help you to avoid many physical problems. For those who suffer from illnesses that are caused by a weakness in this chakra, there are corresponding techniques that will in large measure correct the problem and restore the body's natural equilibrium. The following health problems are related to weakness or blockages in the navel chakra:

Many problems have their roots in the stomach or the digestive or autonomic nervous system.

- Stomach ailments or ulcers
- Heartburn
- Diseases of the liver, spleen, and gallbladder
- Jaundice
- Stomachache
- Disorders of the digestive tract
- Backache
- Nervous disorders
- Obesity
- Anorexia

The Heart Chakra and Good Health

The heart chakra lies in the middle of the chest, level with the heart. Its activity affects the entire rib cage and especially the heart. In almost every culture, the heart is regarded as a symbol for the power of love. Additionally, this chakra regulates blood circulation and blood pressure. Disorders in these areas signal a problem in the heart chakra.

The Healthy Heart Chakra

The lungs are also governed by the heart chakra. Its correspondence to the element of air suggests a natural relationship with the respiratory system. People with strong heart chakras breathe deeply with a regular rhythm. Their circulation is good and their pulse steady, and they are seldom stricken with bronchial or respiratory ailments. By removing blockages that stand in the way of opening one's spiritual heart, one prevents many coronary problems.

In addition to the heart and lungs, the heart chakra influences the shoulders, arms, and hands; the rib cage; and the upper back. It is also closely connected to the sense of touch, since this brings us closer to other people and allows us to comfort and be comforted. Behind many skin disorders lies a related problem: We don't want others to come too close.

Someone with a well-developed heart chakra usually has a healthy heart, strong lungs, and good blood circulation.

Influence on Hormones

On a hormonal level, the heart chakra is connected to the thymus gland, which governs the lymphatic system. The thymus gland produces lymphocytes and antibodies, which are essential components of the immune system.

When the heart chakra is weak, there is an increased susceptibility to illnesses that attack the immune system, including infections, allergies, and even cancer.

When the heart chakra is weak, one has a weakened immune system and is more likely to suffer from infections.

Ailments Related to Blockages in the Heart Chakra

Learn to activate and harmonize the heart chakra through the gentle practices prescribed in chakra work. In this way, you can avoid many illnesses. If you already suffer from any of these illnesses, you can improve your health by undertaking this work. The following ailments indicate a disturbance in the energy level of the heart chakra:

Problems in the heart chakra can cause coronary and respiratory illness. They can also result in a weakened immune system.

- Coronary illness and angina pectoris
- Arrhythmia, heart attack
- High or low blood pressure
- Elevated cholesterol
- Inflammation or infections of the lungs
- Asthma and other respiratory problems
- Colds
- Allergies
- Backache in the rib cage area
- Shoulder pain
- Rheumatism in the arms and hands
- Skin problems

The Throat Chakra and Good Health

The throat chakra is situated in the area of the neck. Its activity affects the area around the throat, neck, and jaw as well as the esophagus and windpipe. The throat chakra is the center of speech and communication. It also influences the upper region of the upper bronchial passages, the breath, and above all the voice.

A strong voice and healthy respiration are signs of a well-developed throat chakra.

The Healthy Throat Chakra

Someone with a strong throat chakra is recognizable by the rich tenor of his or her voice. Such a person breathes freely and will not ordinarily suffer from tonsillitis or any throat inflammation. In addition to its influence on the larynx and vocal cords, the throat chakra also affects the vertebrae in the neck and the shoulders. To a lesser extent it affects hearing, although that is primarily governed by the forehead chakra.

Disturbances in the proper functioning of the throat chakra can lead to a feeling of pressure in the throat or speech defects. Problems with the jaw or teeth also point to a weakened throat chakra, since this chakra supplies the jaw with energy.

Influence on Hormones

The throat chakra is closely connected to the thyroid and the parathyroid glands. The correct functioning of the thyroid is essential for good health. Producing iodine, a key ingredient in the metabolic process, the thyroid gland regulates metabolism and the body's energy level. Not only is the metabolism of protein, carbohydrates, fat, water, and minerals determined by the thyroid, it also influences the nervous system. When it is not in good working order, one can suffer from nervousness on the one hand or a general lassitude on the other. One of the most important functions of the parathyroid glands is the regulation of calcium, which is required for healthy bones and teeth. Calcium also plays a role in healing inflammations.

The throat chakra governs the upper vertebrae and the neck and shoulder area.

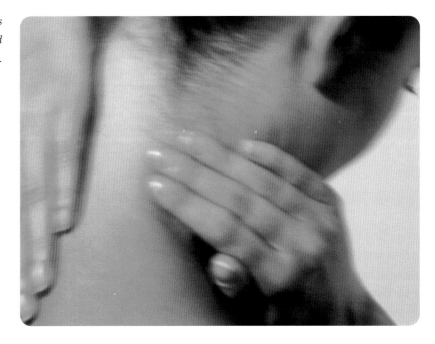

Ailments Related to Blockages in the Throat Chakra

Through the harmonizing effects of chakra work, you can strengthen your throat chakra. For those who already suffer from ailments associated with the throat chakra, such work can be especially beneficial.

Speech defects, sore throats, and dental and periodontal problems can result from a lack of energy in the throat chakra.

If you are prone to any of the health problems listed below, it is time to turn your attention to activating the energies that will strengthen the throat chakra:

- Throat pain
- Tonsillitis
- Speech defects such as stuttering
- Dental and periodontal problems
- Trouble with the vertebrae in the neck
- Neck and shoulder pain
- Stiffness in the neck and shoulders
- Overactive or underactive thyroid

The Forehead Chakra and Good Health

In the center of the forehead, slightly above a point between the eyebrows, lies the forehead chakra, which is also known as the third eye.

The energy of the forehead chakra, which plays a leading role on mental and psychic levels, also influences the body. The brain, particularly the cerebellum, stands in direct relationship to the energy of the forehead chakra.

This chakra regulates the quality of our sensory apparatus as well, above all, that of vision but also hearing and our sense of smell.

The eyes, nose, auditory passages, inner and middle ears, nostrils, as well as the entire hormonal and nervous systems are directly influenced by the activity of the forehead chakra.

The Healthy Forehead Chakra

People with well-developed forehead chakras possess mental clarity, great intelligence, and remarkable powers of concentration. Their vision and hearing are particularly sharp and remain so even into advancing age.

Problems such as poor eyesight, conjunctivitis, migraines and other headaches, sinusitis, chronic colds, and poor hearing or ear infections very rarely trouble people with strong forehead chakras.

People with strong forehead chakras often don't need glasses or hearing aids, even when they grow old.

Influence on Hormones

The forehead chakra is closely related to the pituitary gland, which is the control center of the entire endocrine system. With assistance from electric impulses and transmitters, it regulates the activity of all of the endocrine glands, influencing the immune and nervous systems and thereby our psychological constitution.

Ailments Related to Blockages in the Forehead Chakra

When you gently stimulate and strengthen the forehead chakra through chakra work and remove possible blockages, you give a tremendous

Frequent headaches or migraines can be indications of a blocked forehead chakra.

The forehead chakra influences the nervous system and has an effect on one's spiritual life as well.

boost to your physical and mental well-being. The following problems are the result of weaknesses or blockages in the forehead chakra:

- Headache
- Migraine
- Brain diseases
- Disorders of the eye
- Conjunctivitis
- Poor eyesight
- Hearing impairments
- Inflammations of the middle ear
- Colds
- Sinus problems
- Neurological disorders
- Mental illness
- Schizophrenia
- Learning disabilities and problems with concentration

The Crown Chakra and Good Health

The crown chakra lies at the very top of the head. Its effects are felt throughout the aura; it is the mental and spiritual energy center, but it has a significant influence on the body as well. It does not correspond to any one organ or part of the body; rather, it works to harmonize and protect the entire organism. Its influence is strongly felt in the cerebrum and the eyes and is active in sustaining life on the bodily and cellular levels.

The Healthy Crown Chakra

Normally a strong, healthy crown chakra ensures a long, healthy life. Persistent and chronic illnesses, before all mental and psychic problems, can take hold when the energy in this chakra is blocked.

Influence on Hormones

A strong crown chakra is a guarantee of good health. But if blocked it can result in serious illness.

On a hormonal level, the crown chakra is connected to the pineal gland, which responds to light and regulates the sleep rhythms of the body through the hormone melatonin.

Ailments Related to Blockages in the Crown Chakra

Chakra work can stimulate the crown chakra, thereby protecting against chronic illnesses and promoting the body's own natural healing processes. Here are some of the ailments that are attributable to weaknesses or blockages in the crown chakra:

- Headaches
- Weakness in the immune system
- Nervous conditions
- Paralysis
- Multiple sclerosis
- Cancer
- Mental confusion
- Forgetfulness
- Mental illness
- Depression
- Sleep disorders

7 Chakra Therapy

If you want to activate and develop your chakras, there are two avenues you can take: chakra yoga and chakra therapy. The practice of chakra yoga will be described in chapter 10. Chakra therapy makes use of a number of different approaches. We will be discussing seven different programs to help you to harmonize the energies of each of the chakras.

The many techniques for harmonizing the chakra energies are comprised in seven different programs. All are extremely helpful in resolving the problems accompanying weak or blocked chakras, whether on a physical or a psychic level.

There is a special program for each chakra that will balance and harmonize it.

The Healing Methods of Chakra Therapy

Before turning to actual practices, it will be helpful to provide an overview of the different methods employed in chakra therapy. The treatments that are most effective in harmonizing the energies of the chakras are aromatherapy, herbal remedies, healing with gemstones, and Bach flower remedies. Alternative forms of therapy include vocalization, affirmations, and chakra-energy massage. We also offer some tips for everyday activities.

When you put these techniques into practice, rely first and foremost on your inner voice and intuition. Without any further guidance, you should be able to obtain excellent results. Only in rare cases where severe blockages exist or a person suffers from grave physical or emotional problems should professional help be required. As a general rule, it is best to find your own way. You know better than anyone else what is good for you.

You will find here an overview of different approaches to healing. Although these methods work well in conjunction with each other and are combined in the program, you don't have to use them all. To deal with concrete problems, it is best to devote a period of time in which you can try some or even all of the recommended methods.

Specific programs harmonize and strengthen the chakras.

The Methods of Chakra Therapy Have Significant Benefits

The methods that we suggest are effective and easy to follow.

- They increase our sense of physical well-being.
- They promote psychic equilibrium.
- They are relaxing.
- They purify the chakras.
- They gently stimulate the flow of energy through the proper channels.
- They dissolve blockages in the chakras.

Aromatherapy

The healing properties of fragrances were first discovered in Egypt about five thousand years ago. The same power is recognized and used in modern aromatherapy techniques. Smells can instantly change our moods. The sense of smell is more immediately connected to our feelings and unconscious than any other of the senses.

The olfactory nerve is located in the mucous membrane of the nasal passages. It is directly connected to the limbic system. This control center in the brain stem has a powerful influence on our feelings and hormonal levels.

As we have seen, the chakras also have a significant effect on our emotions and our hormonal system. Just as the chakras influence our mood and feelings, so they in turn influence the flow of energy through the chakras. When, for example, you feel defeated or frustrated, the condition of the chakras will be negatively affected.

Aromatherapy harmonizes our emotions and thus indirectly works to loosen blockages and constrictions in the chakras. Central to this gentle healing approach is the use of essential oils in the form of tiny droplets taken from various plants.

There are great differences in the quality of essential oils commonly available, so you should be careful to select pure, natural oils to use in aromatherapy.

Aromatherapy is a gentle healing technique that harmonizes the senses and helps dissolve blockages in the chakras.

Using Aromatherapy

- Never use undiluted aroma oils, since they can cause allergic reactions in some cases. Be very careful at the beginning to get the dosage right.
- The best way to use the oil is to put a few drops in an aroma lamp.
- You can also use essential oil in a bath or footbath or in combination with chakra-massage techniques. When using it in chakra massage, pour a little oil onto the area around the chakra you wish to stimulate. Use a gentle circular motion to rub the oil into the skin until it has all been absorbed.

Healing with Plants

Medicinal plants have been used in every culture to combat illness and promote health. In the monastic culture of the Middle Ages, the use of plants in healing was particularly widespread. Scientific research has supported claims that many plants have healing powers, and phytotherapy (healing with plants) has now become a recognized therapeutic approach.

In addition to essential oils, plants have many healthful properties. They may contain flavin, saponin, or tannin as well as vitamins and minerals. Many healing techniques make use of these beneficial ingredients. Others work through the so-called synergistic effect, whereby certain healing qualities are produced only by a combination of plants. This leads to greater benefits than can be obtained by using only a single, isolated ingredient. Different herbs and plants can promote health in the body in a number of ways. Some are anti-inflammatory, others antibacterial. They can be used to relieve pain, ease cramps, or reduce fevers. They can have tonic effects or guard against infection and detoxify the body. There are also an array of plants that have beneficial effects on the psyche. They can bring calmness, combat anxiety and depression, and promote good sleep and a general sense of well-being.

The monks of the middle ages were well-acquainted with the healing properties of the plants and herbs in their cloister gardens.

Some healing plants influence areas that correspond to particular chakras. As their healing effect is felt in the body and soul, they also stimulate and regulate the flow of energy through the chakras. The easiest way to get the benefits of plants and herbs is by preparing special healing teas. Some plants, however, are more effective when mixed with wine or milk.

Healing with Gemstones

Using gemstones to heal sickness was a practice known to the Egyptians, Greeks, and Romans. Aristotle was interested in the topic. Hildegard von Bingen wrote about their healing properties. Throughout the world, traditional healers have assembled a great deal of information on the possibilities of using gemstones to treat illness. Gemstone therapy is a subtle, effective healing practice that brings excellent results, even though they have not been recognized by modern medical science.

Working with power, vibrations, and color, gemstones can affect the entire energy system of the human organism. These powers, vibrations, and colors correspond to and resonate with different chakras. Different chakras respond to different gemstones and can be activated and harmonized by them. Gemstone therapy requires trial and error. Not every stone works for every person. It is best to try a few stones and see which works best for you.

The healing power of gems has been recognized since antiquity.

Using Gemstone Therapy

- You can use different gemstones to promote the healing process and help dissolve blockages in the chakras. The simplest and usually most effective method is to wear the stone of your choice against the skin.
- Rough or tumbled stones can be placed directly on the area that corresponds to the chakra you are working on.
- You can use the gem as a touchstone. Its energy will be absorbed through the hand chakras. Or you can set it in a necklace. It is best that the chain be made of gold and worn around the neck.

Healing stones work on one's energy system and the different chakras.

Bach Flower Therapy

Bach flower therapy was developed by Dr. Edward Bach, an innovative and intuitive medical practitioner. It has come to be regarded as one of the most effective methods of alternative medicine. Like homeopathy, Bach flower treatment is a holistic method that targets the circulation of subtle energies in the body. Bach flowers transmit energy. By using essences, one does not deal with plant extracts but rather a vehicle that carries the information within the plant. Mixed in well water, the Bach flowers transmit the healing vibrations of plants. This means that proper attention must be paid to the way in which they are gathered and distilled. Bach flowers should only be harvested on warm, sunny, cloudless days. The light and warmth of the sun play an important role in their efficacy.

Bach flower remedies can be used to combat physical ailments, but they are best known for the help they provide with psychic difficulties. They can be extremely beneficial in treating depression, anxiety, inhibitions, insecurities, and so on. Like chakra work, the Bach flowers harmonize one's state of mind.

Some of the thirty-eight Bach flower remedies can be used with good effect to stimulate the chakras. Certain remedies correspond to specific chakras.

The best results are sometimes found when two Bach flower essences—but not more than two—are combined. The combination reinforces and enhances the healing effect of each of the essences.

Bach flower therapy is a holistic method that can have a profound effect on one's state of mind.

Using Bach Flowers

- The Bach flowers open body and soul and thereby stimulate the flow of energy through the chakras.
- You should take three drops of the particular essence three times a day. It is usually suggested that they be taken shortly before mealtime.
- Place the drops on the tongue and hold them in your mouth for at least a minute before swallowing. You should be able to obtain Bach flower remedies in health food stores or pharmacies that specialize in alternative medicine.

Vocalization

Vocalization is a technique taken from breathing therapy. Each vowel has its own vibration, which resonates in a particular area of the body. Deep vowels such as *u* and *o* vibrate in the stomach or pelvic area. The vibration of high vowels such as *i* are felt most strongly in the head. Through experimentation you can discover how each vowel works on your system. With the exception of the crown chakra, there is a vowel

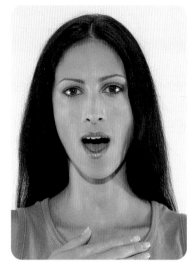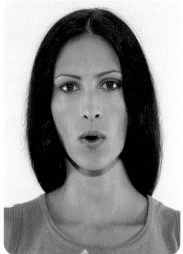

Each vowel stimulates a particular chakra and part of the body.

corresponding to each chakra. The vibratory pattern of each vowel resonates directly with its corresponding chakra.

The vibrations of vowel sounds can activate the chakras.

Using Vocalization

- If you intone a vowel sound for a minute or so and concentrate on the chakra that you wish to affect, you should be able to feel how it is animated and activated. You don't have to sing the vowel. Close your eyes, and breathe in through the nose, then out through the mouth, allowing the vowel you have chosen to sound.
- Don't intone the vowel loudly. Use a low or moderately low voice, but let it vibrate as long as you can and remain relaxed. Repeat for a few minutes to feel its full effect on your body and mind.

Affirmations

Affirmations are powerfully positive statements that are used in different schools of thought. They use the power of language to effect changes in body, mind, and soul. Through the conscious use of language, the unconscious mind can be programmed. Affirmation belongs in the category of hypnotic techniques. Using a monotone, deliberately repeat a short sentence to produce a trancelike state. In this relaxed condition, the positive content of the sentence will have an intensified effect on the unconscious. Thus you plant a seed in the unconscious that can produce a rich harvest in your way of thinking and eventually in your whole attitude toward life. As you repeat a particular affirmation, you are practicing autosuggestion and influencing deeper levels of your being. In the following pages you will find affirmations that are particularly helpful in strengthening and stimulating the different chakras. For example, the heart chakra can be strengthened or harmonized using affirmations that deal with love and compassion. The affirmations are most effective when you whisper them to yourself (or repeat them silently) shortly before bed. When you wake up in the morning is also a good time for affirmations. But you can use them anytime you have the opportunity to relax and close your eyes for a while.

Affirmations are words consciously used to reprogram the unconscious: a kind of self-hypnosis.

The affirmations provided in connection with each of the chakras are only suggestions. By all means, use sentences of your own devising if you wish, as long as you bear the following in mind.

Using Affirmations

- **Affirmations need to be positive. Don't say: "I will not be afraid," but rather, "I am full of self-confidence."**
- **The sentence should be short, simple, and punchy.**
- **Repeat the affirmation at least ten times, though more is better.**
- **Repeat the affirmation silently or whisper it to yourself.**
- **Say the words slowly and draw out the sounds. They should be sounded in a monotone. This enables the unconscious to better absorb the meaning of the words.**

Chakra-Energy Massage

Chakra-energy massage is a spiritually oriented form of massage. Its aim is to stimulate and improve the functioning of the chakras and help in the recovery of one's physical and mental harmony. The term is somewhat misleading, in that regular massage methods such as kneading and applying great pressure to the muscles are not commonly used in chakra-energy massage. It is a much gentler technique than is found in traditional massage practices and is centered around the healing power of touch.

In chakra-energy massage we use the power of the hands to heal the chakras. This is similar to the Japanese technique of reiki.

You can safely and easily use the techniques of chakra-energy massage on yourself, and you can also use them with a partner. This massage is a form of healing through the laying on of hands.

Laying on of hands and various other healing methods that use touch to comfort and soothe were well known in many ancient cultures. Although chakra-energy massage was long forgotten, Reiki, a Japanese form of healing in which energy is transmitted through the hands, has reawakened interest in this way of healing. This technique is widely practiced today. In contrast to Reiki, chakra-energy massage comes from India. It is a form of healing with prana and can be used by Westerners without special training. All that is required is a sensitive touch and the power of your imagination.

Using Chakra-Energy Massage

- To begin, lie on your back and place your hands gently over one of the chakras. Your fingers should be intertwined.
- Place your left palm on the chakra. The left hand is connected to the right side of the brain and the powers of imagination. The right hand should rest lightly on the left.
- Energy will be transmitted through the hand chakras to the chakra you wish to affect.
- To strengthen the efficacy of the massage, you should breathe deeply. At the same time, visualize the color corresponding to the chakra.

The Root-Chakra Program

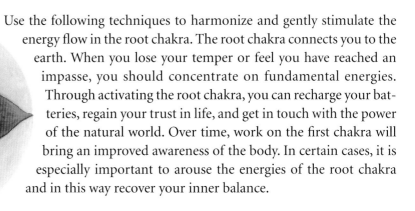

Use the following techniques to harmonize and gently stimulate the energy flow in the root chakra. The root chakra connects you to the earth. When you lose your temper or feel you have reached an impasse, you should concentrate on fundamental energies. Through activating the root chakra, you can recharge your batteries, regain your trust in life, and get in touch with the power of the natural world. Over time, work on the first chakra will bring an improved awareness of the body. In certain cases, it is especially important to arouse the energies of the root chakra and in this way recover your inner balance.

The root-charka program will harmonize and stimulate this chakra, which connects us to the power and strength of the earth.

Checkup: When You Need to Work on Your Root Chakra

- If you feel you've lost trust in life
- If you don't feel at home in your own body
- If you worry about the future and meeting your obligations
- If you feel like you're losing your emotional footing
- If you are easily overwhelmed by life
- If you feel chronically tired and lacking in energy
- If you don't exercise enough
- If you often feel cold or have cold hands and feet
- If your digestion isn't working properly
- If you have problems with your colon
- If you have a tendency toward back pain
- If you suffer from sciatica or throw your back out

The following methods will harmonize the root chakra. It's preferable to combine a number of these techniques, but you can use only a few if you wish. You will get the best results if you are able to devote a period of time to this work. For example, take a week to put all of the suggested techniques into practice.

Aromatherapy

Some essential oils have a stimulating effect on the root chakra. Most effective are cloves, rosemary, cypress, and cedar. Use your intuition to choose the essential oil that suits you best.

For the best results in strengthening the root chakra, one should undergo a week-long course using all the recommended methods.

- Put a few drops of this oil into an aroma lamp several times throughout the day. Let it permeate your living and work spaces. If you are on the move, a few drops in a handkerchief can serve equally well. Breathe in the scent whenever you think of it.
- Rosemary works exceptionally well in a bath. Bathe in warm water. Mix one tablespoon of rosemary with four ounces of cream. Pour the mixture into the bathwater just before you get in. Indulge yourself in a rosemary bath twice a week.
- For a chakra aromatherapy massage, use a mixture of cloves and cypress. Use jojoba or sesame oil as a base. For one tablespoon of base oil, use two drops each of cloves and cypress. Mix together. With the palms of your hands, rub the mixture into your lower back and buttocks with circular strokes until the oil has been fully absorbed by the skin.

Healing with Plants

Valerian, lime blossom, and elder are all healing plants that work to stimulate the root chakra. Elder and lime blossom are also good for warming the body.

- Twice a day, drink a large cup of either elder or lime blossom tea. Add one tablespoon of dried flowers to one cup of boiling water. Cover and let brew for seven minutes. Pour through a strainer.
- It is well known that an infusion of valerian strengthens the system. It is also effective in balancing energies and dissolving blockages in the root chakra. Take three tablespoons of dried and cut valerian root and add to a liter of red wine. Let the mixture stand for ten days, then filter the wine through a clean linen towel. Take two tablespoons three times a day.

In gemstone therapy one should lay the healing stone directly on the skin in the area of the lower back.

Gemstone Therapy

Ruby, hematite, and garnet are the best gemstones for harmonizing the root chakra. Let your intuition guide you to the stone that will work best for you.

- Wear the stone on a gold necklace, or use a touchstone that you rub frequently during the day.
- Ruby works best for direct chakra therapy. Place a ruby on your lower back, preferably in direct contact with the skin. Close your eyes and establish an inner connection with the root chakra. Feel the ruby's effect.

Bach Flower Therapy

Use touchstones by rubbing them from time to time during the course of the day.

Clematis, Sweet Chestnut, and Rock Rose harmonize those aspects of the psyche that are influenced by the root chakra. For chakra therapy, use a combination of any two of these.

- Use the Bach flower remedies three times a day before meals. Place three drops of each essence (six drops altogether) on your tongue. Leave them in your mouth for a little while before swallowing.

Vocalization

Practice vocalization twice a day. Sit up straight, but stay relaxed. Close your eyes. The vowel *u* stimulates the root chakra. Inhale through the nose; as you exhale, intone the *u* sound in a long, drawn-out fashion. Practice this for a few minutes. Feel the vibrations in your pelvic region.

Affirmations

Choose one of the following affirmations and repeat it throughout the day. The best times are right after you wake up and just before you go to sleep. Say the sentence in your mind or whisper it to yourself. Speak the affirmation slowly and calmly. Repeat at least ten times:

- I trust in the power of life.
- I feel at home in my body.
- I am sustained and nourished by nature.

To enhance the power of an energy massage for the root chakra, imagine the energy as a stream of red light that flows through your lower back.

Chakra-Energy Massage

Once a day (but not late at night) you should have a chakra-energy massage for the root chakra:

- Lie on your back. Relax and close your eyes. To stimulate the energy in your hand chakras, rub your palms together in a circular fashion a few times.
- Place your hands to the right and left of your groin. Your thumbs should rest on your pubic bones with the other fingers pointing down.
- Imagine as you inhale that you are taking in prana (life energy). Breathe out as slowly as you can. During the deep exhalation, let the energy course through your root chakra. Imagine that a red stream of light pours through your hands into the root chakra.
- Breathe in and out seven times. As you breathe out, visualize a warm red beam of light flowing from your hands into your root chakra.
- Place your hands at your sides and relax. Remain at rest for a little while to feel the effect.

For an energy massage for the root chakra lie relaxed on your back and place the palms of your hands to the right and left of your groin area.

Activating the Root Chakra in Daily Life

- Exercise regularly. Get physically active. Look for a sport that you enjoy. Easy activities will suffice. You don't have to go in for extreme sports.
- Enjoy a foot massage on a daily basis. Knead the soles of your feet forcefully. This will activate your foot chakras, your reflex zones, and your root chakra.
- Spend as much time as you can outdoors. Take long walks and go barefoot whenever you can.

Walking regularly outdoors in the fresh air is one way of stimulating the root chakra.

- In the morning, bathe your upper and lower legs in cold water. Train a stream of cold water from the feet upward to the thighs and then back down.
- Whenever you can, make direct contact with the earth. Spend time in nature, try to find unspoiled places, meditate under a tree, or work in the garden.
- Wear red clothing and use red fabrics in your home. Place red flowers around the house. Listen to rhythmic music or learn to play the drums.
- Enjoy the sunset.
- These practices will be most effective when engaged in at the time of the full moon.

The Sacral-Chakra Program

The following techniques will enable you to gently awaken the power of your sacral chakra. A harmonious sacral chakra will lend enjoyment and vitality to your life. It connects you to your sensuality and sexuality and allows your creativity to unfold.

Spirituality is not incompatible with enjoying life. On the contrary, one ought to be thankful for the gift of life and learn to fully appreciate one's own being. Take hold of the world around you with the full intensity of your senses. This will prepare the way for inner growth. Cultivating the sacral chakra is always important, but especially so if it is blocked or weakened. If that is the case, then it is imperative for your inner balance that the sacral chakra energies be brought into harmony.

Checkup: When You Need to Work on Your Sacral Chakra

- If you don't enjoy life
- If you don't feel sexually fulfilled or if you suffer from sexual problems
- If you lack appreciation for life and don't recognize its beauty and poetry
- If you are very hard on yourself and put too much importance on discipline and self-control
- If you feel that your creativity is blocked
- If you tend toward jealousy or are preoccupied with feelings of guilt
- If you are prone to back pain
- If you suffer from impotence or lack of sexual appetite
- If you get severe menstrual pain
- If you have bladder or kidney problems
- If your prostate gives you trouble
- If you feel that your physical drives are controlling you

By strengthening your sacral chakra you will increase your joy in living, creativity, and sensuality.

The following techniques work well in combination, or you can choose one that is to your liking. When faced with chronic ailments or psychic problems that may be due to disturbances in the sacral chakra, it is advised that you spend a week's time concentrating on strengthening the sacral chakra using all of the recommended practices.

Aromatherapy

The essential oils we prescribe for harmonizing of the sacral chakra are bitter orange, pepper, myrrh, sandalwood, and vanilla. Make an intuitive choice; use whichever one appeals to you most strongly. Be aware that pepper oil is an especially powerful stimulant. It is best not to use this oil late at night before bed.

- Keep refilling an aroma lamp with a few drops of your favorite oil throughout the day. Let its aroma pervade your surroundings. You can also place a few drops on a handkerchief and carry it with you. Breathe in the aroma frequently.
- For a sensual experience that will stimulate the sacral chakra, take a warm bath. Add a mixture of five drops of vanilla, three drops of sandalwood, and four ounces of cream to your bath just before getting in. Important: Do this only two or three times a week.
- You can also balance the energies of the sacral chakra with an aromatherapy massage. Combine one tablespoon of either avocado or jojoba oil with two drops each of bitter orange and myrrh. Pour the mixture into your palms and massage the area below the navel with a gentle circular motion until the oil is fully absorbed into your skin.

A week-long application of all methods recommended for strengthening the sacral chakra will lead to the best results.

Healing with Plants

Nettle, yarrow, and parsley possess the healing agents that best stimulate the sacral chakra. Nettle strengthens the urinary tract, moderates heavy menstrual bleeding, and improves bladder control.

- Put a tablespoon of nettle or yarrow in a cup of boiling water. Let the tea steep for ten minutes and pour through a strainer. Drink two or three cups daily.
- Parsley has very positive effects. If possible, use freshly cut parsley to ensure that its healthful properties remain intact.

Gemstone Therapy

Hyacinth, gold topaz, aventurine, coral, and fire opal correspond most closely to the energies of the sacral chakra. You will need to listen to your inner voice to choose the one that is right for you.

- Wear the stone on a gold chain for a week.
- The energy of gold topaz and fire opal is especially conducive to the chakras in the hands, so they make very good touchstones.
- For direct chakra therapy, use hyacinth, coral, or aventurine. To harmonize the sacral chakra, lay the stone of your choice directly on your skin. Place it one finger's width below the navel. Concentrate on the sacral chakra and feel how the stone strengthens it.

Nettle, yarrow, and parsley strengthen the organism and, indirectly, the sacral chakra. You should never use parsley during pregnancy.

To activate the power of healing stones, you can wear them on a chain, use them as touchstones or lay them directly on the skin in the area of the sacral chakra.

Bach Flower Therapy

The Bach flower remedies most suitable for the sacral chakra are Oak, Olive, and Pine. These will gently harmonize this energy center. You will get the best results by combining two of the three essences.

Take the Bach flower remedies three times a day before meals. Place three drops on the tongue. Hold in your mouth for a little while, then swish it around and swallow.

Bach flowers have the strongest effect when you combine two of them that correspond to the chakra you are targeting.

Vocalization

The specific vibration in the vowel *o* (a long, drawn-out *o* as in the word *sew*) is particularly effective in stimulating the energy of the sacral chakra. Practice the following exercise twice a day.

Sit up straight and close your eyes. Concentrate. Breathe in through your nose, and as you exhale, let out the long *o* sound. Do this for a few minutes. Pay attention to how the vibration expands in your lower belly.

Affirmations

Choose one of the suggested affirmations, or use one of your own devising on the themes associated with the sacral chakra. Repeat it often throughout the day, ten times at the least. The best time to engage in the practice of affirmation is just after waking up or just before going to bed. Say the sentence silently to yourself or whisper it. Speak each word of the affirmation slowly and calmly:

- I enjoy life with all of my senses.
- I give my creativity and joy in living free rein.
- I lovingly accept my body and my sensuality.

Breathe life energy in and as you exhale let it stream through your sacral chakra.

Chakra-Energy Massage

Try the chakra-energy massage once a day if possible. It will gently awaken the energies in your sacral chakra:

- Lie on the floor on your back, shut your eyes, and rub the palms of your hands together in a circular motion a couple of times to activate the chakras in the hands.
- Put your left hand below your navel in the middle of the belly, and rest the right hand gently on the left. Breathe consciously and slowly into your stomach so that your hands rise and fall. Imagine that you are breathing in life energy, and as you exhale, let it flow into your sacral chakra.
- At the same time, picture an orange-colored beam of energy that streams out of your hands into your stomach with each exhalation. Visualize an orange ball of energy that increases in size with each breath until it radiates throughout your entire belly.
- Hold this image in your mind for seven breaths.
- Put your hands on the floor and experience your body. Pay attention to any changes in how you are feeling. Perhaps you will experience a sense of warmth or well-being in your belly.

In chakra-energy massage you lay your hands on your stomach and the transmit life energy to your sacral chakra.

Activating the Sacral Chakra in Daily Life

Even in everyday life you will find many opportunities to stimulate your sensory awareness.

- Get into contact with water. Take baths, go swimming, or walk by a lake or the ocean.
- Make sure to drink enough liquids, at least two to three quarts of fluid per day. The best drinks are mineral water, juice, or unsweetened herbal teas.
- Explore your creativity, whether with ceramics, painting, or cooking.
- Bring the color orange into your life. Wear orange clothes or scarves; set the table with orange place mats; put orange flowers or a bowl of oranges in your living room.
- Embrace your sensuality. Take aromatic baths, use scented body oils, or take a steam bath.
- Go dancing. Belly dancing, tango Argentina, and salsa all energize the sacral chakra.
- Enroll in a course on tantric yoga.
- Listen to Eastern music or the music of Bach and Vivaldi.
- Use the time of the waxing moon for evening walks and practices that activate the sacral chakra.

Indulge yourself from time to time in an aromatic bath. This will help awaken your sacral chakra.

The Navel-Chakra Program

A strongly developed navel chakra is a fundamental necessity for a strong and stable personality. When you further the development of this chakra, you get a good sense of your abilities and possibilities. It then becomes easier to recognize your true goals in life and gain the necessary willpower to reach them.

The navel chakra connects you to the world of your emotions. It helps you to make gut decisions and to trust your first impressions. When energy flows freely through this chakra, the influence of the fire element will be strongly felt. Fire will awaken your enthusiasm and give you an emotional warmth that can be felt by those around you.

When the energy of your navel chakra is weak or inhibited, you should make it your goal to harmonize and strengthen it. This is especially important if you suffer from any of the complaints that relate to this chakra.

By activating your navel chakra you will strengthen your character and increase your stamina.

Checkup: When You Need to Work on Your Navel Chakra

- If it is difficult for you to express your feelings freely
- If you have a hard time recognizing goals and/or reaching them
- If you give in to others too easily
- If you have a hard time accepting criticism
- If your emotions get the upper hand and you do things that you later regret
- If you suffer from nightmares or insomnia
- If you suffer from anxiety
- If you are prone to stomach problems
- If you have heartburn
- If your stomach feels tight and cramped or you often feel queasy
- If you are overweight or you suffer from eating disorders
- If you have jealous or aggressive tendencies

To harmonize the navel chakra, use one or more of the following techniques. The best results will be gained if you spend a week using all of the suggested practices in combination.

Aromatherapy

Lavender, chamomile, lemon, and anise are all excellent for the gentle stimulation of the third chakra.

- Put a few drops of essential oil in an aroma lamp and let the smell permeate your living or working space.
- A bath using chamomile is especially recommended to balance the energy flow of the navel chakra. For a warm bath, use ten drops of chamomile oil and four ounces of cream. Mix together and pour it into your bath right before getting in. Bathe with chamomile oil no more than three times in a week.
- For a chakra aromatherapy massage, we recommend a mixture of lavender and anise oils. Use jojoba or sesame as the base oil. For every tablespoon of the base oil, use two drops each of lavender and anise. Mix thoroughly, spread onto your palms, and gently massage the area above the navel with this mixture.

Aromatherapy suggests using essential oils in aroma lamps, putting a few drops in a bath, or mixing them with base oils for massage.

Healing with Plants

The healing plants that best support the navel chakra are fennel, chamomile, and juniper.

- The healing power of juniper is most pronounced when the berries are mixed with wine. Add five tablespoons of dried juniper berries to a liter of red wine and let it sit for ten days. Filter out the berries and drink a shot glass of the wine twice a day.
- Chamomile and anise are best used as teas. Use two teaspoons of dried chamomile flowers and two teaspoons of fennel in a cup of boiling water. Let the tea steep for ten minutes, strain, and drink with honey, if desired.

Gemstone Therapy

Citrine, chrysoberyl, amber, tigereye, and yellow jasper are very effective in harmonizing the energy of the navel chakra.

- Use your intuition to choose one of the above gemstones and wear it on gold chain or set in a ring.
- Tigereye and amber make good touchstones. The ancient Greeks treasured tigereye as a symbol of joyous living. Amber is the petrified heart of the evergreen tree. The energy of both stones is exceptionally well received by the chakras in the hands. For the optimal benefit, hold the stone in your hand repeatedly during the day for long periods.
- Citrine and chrysoberyl are particularly well suited for direct chakra therapy. Choose one and lay it directly on the skin about three finger widths above the navel. Concentrate on the energy field of the navel chakra, and feel how and to what extent the stone is affecting the chakra.

The hand chakras take in the healing energy of precious stones and redirect it to the chakra you are working on.

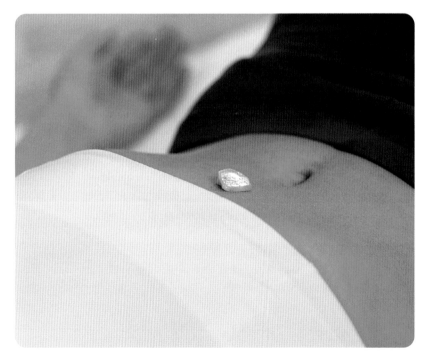

Citrine or chrysoberyl should be laid directly on the navel chakra.

Bach Flower Ttherapy

The Bach flower remedies that have the strongest eaffect on the psychic components of the third chakra are Impatiens, Scleranthus, and Hornbeam. You can choose any one of these, although you will obtain better results by combining two of them. Experience has shown that the best combination is Impatiens/Scleranthus, but the other two combinations can also be effective.

Use the Bach flower remedies three times a day before meals. Place three drops of each essence (six drops altogether) on your tongue. Leave them in your mouth for a little while before swallowing.

Vocalization

Twice a day, practice vocalizing with the vowel sound of the short *o* (as in *ought*). This sound stimulates and harmonizes the navel chakra.

- Sit in a relaxed posture, close your eyes, and let your thoughts come to rest.
- Breathe in through your nose, and when you exhale, intone a drawn-out open *o*.
- Practice this for a few minutes and observe whether you can feel the vibration in the upper part of your belly.

The main effect of Bach flowers remedies is on psychological level. This in turn influences the chakras.

Affirmations

Adopt one of the following affirmations and repeat it a few times a day. The best times to practice are before bed or upon awaking.

Speak the sentence to yourself or quietly whisper it. Say each word slowly and calmly and repeat at least ten times:

- I let my feelings run freely and trust my spontaneous decisions.
- I use my inner strength to make the world a better place.
- Through the power of my will, I can reach any goal.

Chakra-Energy Massage

Try a short chakra-energy massage once a day to consciously send energy to the navel chakra:

- Lie on the floor on your back and close your eyes. Rub your palms together to sensitize your hand chakras.
- Place your hands above the navel on the third chakra. The left hand should lie directly on your stomach with the right resting upon it.
- Breathe into your stomach a few times—let your breath come and go. For seven breaths, picture in your mind that as you inhale you are receiving life energy, and as you exhale this energy is flowing through your hands into the navel chakra.
- At the same time, visualize this life energy in the form of yellow rays flowing out of your hands and into the navel chakra. Now imagine that this part of your body is becoming ever fuller with a healing ball or eddy of yellow energy.
- Lay your hands relaxed on the floor. See if this area of your body now feels more alive, warmer, and more relaxed.

Affirmations work on the unconscious mind. They are a form of self-hypnosis.

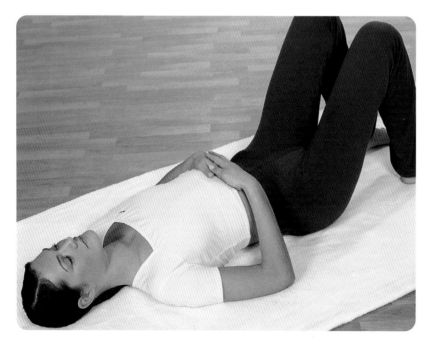

In chakra-energy massage life energy flows through the hands into the navel chakra.

Activating the Navel Chakra in Daily Life

The color yellow stimulates the navel chakra. Wearing yellow clothing and decorating your house with yellow flowers are good ways to bring this color into your life.

- Stay warm, especially when the weather gets cold.
- Make sure that you breathe from your stomach, not from your chest. See that your exhalations are longer than your inhalations.
- Open yourself to the sun's power: enjoy short but regular sunbathing and consciously take in the solar energy.
- Bring the color yellow into your life. Buy yellow clothing, sheets, and place settings. Use lemons as a decorative element in your house.
- Get into contact with the fire element. Try to relax near a fireplace or build a bonfire outside. Light candles in your house.
- Look for things that excite your interest. Make plenty of room for them in your life.
- Romantic music strengthens the navel chakra. Listen to Chopin, Schubert, and Brahms, or go to the opera.
- Learn how to express your feelings. Take classes in acting or mime. Your body has its own expressive language.
- Employ the practices that aim at strengthening the navel chakra during the phase of the waxing moon.

A bouquet of sunflowers will have a soothing effect on the navel chakra.

The Heart-Chakra Program

A well-developed heart chakra enables you to bridge the differences that separate people. As your love and compassion grow over time, you will see that your relationships with others become more satisfying and fulfilling.

By cultivating the heart center, you not only infuse your relationships with greater empathy, you also begin to accept yourself for who you are and recognize your deeper needs and desires more clearly. Only when you are fully aware of what you need and what you want can you truly find yourself.

Engagement with the energies of the heart chakra is for this reason worthwhile for anyone, no matter what their stage in life. The way to freedom lies through the heart chakra. In certain cases, however, it is particularly important to turn your attention to the stimulation and harmonization of the heart chakra.

A strong and harmonious heart chakra will not only make you feel better, it will be felt by everyone around you.

Checkup: When You Need to Work on Your Heart Chakra

- If it is difficult for you let other people into your life
- If you feel lonely or isolated
- If you have relationship problems
- If you are at loggerheads with your partner
- If you have problems sustaining friendships
- If you want to increase your compassion for others and experience a sense of inner peace
- If social situations leave you tired and worn out
- If you have a hard time wholeheartedly accepting yourself
- If you have coronary or circulatory problems
- If you suffer from respiratory problems or asthma
- If you are very susceptible to colds
- If you have serious skin problems

There are many gentle ways to balance the energy of the heart chakra. Here we present some of the most effective methods. You will get very good results when you use two or more in combination. If you suffer from problems connected to the heart chakra, it is best to devote a week to putting all of the following healing methods in to practice.

Aromatherapy

Some essential oils work very well on the heart chakra. Of these, the most highly recommended are rose, jasmine, and tarragon.

- Put a few drops of essential oil in an aroma lamp a number of times during the day. Or let a few drops soak into a handkerchief and breathe in the aroma whenever convenient.
- A bath in rosewater is especially recommended to balance the energy flow of the heart chakra. For a warm bath, use eight drops of rose oil and four ounces of cream. Mix together and pour it into your bath right before getting in.
- For a chakra aromatherapy massage, use a mixture of jasmine and tarragon oils. Use jojoba or sesame as the base oil. For every tablespoon of the base oil, use two drops of jasmine and three drops of tarragon. Mix them thoroughly, spread onto your palms, and massage the area above the heart with a gentle circular motion.

Healing with Plants

A bath with rose oil is especially recommended for harmonizing the heart chakra.

The proper use of healing botanical agents can strengthen your entire organism. Whitehorn, thyme, and melissa work best for the heart chakra.

- Twice a day, drink two large cups of melissa or whitehorn tea. Whitehorn is good for the heart and blood circulation and therefore works indirectly on the heart chakra. Add one tablespoon of dried whitehorn to a cup of boiling water. Let steep for fifteen minutes and strain.
- Melissa also gives support to the heart chakra and is effective when made into a tea. One tablespoon of dried melissa flowers should go into a large cup of boiling water. Let it stand for eight minutes and strain before drinking.

- Thyme honey wine is a most effective elixir for the heart chakra. Use four tablespoons of dried thyme for one liter of red wine. Heat for a little while, adding four tablespoons of honey. Let the mixture stand for one week. Pour the wine through a sieve and take two tablespoons three times a day.

You can activate the heart chakra by placing a piece of jade in the middle of your chest. Feel the stone's energy field.

Gemstone Therapy

Emerald, chrysoprase, jade, and rose quartz are the gemstones that have the greatest harmonizing effects on the heart chakra.

- Once again, let your intuition be your guide in choosing which of these gemstones to use. Wear it on a gold chain against the skin.
- As touchstones, it is best to use either emerald or rose quartz, as their energies are well suited to the hand chakra.
- For direct chakra therapy, use jade. The Chinese considered jade to be the stone of love. Lie relaxed on your back and place a piece of jade in the middle of your chest. Close your eyes and concentrate on the heart chakra. Try to feel how the energy of the stone affects the energy field of your heart chakra.

To directly influence your heart chakra, lie on your back and concentrate on the chakra.

Bach Flower Therapy

Some of the Bach flower essences have positive effects on those aspect of the psyche that are regulated by the heart chakra. The most beneficial of these are Red Chestnut, Willow, and Chicory.

Use the Bach flower remedies three times a day before meals. Place three drops of each essence (six drops altogether) on your tongue. Leave them in your mouth for a little while before swallowing.

Intoning the vowel sound "a" stimulates your entire chest cavity and awakens the heart chakra.

Vocalization

The vibratory frequency of the vowel *a* (as in *father*) stimulates and harmonizes the energy of the heart chakra. Practice vocalization for a few minutes mornings and evenings.

Sit in a relaxed posture and close your eyes. Breathe in through your nose, and as you exhale, intone a drawn-out open *a*. Feel how the sound vibrates through your chest. If you find it difficult to feel the vibrations, place your hands on your chest.

At least once a day you should make some time for a brief energy massage for the heart chakra.

Affirmations

Choose one of the following affirmations. Repeat it often during the day. It is best to practice before bed or upon awaking.

Speak the sentence to yourself or quietly whisper it. Say each word slowly and calmly, and repeat at least ten times:

- My heart is open to giving and receiving love.
- I lovingly accept myself—as I am.
- I give and receive with an open heart and bind myself to all living beings.

Chakra-Energy Massage

For gentle stimulation of the heart chakra, try a short chakra-energy massage once a day:

- Lie relaxed on the floor on your back and close your eyes. Activate your hand chakras by rubbing your palms together in a circle. The left hand should lie palm down in the middle of the chest at the level of the heart with the fingers pointing to the right. Rest the right hand on the left hand. Take a few relaxed breaths.
- Deepen your breathing—especially the exhalation—for a little while. Imagine that each time you inhale, you are taking energy in and that with each exhalation energy is pouring into your heart chakra.
- To intensify the effect, picture this life energy as a green radiance that streams into the heart chakra every time you exhale.
- To take the practice a step further, visualize this green energy in the shape of a ball or whirlpool that fills your chest. Use the power of your imagination, not your will.
- Continue with this practice for the duration of seven breaths. Then rest your hands on the floor and remain quiet for a time so that you can feel the effects of this meditative practice. See whether your chest area feels different from before, whether it seems freer or more alive, and whether your breathing has changed.

Cross your hands over your chest and let life energy in the form of green light stream into your heart center.

Activating the Heart Chakra in Daily Life

Overcoming one's fear of physical contact with other people is a major step towards love, empathy, and personal growth.

- Treat yourself in a loving fashion. Fulfill your desires as far as that is possible. Indulge yourself in things that you truly enjoy.
- Get in touch with the beauty of nature. Take walks through the woods or in pastures and fields as often as you can. Feel the influence of the color green.
- Take loving care of others. Above all, be there to listen to others who need your help.
- Work to develop the inner strength that is needed to show compassion to other people and all living beings.
- Wear green clothing; decorate your house in green. Make sure there are plenty of plants in your home.
- Listen to music that touches your heart.
- Learn to embrace and comfort other people.
- To dispel fears of intimacy, allow yourself to be massaged, or take a course in massage or shiatsu. Or make use of healing techniques that employ the sense of touch such as prana healing or Reiki.
- The new moon and full moon phases are the ideal times for engaging in these practices.

Putting the heart-chakra program into action will improve your relationship with your partner.

The Throat-Chakra Program

A well-developed throat chakra is a prerequisite for the capacity to communicate effectively with other people and express yourself clearly.

People with a strong throat chakra are always looking for the truth. They trust their inspirations, and their forthright way of expressing themselves can provide positive motivation to others. The throat chakra acts as a bridge between the intelligence of the heart and the intelligence of the mind.

In some cases, it is very important to work on the energy of the throat chakra. If it develops along the wrong lines, this can rob you of serenity and inner freedom.

The healing methods we will discuss are especially recommended if you suffer from any of the following complaints.

Checkup: When You Need to Work on Your Throat Chakra

- **If you have a hard time expressing yourself**
- **If you often can't find the right words with which to share your thoughts and feelings**
- **If you suffer from shyness or feel uncomfortable or inhibited in the presence of others**
- **If you say things that you later regret**
- **If you suffer from any kind of speech defect**
- **If you don't feel inspired by your work**
- **If you have a tendency to be manipulative**
- **If you talk other people into the ground**
- **If you have a hard time telling the truth or often find yourself telling white lies**
- **If you suffer from an overactive or underactive thyroid**
- **If you often have sore throats**
- **If you suffer from neck or shoulder pain**

When your throat chakra is strong and free of blockages your heart and head will work together in harmony.

To harmonize the throat chakra, use the following techniques in combination or individually. When the throat chakra is weak, you should consider devoting a week and using all of the methods suggested below, if possible.

Aromatherapy

The suggested essential oils for the throat chakra, eucalyptus, camphor, and peppermint, are very strong and should treated with care. You shouldn't use them in your bath.

For the throat chakra, the recommended essential oils are eucalyptus, camphor, and peppermint. But be careful—these oils are very intense. You should carefully monitor the dosage.

- Make an intuitive choice of one of the above. Put a few drops in an aroma lamp and enjoy its stimulating fragrance.
- A steam bath with a few drops of peppermint oil purifies the throat chakra. Alternate breathing with your nose and mouth. Make sure to keep your eyes closed.
- For a chakra aromatherapy massage, use sesame oil as a base. For one tablespoon of sesame oil, use three drops of the essential oil that you like best. Pour it into your hands and massage it into your neck and shoulders with slow stroking movements, until the oil has been completely absorbed.

Healing with Plants

The healing plants that work best on the throat chakra are peppermint, sage, and coltsfoot. These will balance and stimulate this center's activity.

- Peppermint tea is purifying and increases the amount of prana taken from the air. Drink a large cup two or three times a day. Brew one to two teaspoons of peppermint flower in a cup of boiling water. Let the liquid sit for seven minutes and then strain.
- Sage also makes good tea, but even more effective is sage milk. Heat one teaspoon of dried sage flowers with a small cup of milk. Remove from the heat and let stand for three minutes before straining. Sweeten with a teaspoon of honey. Drink one cup three times a day.
- Coltsfoot protects the neck and throat and eases smoker's cough. For a large cup of tea, you need two teaspoons of coltsfoot. Don't

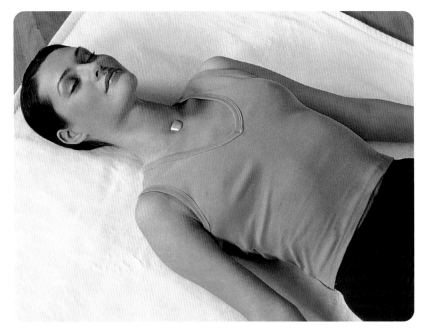

To use gemstones to heal your throat chakra, lie on your back, and place the stone you select in the hollow of your throat.

let the tea stand for longer than five minutes. Drink twice a day after meals.

Gemstone Therapy

The specific vibratory frequencies of lapis lazuli, aquamarine, and topaz are most successful in balancing and gently stimulating the throat chakra.

- Make an intuitive choice from one of these three gemstones. Wear it on a gold chain directly against the skin.
- Lapis is especially recommended for use as a touchstone. In order for its healing energy to be absorbed by the chakras in your hands, hold it in your hands for an extended period several times during the day.
- You will obtain the best results in direct chakra therapy using aquamarine or blue topaz. Lie on your back. The best place to put the stone is in the hollow of your throat. Close your eyes and try to get in contact with your throat chakra. Try to feel the vibrations of the stone.

Gemstones can be worn on a chain, used as touchstones or placed directly on the area corresponding to the chakra you are working on.

Bach Flower Therapy

As noted earlier, Bach flower remedies work on a psychic level, and there is a correspondence between the mental and spiritual aspects that they affect and the seven chakras. The Bach flower essences that best correspond to the throat chakra are Agrimony, Cerato, and Mimulus. You will experience the full benefit of these remedies if you use two of them together.

Use the Bach flower remedies three times a day before meals. Place three drops of each essence (six drops altogether) on your tongue. Leave them in your mouth for a little while before swallowing.

Bach flower remedies should be taken three times a day, always just before meals. Place a few drops directly on your tongue.

Vocalization

The vowel that works best to activate and balance the throat chakra is *a* (as in *game*). Practice vocalization twice a day.

- Sit up straight but stay relaxed. Breathe in through the nose and as you exhale intone a long, drawn-out *a*.
- In order to get the full effects in the area of your throat, continue this practice for three minutes at a time.

Affirmations

Choose one of the following affirmations, or make up an affirmation of your own that corresponds to the theme of the throat chakra. Repeat as many times as you can throughout the day. The best times for this practice are shortly before going to bed and just after getting up:

- I speak from the heart and let the truth be my guide.
- I use the power of words to make the world a better place.
- Every day it becomes easier to express what I think and feel.

Chakra-Energy Massage

You should take time to relax every day with a brief chakra-energy massage. This will have very positive effects on your throat chakra:

- Lie on your back and shut your eyes. Rub your palms together to activate your hand chakras.
- Place your hands gently and without pressure around your throat. The wrist of each hand should touch and rest on the collarbone. Your fingers should be pointing toward your ears.
- Breathe deeply. Imagine that with each breath you are taking in life energy and letting it pour out into your neck.
- To intensify this practice, picture this energy in the form of bright blue rays that stream from your hands into the area of your larynx.
- Keep this image in your mind for seven breaths. Focus on the area of the larynx as it is being filled with healing, bright blue light. You can also visualize this energy as a ball of light.

Before beginning a chakra-energy massage, rub your hands gently together to activate the chakra in your palms.

During the chakra-energy massage visualize as you exhale that life energy in the form of light-blue rays streams in to the throat chakra.

Activating the Throat Chakra in Daily Life

- Occupy yourself with the theme of communication. Try to find the right words to express your thoughts and feelings. Take voice training or a course in public speaking. Learn another language.
- Keep a journal. Write down your daily experiences.
- Expose yourself to the blue colors of the natural world. Look up at the open sky, or if possible spend time at the beach or by the shores of a lake.
- Bring bright blue colors into your life. Wear blue clothing, scarves, and jewelry. Use bright blue hand and bath towels. Place vases of blue flowers in your living quarters.
- Find your voice through vocalization and the use of mantras. Take the time to sing or play a musical instrument. Join a choir. Learn how to express yourself in music.
- Develop the courage to hold to your own opinions. Hold to the truth while preserving a friendly, noncombative demeanor.
- The practices designed for the throat chakra work best while the moon is on the wane.

To recharge your batteries, lie in the grass and look up at the blue sky.

A trip to the seaside can awaken and strengthen the energy of the throat chakra.

The Forehead-Chakra Program

The forehead chakra is the gate that leads to deeper realization and insight. When it is well developed, the power of light will suffuse your being.

With the help of the forehead chakra, you can make use of your powers of intuition and imagination to reach your goals without excessive stress. As long as the sixth chakra is weakened or blocked, you won't be able to attain wisdom or real inner peace.

In the following pages, we will discuss the different techniques that you can use to harmonize the forehead chakra and carefully dissolve existing blockages. Everyone needs to pay attention to and cultivate the energies of the third eye.

Sometimes it is a matter of urgency to address problems that are related to this chakra. You should consider a program directed toward healing the forehead chakra when you suffer from one or more of the following problems.

Embark on the healing program for the forehead chakra, if you are looking to expand your horizons or are having difficulty concentrating.

Checkup: When You Need to Work on Your Forehead Chakra

- If you often have the feeling that life is meaningless and barren
- If you regularly suffer from anxiety or depression
- If you have difficulty giving your fantasy life free rein
- If you can't hear your inner voice or hear it only very faintly
- If you can't find your way, find it hard to get oriented, or don't perceive your path and purpose in life.
- If you have a hard time concentrating and your thoughts seem scattered
- If you are susceptible to headaches and sinus problems
- If you have problems with your eyes or vision
- If you want to bring more light into your life
- If you are striving for a higher realization

In the following pages, we describe the most important techniques for harmonizing the forehead chakra. You can practice those you prefer at any time. As the techniques complement each other, you will get even better results if you combine some of them. Best of all, if your goal is to correct imbalances in the forehead chakra, is to devote a week's time and put all of the suggested techniques into practice.

Be careful when you use essential oils to massage the forehead chakra, as they can irritate your eyes.

Aromatherapy

Some essential oils work especially well in balancing the energies of the forehead chakra. We suggest cajeput, lemongrass, and violet. Make sure to buy oils that appeal to your sense of smell, and go with your gut feelings in choosing the one that is best for you.

- Place a few drops of the oil you select in an aroma lamp at work or at home. If you are traveling, just put a few drops on a handkerchief and sniff it whenever you can.
- For a bath that will bring the activity of the forehead chakra into balance, use violet. Infuse a full bath with eight drops of violet oil mixed with four ounces of cream. Pour it into the water just before getting in the bath. This violet-scented bath should be enjoyed two or three times a week.
- For a chakra aromatherapy massage, you will want to rub one of these oils into your forehead. One warning: This area is relatively close to your eyes. Don't use lemongrass, and follow the recommended dosages carefully.
- Use one drop of violet or cajeput oil mixed with a teaspoon of jojoba or almond oil. Using your index and middle fingers, massage the center of your forehead with this mixture. Rub the oil with a circular motion until it has been fully absorbed. Make sure to keep your eyes shut while doing this, as the oil can be an irritant.

Gemstone Therapy

The stones that have the best effect on the third eye are blue sapphire, opal, and blue tourmaline. Listen to your inner voice when making your purchase, choosing a stone with a dark blue or violet color.

To use gemstones to heal the forehead chakra, place the stone you wish to use directly in the center of your forehead.

- Wear the stone you choose on a chain or use it as a touchstone that you can hold in your hands for extended periods throughout the day.
- Sapphire is the best stone to use in direct chakra therapy.
- Lie relaxed on your back. Place the stone in the middle of your forehead. Close your eyes and make contact with your forehead chakra. Try to feel how the sapphire affects its energy field.

Healing with Plants

Saint-John's-wort, spruce, and eyebright all are effective in stimulating the forehead chakra and balancing the energies in this area. Saint-John's-wort brings light to the soul and is especially good in the dark seasons of the year to drive away sorrow and depression. Ask your health care practitioner, since Saint-John's-wort is effective only when used in high doses.

To help your eyesight and at the same time gently harmonize the functioning of the forehead chakra, use a compress that has been soaked in a tea made from eyebright.

Taken in combination red wine and spruce needles awaken the energy flowing through the forehead chakra.

- Brew a tablespoon of eyebright in boiling water. Let it stand for ten minutes, then strain and let it cool down a bit. Dip a cloth in the tea and lay it on your eyelids.
- To prepare an elixir from spruce, which will invigorate the forehead with new energy, use three tablespoons of dried spruce needles in a liter of red wine. Bring the wine to a boil, remove it from the stove, let it cool, and pour into a bottle. Let the mixture sit for a week, then filter it. Take a tablespoon three times a day before meals.

Bach Flower Therapy

To activate the forehead chakra with Bach flowers, use any two of the following in combination: Crab Apple, Vine, and Walnut.

Use the Bach flower remedies three times a day before meals. Place three drops of each essence (six drops altogether) on your tongue. Leave them in your mouth for a little while before swallowing.

Vocalization

Practice vocalization twice a day. Sit relaxed and close your eyes. Use the vowel sound *e* (as in *meet*). Engage in this practice for at least three minutes. Breathe in through the nose and as you exhale intone the *e* in a long, drawn-out fashion. Concentrate on the third eye.

You should practice vocalization twice a day for at least three minutes.

Affirmations

Choose one of the following affirmations, and repeat it shortly before going to bed or just after you get up. Say the sentence inwardly or whisper it to yourself. Say each word slowly. Repeat at least ten times:

- I am in touch with my inner light.
- I let my fantasy run free.
- I listen to my inner voice.
- I look inward and recognize what is essential.

Chakra-Energy Massage

Once a day, indulge yourself in a brief chakra-energy massage. This will harmonize and gently stimulate the forehead chakra. Follow these steps:

- Lie on the floor on your back and relax. Softly close your eyes. To activate the energy in your hand chakras, rub your hands together with a circular motion.
- Place your left hand gently on your forehead. The right hand should lie on top of your left hand. Your hands should be relaxed. The easiest way is to follow the natural line of your elbows.
- Visualize as you breathe in that you are absorbing healing life energy and that this energy pours into your forehead as you breathe out.
- Imagine that this energy is in the form of dark blue rays that flow from your hands and manifest themselves as a whirlpool or ball of energy.
- Repeat this visualization practice for the duration of seven breaths. Your breathing should keep getting deeper.
- Finally, slowly rest your hands on the floor. Don't open your eyes right away; rather, first feel the activation of the forehead chakra.

After finishing the energy massage for the forehead chakra give yourself enough time to relax and feel its full effect.

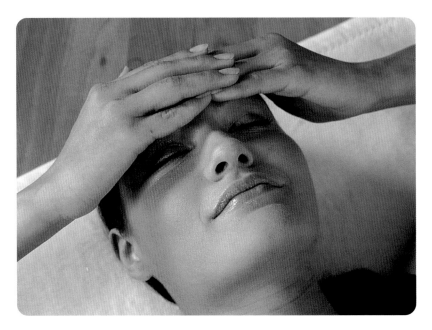

Your hands should rest gently on the forehead.

- Keep your eyes closed.
- Become aware of yourself, and try to feel whether you are experiencing light or warmth in the region of your forehead and whether your head, eyes, and forehead feel better and more relaxed than when you began the chakra-energy massage. Now you can gently open your eyes.

Activating the Forehead Chakra in Daily Life

- Read philosophical and spiritual literature from the Eastern and Western traditions.
- Study the works of the Buddha, Lao-tsu, Plato, Schopenhauer, and other great thinkers and philosophers.
- Keep a dream journal. Write down just after awakening all that you dreamed the night before. Try to interpret your own dreams. The more you study your dreams, the more intense and clear they will become.

An active fantasy life will stimulate the energy in the forehead chakra.

- Try meditating under the stars. Let the stillness and power of the night guide you.
- Let your fantasy take wing. Read fairy tales and mythology, try to visualize crazy things, or, better yet, write a short story of your own. Everything that promotes your fantasy life also awakens your forehead chakra.
- Buy some dark blue clothes. Use towels, tablecloths, and dishes of dark blue.
- The best time to work on the forehead chakra is during the phase of waning moon.

The Crown-Chakra Program

The crown chakra is the awareness center of spirituality and religious sentiment. It is the subtlest of all the chakras, and its connection to the physical body is the most tenuous.

The crown chakra, also called the seventh chakra, is best developed through the techniques of chakra yoga and meditation. It is less affected by naturopathic healing methods, but nonetheless these can work in a subtle way to harmonize the crown chakra.

The best way of enhancing the crown chakra through natural healing methods is to engage in intensive work on all the other chakras. This will inevitable lead to an improvement in the crown chakra.

It is most important to be very careful and gentle with yourself when working with the crown chakra. If you go slowly and cautiously, there will be no danger of harming yourself. Even so, some teachers do not recommend working directly on the crown chakra by oneself. In any case, it is extremely beneficial for the crown chakra to function harmoniously.

You should seriously consider work on the crown chakra if you identify with one or more of the following complaints.

In the harmonization of the subtlest energy center, the crown chakra, you need to proceed with the greatest care.

Checkup: When You Need to Work on Your Crown Chakra

- If you are often depressed and experience a lack of joy in life
- If you feel tired and worn out even though you sleep deeply
- If you suffer from chronic or life-threatening illnesses
- If your immune system is weakened
- If you can find no avenue to higher levels of being
- If you believe that there is no life after death
- If you wish to experience the mystery and strength of silence

The following techniques provide support for harmonizing the crown chakra. If you suffer from concrete problems that are due to blockages in the crown chakra, you should try several of these techniques in combination to increase their positive effect. The best success will be obtained when you take the time to devote a week to this endeavor and try if possible to put into practice all of the suggested techniques.

When you're on the road, just put a few drops of the recommended aromatic oil on a handkerchief and carry it with you.

Aromatherapy

The essential oils of incense and rosewood foster spirituality and provide a good foundation for the crown chakra.

- Put a few drops of either oil in an aroma lamp. If you are traveling, you can use a handkerchief with a few drops of oil and breathe it in whenever you can.
- Enjoy the pleasure of an aroma bath. A hot bath scented with rosewood will have an indirect stimulating effect upon the crown chakra. Mix seven drops of rosewood oil with four ounces of cream. Pour the mixture into the bath just before you get in.

Gemstone Therapy

Diamond, rock crystal, and amethyst have positive effects on the energy field of the crown chakra.

- Amethyst and rock crystal should be used as touchstones. Their energies are well suited to the hand chakras.
- For direct chakra therapy, use a small diamond. Sit as straight as possible and place the stone on the top of your head. (It won't be that easy to balance the stone, and you may eventually have to use your hand to keep it from falling off. But try to keep it balanced as long as you can.)
- Concentrate on your crown chakra and observe how the diamond makes you feel.

Place a healing stone directly on the very top of your head and feel its power.

Bach Flower Therapy

There are Bach flower remedies that strengthen those parts of the psyche that lie within the influence of the crown chakra. The most helpful are Wild Rose and White Chestnut.

Diamonds are very powerful healing agents when placed directly on the crown chakra.

- Use the Bach flower remedies three times a day before meals. Place three drops of each essence (six drops altogether) on your tongue. Leave them in your mouth for a little while before swallowing.

For an energy massage for the crown chakra lay first your left and then your right hand at the very top of your head.

Affirmations

During the chakra energy massage energy flows into your head as crystal-clear or bright violet light.

Choose one of the following affirmations and repeat just as you awake and right before you go to sleep. Say the sentence silently or whisper it to yourself. Make sure to say each word slowly and distinctly. Repeat no fewer than ten times:

- I am fully aware—in my body, thoughts, and feelings.
- The essence of my being is light and peace.
- I open myself to the infinite power of God.

Chakra-Energy Massage

The seventh chakra can also be gently stimulated and harmonized using the technique of chakra-energy massage:

- Lie on the floor on your back. Relax and close your eyes. To awaken the energy of the hand chakras, gently rub your hands together a few times.
- Place your left hand at the very top of your head and place your right hand over the left. Breathe in and out a few times.
- Let your breathing become deeper, and begin to imagine that with each inhalation you are drawing in cosmic energy and with each exhalation that energy is being sent to your crown chakra.
- Repeat this for the duration of seven breaths, while visualizing this energy as indigo or clear light that streams from your hands into your crown chakra.
- Lay your hands relaxed on the floor and become aware of the harmonizing effect on the crown chakra.
- Take some time. Try to heighten your inner awareness so that you can feel whether the energy massage has changed anything, whether you can perceive a difference in your mind and spirit, and whether your thoughts feel freer and lighter.

One of the best ways to harmonize the crown chakra is to meditate in quiet surroundings.

Activating the Crown Chakra in Daily Life

- Open yourself to the power of silence. Practice relaxation, sit silently, meditate, and let your thoughts and feelings become calm. There are many different forms of meditation that can bring you into contact with the power of silence.
- Take up mountain climbing. Go as often as you can to the mountains and look down into the valleys. Open yourself to the energy of mountain peaks.
- Wear white and indigo clothing. Use these colors in your house—as towels, carpets, and dishes.
- Decorate your house with white or purple flowers such as white roses, daisies, white lilies, and campanula.
- Work with your aura (see also chapter 8). By strengthening your energy field, you will also strengthen your crown chakra.
- The best time to undertake these practices is during the phase of the new moon.

8 Prana and the Aura

You don't need a diploma in esoteric studies to activate the chakras. All the exercises and recommendations described in this book are safe and gentle. You can begin them at any time. The proof of their effectiveness will be in the positive changes you feel in your body and mind. Just using your intuition as a guide, you can embark with confidence on the practice of chakra work.

A look, however, at the theoretical bases of the practice can deepen your understanding of how the process works. In this chapter, you will discover the fundamental principles that underlie the teaching on the chakras and learn something about such phenomena as the human aura, the astral body, and the layers of subtle energy of which it is composed. Some basic esoteric ideas will be included to the extent that they have significance for chakra work.

The astral body is composed of subtle energy surrounding the physical body.

A World Beyond the Senses

One fundamental idea that informs the teaching on the chakras is that there is more to reality than what we perceive with our five senses. Dreams pose the question "Where was I last night? Was I lying in bed or walking through the delightful landscape that appeared to me in my dream?" Or you might ask yourself: "What part of myself lay motionless in bed and what part spoke, saw things, laughed, and moved through the dream, all the while taking the dream for reality?" Everyday reality is something quite different from the reality we experience in our dreams. Other levels of reality can reveal themselves in visions, premonitions, meditation, and trance.

The Astral Body

Although one could maintain that there are many levels of reality, chakra teaching distinguishes between two fundamental realities—that of the outer, visible world and that of the world that under normal circumstances remains unseen. Just as there is a visible and an invisible world, so we have a visible and an invisible body. To distinguish between the gross and subtle bodies is most important for chakra practice.

It is only with our inner senses that we can perceive the transcendent reality.

The methods described in this book are spiritual in nature. They serve to harmonize the subtle body. This approach separates the prescribed methods from calisthenics, which are directed to the training and strengthening of the physical body.

Chakra work is not fitness training. It uses spiritual practices to awaken and direct subtle energies. That this also brings harmony to one's physical being is a positive side effect, but it is not the primary aim of the practice.

In chakra teaching, the body composed of these subtle energies is called the astral body. Different esoteric schools call it by different names, such as the etheric, light, or mental body. Some systems further distinguish between different types of subtle bodies, as for example between an emotional and a mental body. For the purposes of chakra teaching, we use the term *astral body* to encompass all of these subtle phenomena insofar as they relate to the physical body.

Ensouling Power

The astral body is not only the polar opposite of the physical body; it is also the spiritualizing power that lends awareness to the physical body. Composed of pure light, it penetrates the material world and is not dependent on space and time.

The nadis are the channels or veins of subtle energy, and the chakras are the energy centers. All of this subtle power works directly on the astral body and then indirectly on its physical counterpart. The following table outlines the differences and the borders of the physical and astral bodies.

Physical body	Astral body
Gross material	Subtle energy
Composed of the five visible elements: earth, water, fire, air, ether	Composed of light that incorporates the seven chakras and is visible in the different layers of the aura
Vehicle for the organs, bones, blood, lymph, muscles, cells, etc.	Vehicle for emotions, thoughts, ideas, and tendencies
Provides the sense of self in everyday life	Provides the sense of self in dream, meditation, and trance states
Corresponds to the earthly sphere	Corresponds to the heavenly sphere

Spiritual Discoveries with the Astral Body

The sense that the end of one's physical existence is not the end of one's inner life can be said to be the underlying impulse of all religions. Those who work with meditation and the practices of chakra work will discover that there is a further existence lying beyond that of the physical body. Chakra work attributes this transcendent experience of being to the activity of the astral body. From the point of view of chakra teaching, the astral body is connected to the earth and the earthly plane only insofar as it is connected to the physical body. The connection between the physical and spiritual bodies is often referred to as the silver cord. The silver cord can be seen as an etheric umbilical cord through which the astral body provides the physical body with energy. While we are asleep, this connection is loosened and we directly touch the astral world in dreams and in deep sleep rest our total awareness. At the point of death, the silver cord snaps and the astral body releases its hold upon the material world. All of the energy that has sustained physical life is reintegrated into the astral body, so that through death the physical body returns to its compositional elements. Chakra teaching ascribes many unexplained phenomena such as extrasensory perception, déjà

The astral body is less closely tied to the material plane than the physical body.

vu, and paranormal powers to the workings of the astral body. Near-death experiences serve as proof of its existence. People who have been declared clinically dead during operations or from accidents and then regained consciousness report similar experiences. Often they are able to describe in detail the operation or what was being said by those around their deathbed. Many speak of experiences of bright light.

The Astral Body and the Chakras

The astral body is the level at which the spiritual development of an individual is determined. It is the soul's body. After death, it survives essentially unchanged, while the physical body is broken down into its constituent parts and set aside. One can look at the chakras as the organs of the astral body. Here, according to chakra teaching, we find the subtle life processes taking place. The chakras unfold and from them radiates life energy that travels through the nadis, the energy channels.

After death all of one's energy withdraws into the astral body. It is, in fact, the body of the soul.

The activity of our chakras stamps our talents, tendencies, and all our personal qualities. According to chakra teaching, they will play as important a role in our next life as they do in our spiritual development in this one. Through the practices of chakra healing, we can decisively engage in the reformation of our astral body and, through work on a subtle energy level, address such character failings as hate, envy, greed, and fear and let go of them. By so doing, we attain inner freedom and a loving awareness that will enrich our future existence. In Hinduism and Buddhism, one encounters in this respect the concept of karma. Simply put, karma is the law of cause and effect. Everything that we do has consequences. If in this life you have been unjust to other people and kept them from the light, you will be betrayed by others in your next life—that is karma. To engender good karma is the most important element of spiritual development. Good acts are the way in which one can influence one's karma for the better. By strengthening your chakras, you can allow energy to flow unhindered through your astral body and you will make a positive contribution to your personality and your spiritual life.

The Aura: The Eighth Chakra

Cultivating the aura is a simple way to increase the effectiveness of chakra work and improve your health. Like the chakras, the different layers of the aura are phenomena of the subtle world. Classical yoga teaching has known about the aura for more than five thousand years. In kundalini yoga, the aura is considered to be of such importance that it is referred to as the eighth chakra.

A practice that consists of work on the aura as well as the chakras is the best way to rid yourself of illness, promote wellness, and develop spiritual balance and inner clarity and strength. When you direct your awareness to your inner and outer energy fields, you will harmonize your astral body in the shortest time. Chakra work and aura work go hand in hand.

Everything we do to activate the chakras will increase the radiance of our aura. And work on aura will in turn help us develop our chakras in a harmonious fashion.

A strong aura is a prerequisite for physical and mental balance.

The Radiant Person

Each person has a unique radiance. No doubt you have friends and acquaintances who put forth positive emanations and have a good influence on those around them. The opposite is probably true as well. There are some people who have something unhealthy or unpleasant about them that you may find hard to define: a negative aura.

The aura depends upon the path that each of us takes. But what makes a strong personality? What is the secret behind personal magnetism? For some it is a matter of external factors. One's appearance, physical composure, facial expressions, and posture are all marked by the aura. Of greater importance are inner factors. Someone who is self-aware and possesses clarity, tranquillity, and happiness—who is, in short, in a state of psychic harmony—radiates these positive qualities. And those who have eyes to see will perceive that such people have bright, shining, pure auras.

The aura is a sheath of energy. Plants, animals, in fact, every living creature has an aura, though it is easier to perceive the human aura.

The Seven Layers of the Aura

In everyday speech, one talks about someone's aura as good or bad vibration. Chakra teaching looks more closely into the phenomenon of the aura. Just as there are seven principal chakras, so the teaching identifies seven layers or shells to the aura. These layers are compound energy fields of varying thickness.

The first layer of the aura corresponds to the level of the physical body. This is the physical aura, the most condensed form of spiritual energy. The seventh layer consists of pure cosmic energy, the level of the Divine. The finer and more ethereal the aura layer, the brighter and stronger its radiance.

The seven shells are not cut off from one another; they interpenetrate and commune with each other. Seers and other sensitive people are able to perceive the aura's layers as bands of color and light.

The aura has often been described as a cloud of light that encircles an individual. The aura is most clearly perceptible around the head, such as the halo seen in images of Christian saints and holy figures. Most representations of Shiva and the Buddha depict them as wreathed in a circle of light to indicate their positive radiance. As we grow spiritually, and our inner power increases, our aura becomes more filled with light. The different colors that the human aura shows are the result of the different vibratory frequencies of each layer. Chakra teaching distinguishes seven layers.

The First Layer

The first level of the aura contains the densest energy. It corresponds to the boundary of our physical being, our skin. In Sanskrit, this layer is called *annamaya kosha*, which means "shell of nourishment."

This shell corresponds to the five elements that make up the physical body (earth, water, fire, air, and ether). It governs the major phases of earthly existence: birth, growth, aging, and death.

The Second Layer

The second layer of the aura is the vital or etheric shell. It adjoins the etheric body. In Sanskrit, it is called *pranamaya kosha*, the "life shell." As it is very thick around the surface of the skin, it is perceived as a second etheric body or etheric double. This layer regulates the body's energetic processes: body temperature, circulation, metabolism, hormonal secretion, and respiration. Hunger and thirst, the sensation of hot and cold, and the self-preservation instinct are all impulses connected with this second layer.

Gods and enlightened beings are portrayed surrounded with a cloud of light. The haloes of saints in Christian art are representations of the aura.

The Third Layer

The so-called emotional shell is the boundary of the emotional body. The label is somewhat misleading, since it is concerned not only with emotion but with thoughts, desires, dreams, and other aspects of the inner self. The Sanskrit name *manomaya kosha* is better translated as the "psychic shell."

The third aura layer affects our thoughts, our unconscious, and the five senses. It also influences our moods.

The Fourth Layer

The fourth layer, known as the mental shell, forms the boundary of the mental body. This corresponds to the more refined aspects of the personality. Mental clarity, the world of ideas, intuition, and decisiveness all belong to this level. In Sanskrit, this layer is called *vijnanamaya kosha*, "the shell of knowledge."

The different layers of the aura progress from the world of phenomena to the level of the Divine.

The Fifth Layer

The causal shell bounds the causal body. In spiritually developed people, this can be a mile wide. The causal shell is the last visible layer of the aura—the two highest levels are pure spirit and imperceptible even to the spiritually gifted. The Sanskrit name for this layer is *anandamaya kosha*, "the shell of pure bliss." Joy and happiness are the predominant feelings associated with the experience of this layer. The causal shell is a boundary line. Below it lies the earthly sphere; above it, the Divine.

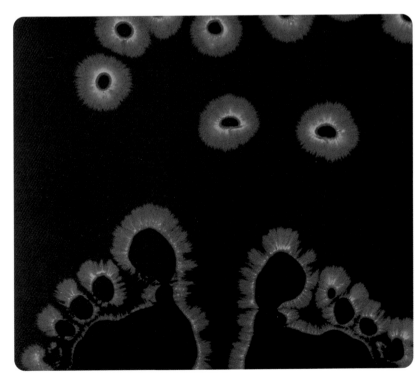

Kirlian photography can render the auras of living creatures visible.

The Sixth Layer

The sixth layer is that of the soul. Its Sanskrit name, *jiva*, means "the individual soul." Spiritual light and the cosmic vibration are phenomena belonging to the sixth level.

The soul shell cannot be perceived by the senses. In a deep meditative state, we can, however, feel it as inner light and vibration.

The Seventh Layer

The highest layer of the aura is the heavenly or divine shell. This is the level of one's divine self. The nature of this level is that of the omnipresent self or God. Only enlightened beings attain awareness of this level.

The highest level of the aura, the seventh layer, can only be perceived through the experience of enlightenment.

Strengthening Your Aura

There are many things you can do to make your aura stronger. All meditative techniques strengthen the aura. Yoga and chakra practices intensify your etheric radiance—even when you are not focusing on the aura. There are also particular techniques you can use that specifically address these subtle layers of your being and can instill them with new energy.

The Protective Function of the Aura

A strong aura will protect you from destructive and aggressive people and vibrations. At the same time, it will enable you to send positive energy out into the world. Practical work on the astral body is concerned only with the first five shells of the aura. They compose the individual aura—the electromagnetic field that envelops the physical body in a cloud of light. When seers describe their perception of the aura, they are always referring to these five levels, since the two highest shells of the aura are pure spirit and beyond the reach of the most refined senses.

Highly sensitive people describe the auras of plants, animals and people as clouds of light of various colors.

The shells of the aura that are visible to such sensitive people can also be seen through the medium of Kirlian photography (see picture on p.178). The Russian electrical engineer Semën Kirlian invented a special photographic process that reveals different-colored halos, thus providing information about the spiritual condition of the person being photographed. The aura of a person who is downcast or depressed, for example, will be less distinct than that of someone in a positive frame of mind.

A strong aura acts as a protective shield against hostility and negative influences.

Our physical and psychic condition expresses itself not only through the chakras but through the aura as well.

At the same time, we can make positive improvements to our health and state of mind by becoming aware of our chakras and aura and working on their development and radiance.

People who have developed a strong radiant energy field cannot be easily thrown off course. Their aura protects them from the negative influences that come from their environment.

In fact, we can think of the aura as a kind of spiritual protective screen. One can perhaps recall the Starship Enterprise on the TV series *Star-Tre*k and Captain Kirk calling for all energy to the shields when under attack. In a similar way, the aura acts as a protective screen. Just as the body's immune system defends it from potentially harmful viruses and bacteria, so the aura protects us from the damaging negative thoughts and emotions that encroach on us from without.

Attuning Your Perceptions

In order to activate your aura, you need to sensitize your awareness to receive subtler vibrations. Normally we are focused on the everyday world of the senses. But with careful attention, we can begin to feel the presence of etheric power.

In all likelihood, you already have some experience of subtler energies and the phenomena of the aura:

- Have you had the sensation that someone standing behind you is looking at you?
- Have you ever felt that something is making you uneasy, without any clear reason for that feeling?
- Do you walk into a room and feel that the atmosphere is heavy? Or perhaps the opposite, that it seems light and free?
- Have you ever experienced telepathic communication, for example, picked up a telephone to call a friend and at that moment the phone rang and your friend was on the line?
- Have you ever felt the presence of someone who is in actuality miles away?
- Have you ever seemed to feel or see energy flowing between a mother and child or between two lovers?

Positive work on the astral body will also harmonize the body and mind.

Learning to pay close attention to such experiences is the ideal preparation for beginning work on the aura and chakras.

Gathering Your Energy

Anything that robs you of energy depletes your aura. On the other hand, whatever steps you take to promote the free flow of energy will enhance your aura's radiance.

Avoid people who leave you feeling drained. If after spending time with an acquaintance, friend, or family member you feel worn out or dragged down, you might consider staying away from that person for a time.

In the *Hatha Yoga Pradipika*, an important early text on the practice of yoga, it is written: "Too much food and too much stress, talking or swearing too much, incorrect practice and bad people—these six things darken the light of the soul." One might put it another way and say that these six things interfere with the development of the chakras and aura. Stay away from things that steal your energy.

Taking Care of Your Body

Often people following a spiritual path will neglect their physical bodies. They become more interested in developing magical powers than in occupying themselves with the mundane needs of everyday life. In yoga, however, one is taught to pay careful attention to the body, since it is the temple of the soul.

Avoid anything that robs your energy: junk food, stress and overwork, gossip, and chaotic or destructive people.

Our bodies are gifts from God, providing an opportunity for spiritual growth through becoming fully involved in life on this planet. To strengthen your aura, you have to take good care of your body. Its demands are basically modest. All you really need to do is take some time each day to care for it. Stay active; eat fresh, nutritious foods; and get plenty of fresh air and enough rest.

Choosing Your Own Path

It is up to you to decide what you want to focus your attention on, what is important to you, and what qualities you want to develop. At the beginning of every journey, one must make a conscious choice.

Your aura provides you with an invisible shield that protects you from destructive powers. It is a permeable membrane that provides separation between the inner and outer worlds but also makes exchanges between the two possible.

The secret of a radiant aura lies in this: You must consciously build up the strength of your love, trust, and peace. Send positive thoughts into the world and defend yourself from the negative powers of hate, envy, and greed so that they don't gain a foothold in your life and spirit.

Take care of your body.
Fresh air and exercise
will strength your aura.

How you direct your consciousness will determine what powers you send out and what powers you take in. If, for example, you spend your time gossiping and bad-mouthing people, you will diminish the light and radiance of your aura. Even if you have a positive attitude toward others, you will darken your soul's light if you devote your attention to the sensationalism and horror stories peddled by the media.

Every day you face two important decisions: what effect you want your speech and actions to have on the world around you, and what impressions and vibrations you want to be receptive to. This second idea means that there are some impressions from the outside world you will have to shut out.

It is not only the big things in life that are important. Less dramatic choices influence the paths that we take. It makes a difference whether you eat fast food or fresh fruit, vegetables, and whole grains; whether you read spiritually uplifting books or the tabloids. You need to choose between thought-provoking, inspiring movies and horror or slasher films, between heavy metal and Mozart, between gossip and respect for others.

Every time you choose wisely, you fortify your soul, increase your serenity and inner peace, and strengthen the energy of the chakras. And this will be reflected in the radiance of your aura.

The secret of a radiant aura is to send constructive energy out into the world and not take any destructive energy back into yourself.

Live Intensely

The more alive you are, the more radiant and alive your aura. The aura is not only dependent on one's personal maturity. It underlies the changing moods and states of mind that are a normal part of life. Even the most energetic people sometimes feel worn out. But as you begin to feel better, your feeling for life will improve. Don't allow your days to become gray and monotonous. To be fully alive, you need to break old patterns and try new things.

Everyone feels down at times. But strive not to let your negative moods get the better of you.

If you want to possess a radiant aura, you can't remain a creature of habit. You need to develop your potential. Learn a language, read challenging books, continue your education. Take up folk dancing or painting, or learn to play a musical instrument. Awaken your creativity and find ways to express the things you feel.

This is the way to overcome blockages in the astral body. To live fully, you need more than good physical health; energy needs to flow though your mind and spirit. Follow your intuition, listen to your inner voice, and do things that bring you joy.

Learn to perceive your aura. Concentrate on your body and try to sense its boundaries.

Exercises for Your Aura

All yoga and meditation exercises strengthen the aura, but some techniques are specifically intended to recharge its energy. These exercises can be done in between daily activities, especially when you are feeling exhausted or dispirited. When your aura is strong, your interactions with other people will be positive. These exercises can help you prepare for an important meeting, whether for business or socially.

Below are four techniques that form an effective program for recharging your aura. You do not have to follow the whole series. One exercise is enough to provide a quick boost of energy. It is better to concentrate fully on one technique than to do them all without deeply focusing on any of them.

Exercise 1: Aura Awareness

With some work, you can learn to be aware of your aura in the normal course of a day. In order to do so, you need to sit back, relax, and concentrate on getting in touch with your aura. It is only by concentrating on your aura that you can feel it become radiant.

Choose any of the practices listed below or engage in an intensive program for your aura by using all four of them.

- Sit on the floor in a lotus position. You can also sit on a chair. The important thing is not to lean against anything but to use the strength in your back to support your body. Close your eyes and relax. Allow your mind to come into stillness, and fully concentrate on your body.
- Try to feel your body's outer extremities. Focus and be aware of your feet and legs, buttocks, back, hands and arms, abdomen, chest, shoulders, and finally your head and face. Be aware of the skin surrounding the different parts of your body. Be aware of the borders of your body, where physical sensation ends, if it stops with the skin, or if it feels as if the body generates a fine envelope that extends beyond it.
- Try to feel an awareness of your skin as reaching beyond itself into space. Do not strain yourself. There is nothing that needs to be done or created in this respect, only an awareness of where your boundaries lie. These can change from day to day.

- Notice where you feel an awareness of the borders of your body, where you cease to experience, to feel, and to be. Consider whether your skin really is the border or if you can conceive of your body as extending beyond it. The more relaxed you are, the easier it will be to find that you literally grow out of yourself. Perhaps you will feel that you extend further and are freer as you concentrate on the ethereal boundaries.
- Stay with the exercise a little bit. Enjoy the feelings of expansiveness, openness, freedom, warmth, and being alive.
- End the exercise by becoming aware of the floor. In order to fully return to earth, be conscious of the weight of your body. Breathe deeply in and out, open your eyes, and stretch toward the floor.

Try to feel you aura and step beyond the limitations of your physical being.

Exercise 2: Perceiving Your Aura with Your Hands

- Sit in a comfortable position. Rub your palms together in a circular motion. Close your eyes and try to feel your aura with your hands at certain parts of your body.
- Begin by placing your hands on your stomach, with one palm above your navel and the other below it. Feel the contact between your hands and your stomach. Now bring your hands an inch away from the surface of your stomach. See if you can still feel the contact when your hands are no longer touching your body.
- Slowly move your open palms away from your body. See how far away you can move your hands before you no longer feel your body radiating.
- Use your hands to try to feel your aura in your abdominal region. Your hands will feel that with each exhalation something is directed away from the body, and that with each inhalation something is directed toward it.
- In time, you will come to be aware of how far your aura radiates and that your arms may not be able to reach far enough to encompass its expanse.
- Repeat the exercise in your chest area and then at your head. Rest your hands on your chest, on your face, and behind your head. Slowly move your hands away from the surface of your body. Hold them incrementally a bit farther away. Notice how far away your hands can be removed before they stop feeling your body.

Exercise 2 will help you sense your aura using the palms of your hands.

Exercise 3: Sending Light to Your Aura

Light is the main attribute of the aura. The clearer, brighter, and stronger your aura is, the better you will be protected from external negative influences. By doing these visualizations, you will be able to purify your aura and free it from harmful influences.

With your hands try to feel the expanse of your aura at different parts of your body.

- Sit on a chair or on the floor. Close your eyes. Relax. Let go of the draining thoughts and feelings of everyday problems. Channel your consciousness into the here and now. Let your breath flow freely. Use only your breath to support your ability to visualize.
- This exercise has two phases. As you inhale, you take in universal light. As you exhale, you let the light of your aura shine.

- While inhaling, imagine that you are taking in light and energy from the universe. Use your inner eye to see how this healing light flows in from above and how it flows through your head to your chest area and collects in your heart chakra.
- While exhaling, imagine that the light from your heart goes through your entire body and radiates into your aura.
- Breathe in and out seven times. While you breathe, visualize that the light from above is concentrated in your heart chakra, which is sending it to your aura. Do not strain yourself. Stay relaxed.
- In the beginning, if you find it difficult to imagine the light, you can also visualize it as golden rays traveling through your heart center and making your aura shine. The ability to visualize develops quickly. With a bit of patience, the imagery will become brighter and more colorful.
- The best indication that you are doing the technique correctly is that fears and sad feelings disappear and you feel freer, filled with life, and whole.
- It is not necessary to do this exercise for longer than seven breaths. The outcome is determined by the intensity, not by the duration.

Imagine that you are taking into yourself energy from the universe in the form of yellow rays of light and let them stream out through your aura.

Exercise 4: Supercharging Your Aura

- Stand with your legs apart. Make sure that the soles of your feet rest completely on the floor.
- Your toes should be pointing slightly outward. Relax your face and shoulders and let your arms dangle at your sides.
- Be aware of your connection to the ground. If your knees are slightly bent rather than locked, you can more easily feel the energy of the earth flowing through your body.
- Breathe through your nose and feel how it connects to the movement of your arms. Then deeply exhale.
- Inhale and bring your arms forward, away from your sides, with the palms facing out. Slowly move your arms up until they are over your head, until your hands join; your palms are pressed together, and the tips of your fingers meet. Stay in this position and breathe out.
- With the next breath, separate your palms and once again let your arms sink down to your sides.

Recharging the aura: Inhale and let your arms drop to your side. Then with your next inhale raise them above your head.

- Stretch your arms and hands. Assume the starting position and breathe out.
- Continue the cycle by lifting your arms and holding them up over your head, then letting them sink down again until they hang limply at your sides. Breathe deeply while bringing your arms up and down, and again at each ending point. Repeat this cycle a total of seven times.
- To energize your aura, it is not enough only to concentrate on the movement of your arms. You need to incorporate visualizations as well. Keep your eyes closed while you do the exercise and picture the following:
- While your arms are moving up and down, visualize that the energy from the earth is moving through your whole body.
- Exhale when you hold your arms over your head. Visualize the earth energy filling your aura and strengthening it.
- Inhale while lowering your arms and imagine that you are gathering molecules of light from the universe.
- Exhale when your arms are hanging loosely at your sides, and visualize that the universal energy in your body travels though its borders and enters your aura.

In order to recharge your aura, imagine while you are practicing exercise 4 that all of the cells of your body are being infused with cosmic energy.

- Now perform the four phases of this exercise in a continuous flowing movement. Above all, make sure that you move your arms slowly and gently and that your breathing is unobstructed. After you have repeated the cycle seven times, lie on your back for a short time and experience the effect of the exercise.
- Notice whether something has changed and if you feel more carefree, energetic, or relaxed than before. Consider whether you can perceive your aura, how your body feels now, and if your thoughts and feelings have changed.

Prana: The Cosmic Life Force

The concept of "prana" is derived from yoga philosophy and means "cosmic energy."

Chakra exercises activate the vitality in your body, mind, and spirit and promote integral development. The concept of prana plays an important role in this process. It stems from the yogic tradition and means "cosmic energy." Prana is the primordial force of all natural phenomena, the subtle energy, the vital essence found in all things. Swami Vivekananda says, "Everything that you can see in the universe that is animated, that moves, or is alive is a manifestation of prana. All of the tangible energy in the universe can be called 'prana.'"

Prana Is Everywhere

Prana is the active principle of life. We all live in an ocean of prana; night and day we are engulfed in this free-flowing universal life force. Prana permeates the entire cosmos. Its workings can be observed in nature, as heat, magnetism, or electricity. Prana is in water, air, food, light, and sun. We are constantly taking in prana, although most of the time we are unaware of it. Prana is therefore essential for human life. It animates all of our cells and protects them. It supplies energy to our mind and spirit. A good supply of prana ensures vitality, happiness in life, harmony, and health. A deficiency of prana causes physical and spiritual problems.

Only when prana can flow unhindered through our astral bodies, through the nadis (see pages 199–200) and through all the chakras are we physically and spiritually harmonized with the universe. A main component of yogic practice is the ability to consciously harness and store cosmic energy. Some yogis have achieved total control of prana. Through this they develop magical powers and are, for example, completely inured to pain. They also gain the ability to heal themselves and others.

As long as it is fresh to some extent, the air that we breathe is highly enriched with prana. Therefore, breathing exercises are often used to absorb prana. The Sanskrit term *pranayama* is a combination of *prana* (primordial cosmic energy) and *yama* (control or expansion).

Pranayama techniques depend less on breathing and much more on the correct application of our awareness.

By controlling the flow of prana some yogis can make themselves impervious to pain.

Stimulating the Flow of Prana

The power of our thoughts and especially the power to visualize are the best instruments to harness prana and to stimulate its flow through our bodies. *Pranayama* is often mistranslated as "breathing exercises," but what it really means is "control of prana." Visualization and meditation techniques are fundamentally pranayama exercises, but they also serve to increase the absorption of prana.

Swami Sivananda also refers to the connection between prana, breathing, and awareness: "Through the control of the physical act of breathing it is possible to govern the subtle nature of prana. This leads to a mastery of awareness, which would not be possible without prana. Subtle prana is closely connected to awareness."

Through breathing we can harness a lot of life energy, prana, but this can happen only when, in the process, unconscious breathing becomes conscious. Mechanical breathing merely increases the supply of oxygen. We can make contact with subtle energies and harness them through conscious, meditative exercises and use them for our personal development. This functions exactly the same way as chakra work.

How to Awaken Your Life Energy

Only when you have become a master of life energy can you grasp the spiritual dimension. The more prana you harness and store, the faster you will be able to develop all your chakras.

When you have a lot of prana at your disposal, your nerves, hormones, and immune system function optimally. A high level of prana is synonymous with outstanding physical health, mental tranquillity, and spiritual clarity. A deficiency of prana can result in physical aiilments and exhaustion as well as depression, anxiety, and low self-esteem.

By learning to consciously absorb and store prana, you can promote the development of your chakras.

There are many possible ways to harness and store prana. This book describes breathing, meditation, visualizations, and chakra-yoga techniques. But daily life also provides many easy opportunities to attract and strengthen prana:

- Get sufficient sleep. When possible, go to bed before midnight and wake up at sunrise.
- Exercise regularly. Go for a walk, ride a bicycle, or go swimming. Be careful not to overexert yourself, and avoid extreme sports.
- Relax at different times throughout the day. Allow your entire consciousness to rest for short periods. Practice the art of stillness.
- Eat healthful, vitamin-enriched foods. Pay attention to the way you eat. Chewing thoroughly increases the amount of prana you take in.
- Abstain from alcohol, nicotine, and other drugs. Avoid fatty foods and take care not to overeat.
- Guard against external negative influences. Protect your body against cold, damp, and drafts.
- Limit your exposure to radio, television, magazines, and the Internet.
- Regularly expose yourself to light and sun. Be careful to take in the right amount. Short sunbaths quickly build up prana, but overexposure drains and endangers the body, which depletes prana.
- Avoid stress wherever possible and try to enjoy life vigorously.
- You can use your powers of concentration and visualization to maximize the absorption of prana. You don't need to do anything special; just try to maintain a level of awareness.

*Awaken your life energy
and you will feel full
of vitality and zest for life.*

- Pay attention to how your daily activities influence the absorption of prana and how this energy is divided up throughout your entire body. In this way, a walk in the woods, a short sunbath, even a nap can be a true prana treatment.

*Picture that you
are taking in prana
in everything
that you do
and feel it flow
through your body.*

Exercise: Prana Breathing

Naturally, in addition to all these pointers, there are particular exercises meant specifically to harness prana. The following yoga breathing exercises will help you to rejuvenate your powers within a short period.

Breathing rhythmically is essential. In yoga, there are often specific rhythms for inhaling and exhaling that infuse the body with energy and at the same time calm the mind. Prana breathing is done in three phases: inhale–hold the breath–exhale. These three phases are set to the proportion of 4:4:8. That is, inhale for four seconds, hold the breath for four seconds, and exhale for eight seconds.

Holding your breath is one of the best ways to take in a lot of prana. Holding the breath for long periods, however, is recommended only after years of practice and under the guidance of an experienced teacher, or it can cause more harm than good. Holding your breath for a few seconds, as in this exercise, is not dangerous at all.

- You can do this technique either sitting or lying down. Close your eyes and relax your body and mind. Then begin prana breathing. Inhale for four seconds, hold your breath in a relaxed manner for four seconds, and then exhale for eight seconds. It is important to inhale and exhale only through your nose during this exercise.
- Take care that the air flows through your nose as gently and as quietly as possible. Stay completely relaxed.
- Repeat the breathing cycle 4:4:8 seven times altogether. Notice that with each breath, your life energy absorbs prana. Each time you hold your breath, imagine that prana is flowing throughout your body. With each exhalation, release any preoccupations or depressing thoughts.
- After you have repeated the exercise seven times, take time out to feel its effect.
- You can also apply this technique at any time throughout the day, but don't do it more than seven times in succession.

In the practice of prana breathing don't hold your breath too long. You can take prana in by holding it for a just a few seconds.

Exercise: Prana Mudra

Specific hand and finger positions called *mudras* are used in yoga to produce positive states of awareness. Among the mudras that give energy, the prana mudra is perhaps the most effective. This hand position supports the flow of prana in the astral body. You can do the following mudras at any time during your daily routine. It would be best for you to withdraw to a quiet place and to follow the exercise very consciously. Prana mudras are formed with both hands placed in the same position:

- Place your hands in front of you so that you can see your palms. Extend the index and middle fingers. Bend your thumb, ring finger, and little finger, and gently bring together the tips of these three fingers so that they form a circle.
- Assume this finger position with both hands. Rest the backs of your hands on your thighs, and stay in this position for at least five minutes. All you need to do is relax and observe what happens. You will notice that through this hand position, your body charges itself with energy.

Certain hand positions, called mudras, aid in the practice of prana breathing. The mudra shown here supports the flow of prana and increases your level of energy.

Exercise: Storing Prana

Yogis have discovered that the solar plexus is the part of the body where most prana is stored. The solar plexus is a nerve center in the upper abdomen that corresponds to the navel chakra.

The mudra shown here for the left hand should be duplicated by the right hand as well.

Fire is the element of the navel chakra. It symbolizes the dynamic power with which the region of the solar plexus supplies energy to the whole body. While your awareness seeks to direct prana to your solar plexus, you can store the energy you absorb and then engage it, for example, in the healing process (see pages 197–198).

- Sit in a comfortable position and close your eyes. Gently place your left palm over the center of your stomach. Place your right palm over your left hand. Relax and breathe in and out. Focus your whole attention on your navel chakra. Seek to identify this well of energy in your body.

As you inhale draw in prana; as you exhale let it stream through your solar plexus.

The solar plexus, to which the navel chakra corresponds, is where most prana is stored.

- When you have made good contact with your navel chakra, begin to visualize. Imagine that with each breath you are taking in cosmic life energy from the environment. Allow the prana to slowly fill your solar plexus.
- Use your breath to envisage how this life energy is now distributed within your navel chakra.
- This exercise will be easier in the beginning if you imagine prana to be a bright yellow light. As you inhale, you take it in. As you exhale, it is distributed through the region of your solar plexus and becomes brighter at the same time.
- Stay with this image for a few minutes. Be conscious of how your body slowly fills with this new energy. Be aware of whether your thoughts and feelings change.
- Simply observe what happens when you patiently stay with this visualization.
- Slowly remove your hands from your midriff and place them on your thighs.
- End the exercise and open your eyes.

Exercise: Prana Healing

The more control you achieve over your prana, the better you can use this power to support the healing process. In time it becomes easier to develop a feeling for cosmic life energy. You can help yourself and others to store prana and channel awareness.

Though you should not expect too much in the beginning, the results of prana healing are astounding. Experience is needed in order to activate this powerful therapeutic energy.

Once you have a reservoir of prana to draw upon, you can use it to heal yourself and others.

- When using prana to heal yourself, sit or lie down comfortably. The Storing Prana exercise is the first phase of Prana Healing. As described on page 196, place both hands over your stomach at the top of your solar plexus. Imagine that each time you inhale you are taking in prana and that this prana is being stored in your navel chakra.
- Take some time to draw breaths that charge your whole navel chakra with healing energy. Again, imagine this energy as bright yellow light.
- For the second phase of this exercise, rest your hands comfortably on your thighs. Keep your eyes closed. Each time you inhale, concentrate on the energy that is collected in your navel chakra. With each exhalation, send this prana to the region of your body that you want to empower.
- With help from your powers of visualization, you can channel prana to every part of your body. You can conduct it to a sprained ankle, a skin inflammation, or a part of your back that hurts.
- Each time you inhale, make conscious contact with the power in your navel chakra. With each exhalation, direct this energy to a sick organ or a weak part of your body. Perform this visualization for at least five minutes. During this time, for example, you can imagine the current of healing light, which flows from your navel chakra to the afflicted area.
- Gradually you will sense how this new energy radiates to weak areas. Throughout this exercise, maintain a strong desire to heal yourself. Don't think about the rest of your body. Ask your inner doctor to use prana, the best possible means to heal your body. Stay patient and calm.

Exercise: Prana Healing with a Partner

By sharing prana
with others you
increase rather
than diminish
your own store.

Naturally, you could use the techniques provided for Prana Healing exclusively for your own healing and to recharge your own restorative energy, but you can also use these techniques to help others:

- First, gather as much prana as possible in your navel chakra. Rest one hand on the upper part of your stomach and the other on the afflicted body part of the person who is ill. Exhale and let the cosmic life energy in your solar plexus slowly flow to the weak area of your partner's body.
- Remain totally relaxed and work with visualizations rather than using your will.
- Because the cosmic life force is inexhaustible, you will not deplete prana by employing this technique, but quite the opposite! When it is done correctly, not only will the patient have more energy and feel stronger, but the exercise will empower you as well.

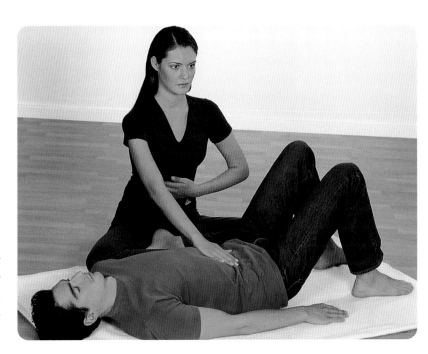

To practice prana healing put one hand on your solar plexus and the other on the affected area of the person you are working on.

Nadis: Channels for Life Energy

Prana, the cosmic life energy, supplies the body with power and vitality. The chakra teachings are the consequence of setting prana in motion through the astral body. This is not done randomly but by conducting it through subtle pathways. These subtle channels are called *nadis*. (Sanskrit: *nad*=flow) According to the yogic tradition, there are 72,000 nadis. Some texts cite the count as even more, naming as many as 350,000.

Nadis form a fine network of pathways that extend throughout the entire body. Each chakra is the hub for thousands of nadis, which radiate from the chakra and flow forth. Many spiritual traditions have depicted this as a flower. Chakras are frequently described as flowers with petals.

The theory of nadis has a certain resemblance to a concept found in Chinese medicine. The pathways of prana energy are similar to meridians. Prana corresponds to *chi*, which in Chinese medicine is equivalent to universal life energy. There are also differences, however. Neither the quantity nor the location of the nadis corresponds to meridians. The meridian teachings are fundamental to the practice of medicine, but the theory of nadis and chakras applies specifically to spiritual practice.

The goal of many styles of yoga is to stimulate the flow of energy through the nadis. The exercises and remedies in chakra work unblock the nadis. It follows that every chakra is the focal point of thousands of nadis, and the revival of chakra energy always has a purifying effect on them.

Prana circulates in the astral body through the nadis, channels for this subtle energy.

The Three Main Nadis: Ida, Pingala, and Sushumna

It is virtually impossible—and also impractical—to concern yourself with all of the 72,000 nadis in your body. There are three main nadis that are particularly significant and play a large role in regenerating chakra energy. They are: *ida*, *pingala*, and *sushumna*. When energy can flow unhindered through these three main nadis, the chakras can be freely expanded.

The free of flow of prana through the three principal nadis is a precondition for the mastery of worldly and spiritual life.

Ida is the astral channel through which negatively charged currents of energy flow. Ida represents the feminine pole, which also binds together the energy of the world. In Chinese philosophy, it is called yin energy.

The root chakra is the point of departure for ida. It starts in the spinal column and ends in the left nostril.

Pingala is the positively charged energy in the body. It corresponds to the energy of the sun and is classified as a masculine or yang aspect. Pingala also originates at the root chakra, and it ends in the right nostril.

The two energy channels ida and pingala cross the chakras as they travel up along the spinal column. In this way, both encircle the main channel, sushumna. Sushumna corresponds on the physical plane to our spinal cord and flows in a spiral directly through the spinal column.

Like ida and pingala, sushumna is a subtle energy path in the astral body. It is not the same as the spinal cord.

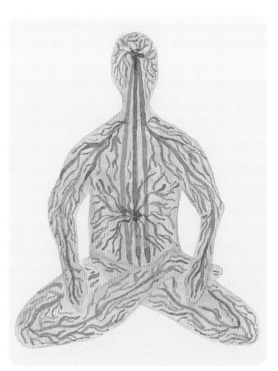

Prana, cosmic life energy, flows through the entire body on a fine network of pathways.

The astral channels ida and pingala supply the whole human organism with all the energy required for life on earth and for all of the tasks necessitated by the material world. This is in contrast to sushumna, the astral channel within the body, which has a special meaning for one's spiritual development. When prana energy can only flow through ida and pingala, one is imprisoned within the material realm of time and space.

Exercise for Balancing Your Nadis

The flow of energy in the sushumna nadi is stimulated through meditation, yoga techniques, and chakra work. This leads to a higher level of awareness. In India, the sushumna channel is also represented as the Brahma nadi, the path that leads to God. (Brahma is the highest god in the Hindu pantheon.) The following exercise balances your nadis.

The teachings of yoga are concerned with energy. Energy flows through ida coolly and peacefully (yin), while pingala energy warms and activates (yang). An excess of ida, which is the negative energy pole, results in tiredness, listlessness, depression, and poor circulation. An excess of energy flowing through pingala, the positive pole, can lead to nervousness, irritability, insomnia, and heart problems. Through the following breathing techniques, you can create a balance between these two poles. In a seated position, breathe through both nostrils for a few minutes.

- **Moon breathing:** Sit in a comfortable position with your back straight. Close your eyes. Put your right hand on your nose, and close your right nostril with the tip of your right thumb. Now breathe in and out in a regular rhythm through your left nostril. Do this for at least five minutes.

    Use this form of breathing when you are suffering from nervousness, insomnia, or anxiety or to soothe yourself for any other reason. You should also do moon breathing several times a day if you suffer from inflammation, high blood pressure, a defective heart, or aches and pains.

- **Sun breathing:** Sun breathing is also performed in a seated position. Close your eyes and put your right hand on your nose. Close your left nostril with the ring and little fingers of your right hand. Breathe exclusively through your right nostril. Do this exercise for at least five minutes whenever you are lacking energy. Sun breathing is recommended for when you are tired, exhausted, downcast, or anxious. It is also advised for low blood pressure, dizziness, weak circulation, or digestive problems.

Sun breathing is breathing through the right nostril; moon breathing is breathing through the left nostril.

Kundalini: The Sleeping Serpent

Sanskrit, the ancient Indian language, uses images to illustrate many concepts. The sages and Brahmans knew that for most people, symbols were easier to understand than complicated definitions. This is the case with the term *kundalini*, which means "serpent power." Behind the image lies the secret of spiritual development and the deepest sense of what it is to be human.

When kundalini is awakened all of the chakras are in turn activated and connected with each other.

The Meaning of Serpent Symbols

In ancient India, the dominant interpretation of kundalini was that it is a coiled serpent that sleeps in the root chakra at the base of the spinal column. When kundalini is awakened, it climbs up the spinal column through the sushumna channel. As it travels, it activates and binds together all the chakras, one after the other. Kundalini reaches its goal when it arrives at the crown chakra. The main theme of the kundalini theory is that of self-development. Kundalini is nimble, as fast as lightning, and flexible. It stands as an ancient symbol for the enormous potential for growth that every person has.

Kundalini is represented as a coiled serpent, symbolizing human spiritual potential.

A snake's body has a great many vertebrae, anywhere from one hundred to three hundred. (Humans have thirty-three vertebrae.) In yoga, the spinal column symbolizes the potential for personal development. In hatha yoga, the mobility of the spine is extremely important. The chakras also have a great deal to do with the developmental process, and their location corresponds to the length of the spinal column. The serpent sleeps; it is wound up in a coil, which does not unwind. The sleeping serpent, the creative energy, must unwind and set itself in motion. Then it travels upward through the sushumna channel, from the material world to the spiritual. The root chakra in which it rests contains the grossest energy, and the crown chakra, its goal, contains the subtlest.

The ascent of kundalini, which is equivalent to spiritual development, is accompanied by pleasurable sensations. People dedicate themselves to years of meditation or other spiritual methods, but even though they experience great happiness and satisfaction, they are still unable to attain a state of bliss.

In reference to this, Swami Vishnudevananda says, "When the coiled-up energy (kundalini) ascends through sushumna and, in the process, travels from chakra to chakra, the yogi experiences every form of knowledge, power, and bliss."

As long as kundalini energy is awakened gently and carefully, a pleasurable state of awareness accompanies it. The flow of energy, which streams through the sushumna nadi, activates the other nadis, ida and pingala. This results in good health, a strong immune system, and relief from aches and pains and other physical ailments.

The awakening of kundalini has an even higher goal than good health. Ultimately, the creative human life force should be animated and bound together with cosmic consciousness in the unification of the individual self with the Divine. When this unification takes place, one experiences illumination. In yoga, this state of the highest level of consciousness is termed *samadhi*. It corresponds to the mystical marriage of the Western tradition, the union of humans and God.

In order to take full advantage of kundalini's creative power, energy needs to flow freely through all of the chakras.

Shiva and Shakti Energy

The unification of primordial masculine and feminine energy is the goal of awakening the sleeping kundalini. This is the only way for humans to transcend duality and enter into divine unity. Only those who know both poles and enjoy both the masculine and feminine aspects of themselves, in whom yin and yang are unified, can overcome duality and arrive at a state of completeness.

In the kundalini teachings, Shakti is the creative force, which is viewed as an active aspect in which yin and yang are unified. Shiva represents pure consciousness, or the calm aspect of kundalini. Shakti corresponds to the feminine pole and Shiva to the masculine. Shiva (in Sanskrit, "the Benevolent One") is considered to be the omnipotent ruler of the world and the embodiment of masculine energy.

Shiva is one of the main gods of the Hindu pantheon. He stands for the cosmic awareness that is within the highest chakra and also for the principles of knowledge and awakening. Shakti (in Sanskrit, "Power") symbolizes the primordial feminine principle. As Shiva's polar opposite, in mythology, Shakti emerges as Kali, the terrifying and dramatic destroyer, especially in contrast to Parvati, the loving and charitable maternal goddess. Shakti symbolizes the life force that animates all matter and creates nature.

The Indian goddess Shakti embodies the power of life, the god Shiva stands for awareness and awakening.

The lowermost chakra in the astral body is situated at the base of the spinal column. This is the seat of Shakti energy. It is the center of coiled-up kundalini, which is also known as Kundalini Shakti.

Shakti is the mother of all things. Thanks to her limitless generative power, Shakti can create the world. She generates the entire visible universe and the five elements. Her power flows from the eternity of time immemorial, from infinity in the plane of time and space.

Through the union of masculine and feminine primordial energies, symbolized by Shiva and Shakti, one attains union with the divine.

Exhausted by this creative process, the primordial heavenly mother reposes in the form of Kundalini Shakti, symbolized by the coiled serpent.

In this myth, humanity's potential is conveyed in words. Within everyone lies the embryo of the power that brought the universe into existence. When we succeed in activating this primordial female energy, we can liberate our consciousness from the material world and connect to divine power. The fundamental spiritual task for humans is to awaken the sleeping kundalini to new life in order to enable the free-flowing unity with the divine spring that resides in the crown chakra.

Gentle Interaction with Serpent Power

We have many opportunities to embark on a spiritual journey and to undertake a search for our true self. We can look for a guru, buy books with a spiritual theme, learn yoga or tai chi, practice different forms of meditation, or work with our chakras. By awakening kundalini energy, there is the possibility of returning to the essence of being.

Many yoga techniques, specific breathing exercises, or body positions, for example, are used to purify the astral body and stimulate the flow of prana energy.

Swami Vishnudevananda writes, "Through asanas (body positions) pranayama, mudras, and meditation, hot energy is produced and directly conveyed to kundalini. Only through prolonged exercises can sushumna be cleansed of all impurities. This enables kundalini Shakti to travel without difficulty through the sushumna channel until it arrives at the *sahasrara* chakra (crown chakra)."

Over time, through chakra yoga, kundalini power will be awakened. Of course, in chakra work we do not directly engage kundalini, but, through the application of various techniques, we activate the chakras and bring kundalini into balance. All chakra work purifies the astral body and frees the energy paths from blockages. When the path is unobstructed, kundalini energy can gradually and naturally be set in motion, gently and entirely without force.

Intensive chakra work balances all the chakras and makes it possible for the power of Kundalini to flow freely through the energy paths.

A Word of Caution

It is advisable to avoid intensive techniques to develop Kundalini energy, in particular, special breathing techniques. You will not find those practices in this book.

Westerners should not overly fixate on awakening kundalini energy. Some very intensive yoga techniques are directed toward kundalini energy. These involve breathing techniques that call for long periods of holding the breath. These exercises are dangerous for those who are not trained and should only be performed under the supervision of an experienced teacher. Even for an experienced teacher, these exercises are not entirely without risk. In Western circles, a lot of people experiment with traditional yoga practices that should be done only after a very long period of preparation. Students of yoga must spend years purifying themselves before undertaking these exercises.

This self-purification entails years of not eating any meat or drinking any alcohol. It also requires freedom from spiritual poisons such as envy, selfishness, and lust.

Only after this long preparation may yogis even begin to apply pranayama or kundalini techniques.

In the following table are the five forbidden things (*yamas*) and the five commandments (*niyamas*) that absolutely must be heeded before this practice can be started.

Yama and Niyama: Ten Steps of the Path to Happiness

In his Yoga Sutras, the Indian sage Patanjali formulates the most important and ethical rules of yoga. His ten recommendations

Yamas: The Five Forbidden Things, or Rules for Moral Discipline	Niyamas: The Five Commandments, or Rules for Self-Discipline
Renunciation of power	Purification of the body
Renunciation of lying and deception	Contentedness
Not stealing	Frugality
Moderation in all things	Study of sacred texts
Nonattachment	Conscious orientation toward the Divine

illustrate the requirements for all who have made an earnest decision to follow the spiritual path. Following yama and niyama, the ten steps of the path to happiness, is a good method for removing the barriers to a spiritual path.

Experience has shown that taking yama and niyama into consideration is also very helpful for chakra work. Directly as a result of the untoward habits that yama and niyama advise against, the same spiritual blockages occur that hinder the unfolding of the chakras. There are innumerable possibilities in everyday life to orient oneself toward these rules.

Gently and Without Strain

At this point, we must again issue an emphatic warning against possible injury. If you seek to awaken kundalini energy through extreme ascetic exercises or forceful breathing techniques, you must seriously assess the possibility of physical and spiritual injury! Indeed, in principle it is possible to forcibly direct kundalini energy up through blocked chakras, but the results can be very unpleasant and can cause severe side effects. Fever, shivering, chronic exhaustion, and mental confusion are symptoms that energy is out of control and has been called forth inappropriately. With chakra work, you should take the following into consideration:

Avoid all techniques that promise to develop your Kundalini energy quickly.

- In chakra work, we handle the energy of our astral bodies cautiously and gently. Relaxation and understanding are good for our chakras.
- Through pleasant visualizations, simple body positions, and gentle breathing exercises, our chakras can regain their original harmony.
- When we conduct ourselves in a loving manner and follow our path patiently yet unwaveringly, we create the best condition for a harmonious spiritual awakening.
- In this way, we propagate and sow the soil. We need to accept that the flower of awakening requires its own time to bloom. It can sometimes be better to allow things to assume their natural course rather than force them.

9 Hand and Foot Chakras

In chakra yoga, the hands and feet are considered microcosms of the body. The fact that the entire organism can be indirectly stimulated through the hands and feet is also made use of in reflex zone therapy. The handling of the soles of the feet and the palms of the hands is a very pleasant and relaxing experience for most people. Massaging these areas of the body reflexively aids the healing of numerous illnesses. The hand and foot chakras are characterized as secondary chakras. They are connected to the primary chakras. When we gently stimulate the chakras in the hands and feet, we are able to promote the unfolding of other chakras.

Hand chakras are located the middle of your palms. They are the centers of awareness of your hands.

The Hand Chakras

Cave paintings dating from the ice age show that as long ago as prehistoric times, the hand held great symbolic meaning. Ritual hand gestures are evident in all sacerdotal cultures. In Indian mythology, the hand symbolizes holy acts. Some effigies of Shiva show the Indian god with radiant palms. Also in Indian temple dancing—Bharata Natya—specific gestures are used to convey such feelings as sadness and horror as well as love and inner peace.

Buddhist iconography depicts the bodhisattva Avalokiteshvara with a thousand arms, with an eye on each of his thousand palms. Avalokiteshvara represents compassion and wisdom (symbolized through the eye) manifested in action (symbolized through the hand). One important function of the hand is to put something into motion, and another is to touch. Hands also symbolize capability, something to be done in the world, something to grasp and to put in motion, as seen in the gift of some sages to touch and to heal.

The hand chakras are the centers of awareness of the hands. They are located in the middle of the palms. Men and women with second sight describe them as radiant turquoise swirls. When we are aware of our hand chakras, we can develop the power to heal.

With our hands we come into contact with the world. Hands express safety, tenderness, and caring. People who have the capacity to heal others have hand chakras that are well developed. The Christian tradition stresses the power of hands to heal, as does Reiki. Many yoga masters also have the ability to transmit life energy to others through their hands. In these instances, the radiant power of the hand chakras is so great that it can be perceived by exceptionally sensitive people. The hand chakras relate to the heart chakra. From the loving heart flows the power that the hand consciously puts into motion, to touch and treat others in a healing way. Every technique that stimulates the heart chakra strengthens the flow of energy in the hand chakras. Conversely, hand-chakra exercises have a positive effect on the heart chakra.

The hand chakras and the heart chakra are directly connected. Work on the one stimulates the other.

Awakening the Hand Chakras

All of us can develop our hand chakras and consequently our powers to heal. Prana, the universal life energy, can be consciously channeled through the palms. As preparation for prana healing (see page 197) and the chakra-energy massage (see page 129), there are exercises to greatly stimulate the hand chakras. In order to develop the healing power of your hands, you must sharpen your awareness of them:

- Be aware that throughout the day you touch a lot of things with your hands. Focus your attention on all the things with which you come into contact.
- Artistic pursuits like pottery and sculpting as well as activities such as gardening connect your hands to the earth element.
- Tai chi and qi gong strengthen the power of your hands to radiate by themselves. Classes in these methods are widely available.
- Learn an instrument. Playing the piano, flute, or guitar improves manual dexterity, making it easier for energy to flow through the hand chakras.
- Practice massage techniques. Classic massage, shiatsu, and all of the chakra-energy massages are useful ways to become familiar with the art of healing and to develop the hand chakras. Chakra work also includes exercises for activating the hand chakras.

With a sensitive awareness of your hands, you can develop the powers of healing.

Exercise: Sensitizing the Hands

- Place your hands flat, one on top of the other. Direct your concentration to the contact of your palms.
- Be aware of each individual finger and how the large and small balls of your hands touch each other. The contact will be more noticeable in some places than in others.
- Gently rub your hands together in circles. Do not apply too much pressure while you do it.
- Put the palms of your hands gradually, cautiously, and very slowly back together, one on top of the other. Try to bring your hands together, holding them as far apart as you can while still being able to perceive the energy between them. Experience where the borders lie, how far you can move one hand away from the other without losing the contact between your palms.

There are many exercises that you can do in order to awaken the awareness of your hands.

Imagine that there is a ball of light between your hands that is becoming ever larger and stronger.

Exercise: Holding a Ball of Light in Your Hand

- Hold your hands about an inch apart, one above the other. Your palms should be facing each other. Relax. Breathe deeply in and out and gently close your eyes.
- Open and close your fists a few times. Stretch and extend your fingers.
- Open your hands and hold them in front of your body as in the starting position.
- Be aware of how energy builds up between your palms.
- Imagine that now you hold a small ball of light between your hands. Slowly make it bigger and be aware of the space between your palms, which are still positioned one over the other.
- Visualize that the ball of light between your palms is becoming bigger and more powerful. Imagine the ball of light as turquoise-colored.

The goal of this exercise is to increase the radiance of your hand chakras, and to learn how to feel them and use them to heal.

- Now turn the ball of energy. Bring one hand over and the other under, rotating the right palm under and the left over in a turning motion.
- Be aware and experiment to see how far apart you can move your palms without losing the feeling of warmth and the current of energy.
- After you practice this exercise for some time, your awareness of the ball of light and the radiant power of your hand chakras will increase.

Exercise: Supercharging the Hand Chakras with Energy

This exercise increases the flow of energy in the hand chakras. You can do it while either sitting or lying down.

Both at the beginning and at the end of this exercise, hold your left hand in front of your forehead and be conscious of the effect.

- Raise your left hand in front of your head. Your palm should face your forehead, about an inch away.
- Now place your hand on your stomach, just above your navel. This is the location of your navel chakra.
- Place your right hand on top of the left.
- Be aware of the contact with your navel chakra. Breathe in and out, deeply and slowly, seven times. Notice that each time you inhale, your stomach arches out a little bit. Imagine that your breath flows out from your stomach and into your palms. Further imagine that the warm, healing energy from your navel chakra flows out into your palms.
- After seven breaths, gently remove your hand from your stomach and slowly direct your left hand to your forehead once again.
- Notice the difference from a little while ago. Feel how the warmth from your hand chakra flows into your forehead chakra. The flow of energy is not necessarily expressed as warmth. It can also be noticeable in the form of tingling or a light pressure. Often this exercise results in experiences of light. In any case, the feeling produced by the current of life energy should be pleasant and comfortable.

When energy flows between your hand chakras, and then to the other chakras, it creates a pleasant sensation.

Mudras for Inner Peace

Mudras are special finger or hand positions that result in specific feelings. Many mudras deepen meditation.

The word *mudra* is a Sanskrit term meaning "that which brings peace." Although various body positions may be described as mudras, the term refers mainly to hand gestures and finger positions. Mudras are significant in Indian dance, and they also have meaning in yoga. Specific finger and hand positions facilitate the anchoring of peaceful feelings in the subconscious. When you form a mudra with your hands, you assume an inner posture of serenity, creating a connection between the physical hand position and a tranquil state of mind.

After you have repeated these techniques a few times, assuming the hand positions will release an unconscious impulse that will evoke a state of serenity. For over a thousand years, meditation practices in many cultures have been reinforced by mudras. Gestures of greeting are also mudras. When the hands are folded in a posture of prayer, it is easy to direct one's spirit to the higher spheres. Through reflexive energy cycles, mudras have an effect on body and spirit. Some mudras have a calming effect; others soothe pain or stimulate the life forces. The following mudras are suitable for awakening the hand chakras.

You can awaken your hand chakras with sun and moon mudras. In them the positions of your right and left hands are not identical.

Exercise: The Sun Mudra

The following hand positions relate to sun energy. They loosen blockages in the hand chakras and stimulate the organism.

- Extend the index, middle, and ring fingers of your right hand. Bend the thumb and little finger to form a circle. The tip of the thumb should rest gently against the tip of the little finger.
- The position of your left hand is slightly different. Make a ring with your thumb and index finger. The fingertips should rest together gently. The middle, ring, and little fingers should be extended.
- After you have assumed this mudra, rest your hands on your thighs. The palms should be turned upward.
- Close your eyes, relax, and breathe. Concentrate on your hands and try to be aware of how this mudra affects your sense of attunement.

The moon mudra will siphon off a superabundance of energy and lead to sense of well-being.

Exercise: The Moon Mudra

The effect of the moon mudra is especially soothing and balancing. The flow of energy in your hand chakras is gently harmonized. Surpluses of energy, evidenced by anxiety, nervousness, or irritability, can be drained through the hand chakras.

- The moon mudra is the mirror image of the sun mudra. This time, touch together the thumb and index finger of your right hand while the other fingers remain extended. The left thumb rests against the little finger, while the index, middle, and ring fingers of the left hand are extended.
- Take up the hand position, close your eyes, and let your thoughts rest.
- Imagine that with each breath, stress is sent out through your palms. Try to be aware of the effect that the moon mudra has on your body and mind.

While the sun mudra stimulates your hand chakras and the rest of the organism, the moon mudra has a balancing and calming effect.

The Foot Chakras

The foot chakras are directly connected to the root chakra and bind us to the earth. They are located in the middle of the soles of the feet.

The foot chakras lie in the middle of the soles of the feet. Sensitive people describe them as dark red swirls of light. Through the foot chakras, we can be aware of contact with the earth. Even without our realizing it, there is always an exchange of energy between ourselves and the powers of the earth. The foot chakras play a determinative role in this exchange. When the energy in the foot chakras flows freely, we feel we stand firmly on the ground and are supported by the earth.

The foot chakras are directly connected to the root chakra. The energy of the earth is further conducted from the foot chakras to the root chakra. A conscious connection with the primal power of the earth is the best foundation for spiritual growth and good health. One's health can be deduced from the state of the feet. We all know that warm feet indicate good health; cold feet often herald a cold.

Foot Reflex Zones

Reflex zone therapy is centered on the feet. Even though reflex points were already known in ancient cultures such as the Maya or in Indian Ayurveda, the concept of reflex zone therapy is generally equated with modern reflexology, which originated at the beginning of the twentieth century.

Its founder, Dr. William H. Fitzgerald (1872–1942), discovered that pressure on specific points can relieve pain and that specific zones of the feet correlate to some extent to the various organs of the body. On different places of the body there are interrelated zones with pressure points that correspond to specific organs and glands. The best-known reflex zones are located on the feet. The massaging of one point can relieve pain and strengthen the organs. The masseur Eunice D. Ingham-Stopfel later built foot reflex massage into an established form of therapy that is utilized today by many alternative health practitioners. Despite their similarities, chakra teachings and reflex zone therapy have different conceptual bases. In ancient India, the feet, and particularly the soles of the feet, were held to be mirror images of the body. The foot reflected the whole body.

The gentle stimulation of the chakras in the hands and feet promotes the development of the other chakras.

In keeping with the spiritual law "as above, so below," it was thought that all of the seven main chakras could be stimulated through the feet. The reflex zones and the chakra teachings are unified on some points, for example, that the toes and the upper region of the foot correspond to the head and the upper shoulders; that the middle region of the foot corresponds to the lungs, chest, arms, thyroid gland, heart, and windpipe; and that the lower part of the foot is connected to the digestive organs and the pelvic region. The lower part of the sole of the foot, the area around the heel, corresponds to the bladder, rectum, sacrum, coccyx, and sciatic nerve.

All seven chakras are represented in the foot chakras and can be stimulated by working on the feet.

Therewith, from above to below, all seven chakras in the body are to some extent replicated in the soles of the feet. The root chakra corresponds to the underside of the heel, the heart chakra to the middle of the foot, and the crown chakra to the upper area, the toes.

Awakening the Foot Chakras

The foot chakras correspond to the root chakra. All of the actions that activate, stimulate, and strengthen the root chakra (see page 130) contribute to the development of the foot chakras. The inverse is also true. There are also many other techniques that stimulate the foot chakras and loosen energy blockages in them:

- Go barefoot as often as possible. The foot chakras can be animated only when they have contact with the earth. This contact is often cut off when we wear shoes and walk on paved streets. Take every opportunity to walk barefoot over meadows, beaches or pebbles, or through the woods.
- Keep your feet warm whenever possible. During the cold seasons of the year, take warm footbaths regularly. Warm feet are excellent protection against infectious diseases.
- You can put drops of essential oils, like rosemary oil or vetiver, into the hot footbath.
- Every day do a few special gymnastic exercises for your feet. For example, put a hand towel on the floor, grasp it with your toes, and try to lift it. Or lie on your back with your legs extended at an angle and rub the soles of your feet together.

In order to activate your foot chakras, be aware of the connection between the soles of your feet and the earth; imagine that there is an exchange of energy between you and the earth.

- Learn about foot reflex zone massage. There are a lot of courses and also good books that convey the basics.
- On a regular basis, vigorously massage the soles of your feet, from the heels upward to the balls of your toes. It is best to use your thumbs. Hold one foot at a time, and rub each zone of the foot for as long as it takes to warm the whole sole of the foot and fully supply it with blood.
- Foot massages are even more effective when you apply essential rosemary oil. Make a massage oil with a ratio of four drops of rosemary to one teaspoon of base oil. (Almond oil is suitable for the base oil.) Then massage this oil deeply into the soles of your feet.

Exercise: Awareness of the Connection to the Earth

In summer, do this exercise in a field, in a forest, or at the shore of the ocean or a stream. During cold weather, you can do it at home on a thick carpet. The important thing is to begin by removing your shoes and socks and warming up your feet with a short massage.

You activate the chakras in your feet when you make conscious contact with the ground upon which you stand.

- Stand up straight. Your feet should be apart, about the width of your shoulders, with your toes pointed out. Relax your knees. Stretch your neck slightly so that your chin extends toward your chest. Try to stand as straight as possible.
- Focus your attention entirely on the soles of your feet. Make conscious contact with the ground.
- Enjoy this position and release all the unnecessary tension from your muscles.
- Form an internal image of your foot chakras. Imagine a small swirl of light that goes from the soles of your feet into the earth. The easiest thing is to visualize this light energy, which springs from the middle of the soles of your feet, as dark red rays.
- With each exhalation, use the power of your imagination to send a little bit of power into the earth. In this manner, you give a little bit of your spiritual energy as a gift to the earth that holds and nourishes you. In time, you will be able to observe that it becomes a flow of energy. The more you are prepared to give, the more power you will receive back from the earth. Enjoy this exchange of energy.
- Finally, imagine that the holy power of the earth goes through your foot chakras and into your legs. From there it flows into your root chakra, and finally throughout your entire body.
- End the exercise by lying on your back for a short while and feeling its effects.

10 Chakra Yoga

Through the chakra-yoga exercise program, all seven chakras are strengthened, developed, and activated. The antecedents of chakra yoga can be found in hatha yoga and kundalini yoga. While hatha yoga concerns itself with the health and welfare of the body, kundalini yoga is directed toward spiritual development. Chakra yoga combines these two aspects. The techniques of chakra yoga promote the flow of energy in the subtle body and nourish the chakras and relieve them of blockages. When energy circulates freely through the astral body and the chakras, this will lead to positive effects in one's physical body and psyche. The benefits include strengthened immune and circulatory systems, healthier organs, inner peace and tranquillity, and spiritual clarity.

There exist yoga programs corresponding to each of the seven chakras.

Chakra yoga consists of physical postures and techniques for breathing, relaxation, and meditation. There is a special program for each of the seven chakras. To strengthen one of your chakras, you should follow the program for that chakra for seven days. After that you can go on to the program for another chakra.

To stay with one chakra for a longer period is only recommended if you suffer from very serious blockages. And even in that case you should continue with one chakra program for no more than three weeks at one time.

To ensure the even and harmonious development of all the chakras, make use of the entire range of the recommended practices.

The simplest way to begin is by working on each chakra in turn for one week, starting with the root chakra and ending with the crown chakra. After forty-nine days, repeat the cycle beginning with the root chakra.

Before You Start

Here are a few simple rules as a preparation for chakra yoga that will help you to avoid mistakes and get the most out of your practice. Here are the most important guidelines:

Chakra yoga is not a sport, nor is it a competition. Relax and only do as much as you can.

- You don't need a lot of space to practice chakra yoga. Find a place where you won't be disturbed. Use a thick wool blanket or a yoga mat. Air out the room before you begin, but make sure it is not too cold. It's easier to relax in a warm room.
- The atmosphere needs to be calming. Turn off the telephone. Light a candle. Put flowers in the room. Using an aroma lamp with an essential oil that corresponds to the chakra you are working on is also of benefit.
- Wear comfortable clothes: loose plants, t-shirt, or sweats. If the room is warm enough, practice barefoot.
- The best time for chakra yoga is early morning, before breakfast. That way you feel its energy all day long.
- You can do yoga at almost any time of the day, as long as you wait for two hours after eating before beginning your practice.
- Since chakra-yoga techniques will sometimes strongly activate physical and mental energy, it is advisable not to practice late at night.
- Doing the chakra-yoga exercises once a day is sufficient. If you like, you can engage in some relaxation and meditative practices in the evening.
- Remember, yoga is not gymnastics. It does not require force, nor is it a performance.
- Stay relaxed in all positions. Avoid pain and never overestimate your own flexibility by stretching further than is comfortable. Direct your attention within. Close your eyes whenever possible, and breathe deeply through your nose while holding each position. Relax briefly in between each step of the program and

Concentration means focusing your energy. It requires physical and mental calm.

feel its effects.

A sign of progress along the path of yoga is being able to hold poses for longer periods of time and keep your body, thoughts and emotions still while doing them.

Important Warning

Never practice yoga if you have a fever or an infection, after surgery, or if you are suffering from a severe illness.

Be very careful exercising in the following situations:

- If you suffer from back pain, sciatica, slipped disks, or vertebral problems, do not engage in the exercises that might overtax the spine, such as the crocodile pose (page 241) or the head to knee pose (page 242).
- During your menstrual period, avoid postures that put pressure on the stomach, such as the child pose (page 266), the modified head stand (page 271), and the wind-relieving pose (page 238).
- If you suffer from varicose veins, don't remain cross-legged or in the lotus pose for long periods.

The Seven Steps of the Chakra-Yoga Program

The yoga program for each chakra consists of seven steps that should be taken in order.

Each chakra has corresponding positions (asanas), breathing exercises (pranayama), hand positions (mudras), and meditation practices that are particularly effective in stimulating the energy of that chakra. Even though each program consists of different practices, they all partake of the same form. The programs for each are composed of seven steps that should always be followed in order.

Step 1: Preparation

Start with a five-minute period of relaxation for body and mind. Step back from your daily life and free your mind of extraneous thoughts. Now you are ready for a brief warm-up.

Special mudras that correspond to the chakra-yoga exercises deepen concentration and can be used in prayer as well.

Steps 2, 3, and 4: Asanas

After the preparation come three asanas, body postures or exercises that influence the flow of prana and stimulate the targeted chakra.

Step 5: Pranayama

Next is a breathing exercise. This brings the life energy that has been generated through the practice of the asanas to the chakra you are working on.

Step 6: Meditation

In chakra-yoga meditation, we use a combination of special mudras and mantras that correspond to each chakra.

Step 7: Relaxation

The last step consists of deep relaxation of body, thoughts, and feelings. Visualize the energy flow into the chakra you are working on, and see how it harmonizes and heals all of the areas that are governed by this chakra.

The program for each chakra begins and ends with a period of deep relaxation. At the beginning of the practice rest for five minutes; at the end of the practice rest for ten minutes.

Deep Relaxation and Warm-up Exercises

To avoid repetition, all of the elements that are repeated in each of the programs will be described only once. This is particularly the case for the deep relaxation and warm-up exercises.

Deep Relaxation

Many of us have a hard time relaxing. The inability to relax can lead to tiredness, even exhaustion, nervousness, and moodiness. The importance of relaxation and rest is widely recognized, but few of us know how to really relax. Yoga is one way to do so. Breathing and body exercises harmonize mind and body and dissolve tension. Each chakra-yoga program begins and ends with a period of deep relaxation.

We use the same relaxation technique to begin and end your practice. The only difference is that the beginning period of relaxation should last five minutes, but you should give yourself ten minutes of relaxation at the end of your practice. In the last phase of the program, you need time for the organism to recover from all of the stimulation that occurs during the practice. To augment the effect of deep relaxation use the visualization techniques described above.

Before and after your yoga practice you systematically relax all of your muscles, which calms both body and mind.

The Practice of Deep Relaxation

● Lie on your back, face up, with your legs and feet apart. Place your arms next to your body with hands facing up. Close your eyes, let go of tension, and let your breath come and go.

It is very important not to skip the relaxation periods before and after your practice.

- Check your position. Are you aware of any tension? Feel the weight of your body on the floor. You can use the outbreath to release tension from your body and mind. Each time you exhale, imagine that you are letting go of all stress. Now you can begin relaxing your muscles.
- Lift your right leg a few inches off the floor. Tighten the muscles in your foot, calf, and thigh. Hold this tightened position for four seconds. Then let your leg drop and relax your leg completely. Repeat this three times.
- Now lift your left leg a few inches off the floor. Tighten the muscles in your foot, calf, and thigh. Hold this tightened position for four seconds. Then let your leg drop and relax your leg completely. Repeat this three times.
- Now tighten your buttocks. Hold for four seconds and relax. Repeat three times.
- Lift your right arm and make a fist. Tighten your lower and upper arm, hold for four seconds, and then let your arm drop and relax. Repeat this three times, then do the same with your left arm.
- Direct your awareness to your abdomen. Push your lower back toward the floor and at the same time tighten your stomach muscles. Hold this position for four seconds and then let all of the tension in your abdomen and lower back dissipate. Repeat three times.
- Now pull your shoulders up toward your ears. Hold this position for four seconds, then let your shoulders drop. Repeat three times.
- Now lift your head an inch from the floor, keeping your neck muscles tight. Clench the muscles in your face. Then relax your neck and face and let your head fall gently to the floor. Repeat three times. Turn your head slowly left to right a few times and then let it rest at center.
- Now that you have tightened all of your important muscles, turn your attention once again to the heaviness of your body and the way it lies upon the floor. Enjoy this feeling of relaxation and observe how your thoughts and feelings become increasingly peaceful.
- Finish your deep relaxation by stretching your arms over the head. Stretch your whole body and slowly open your eyes.

At the end of the period of deep relaxation your thoughts and feelings will be calm and your whole body will feel relaxed.

Warm-up Exercises

The initial period of deep relaxation should be followed by warm-up exercises that will loosen and stretch your body.

The following techniques are helpful preparations for the chakra-yoga programs discussed below. If you run short of time, you can omit them and go right into the yoga exercises.

The warm-up exercises will make your muscles, tendons, and joints more flexible. The spine also will become more flexible. A healthy spine is fundamental for the development of the chakras, because all of the chakras, with the exception of the crown chakra, lie along the line of the spine.

Exercise 1: Backward Roll

The following exercise massages your entire back and improves the blood circulation in your back muscles. It helps those who suffer from back pain and tension. Be sure to lie on a soft surface when you do this exercise. If in doubt, put another blanket under you. Make sure that you have enough space behind you so that you can roll back without bumping into anything.

In the second stage roll back vigorously so that only your upper back is in contact with floor.

In the first stage of the backward roll lift your feet a bit off the ground, round your back and try to keep balanced.

- Sit on the floor with your legs together, knees slightly bent. Cross your hand behind your knees.
- Lift your feet a little off the ground and try to maintain your balance in that position. When you are able to do this, pull your knees toward your chest and make your back as round as you can.
- Rock lightly back and forth. With a strong swing backward roll back until only the upper part of your back touches the floor and then roll back to the starting position.
- Roll gently in this way back and forth a few times. In time you will find that you need less force and you will have more control over this movement.

The warm-up exercises, cow and cat, massage your back, keep your spine flexible, and stimulate all the chakras.

Exercise: Cow and Cat

The following exercises lends flexibility to your spine and stimulate all of the chakras.

- Kneel on all fours with your hands under your shoulders and your knees under your hips. Your arms and thighs should be straight. The tops of your feet, your knees, and your palms should touch the floor. Your spine should now be parallel to the floor.

In the cat pose arch your back upward and let your head hang down.

In the cow pose you let your spine drop, so that your back is concave.

- Inhale deeply and at the same time form the cow position. This is done by arching your back downward. Lift your head as if you wanted to look up at the ceiling. Feel your spine in this position.
- Exhale deeply and form the cat position. Do this by arching your back upward. Pull your head in. Feel the stretch in your back.
- Move smoothly between the two postures and combine this with the soft flow of your breath. Each time you lift your head and hollow your back, inhale. As soon as you go past the straight position and arch your back upward, breathe out.
- Repeat this exercise, and then lie on your back and relax.

Most people nowadays have tense shoulders and stiff necks. Neck exercises reduce these tensions.

Exercise: Neck Roll

The neck and shoulder muscles are the site of a lot of tension for people who work mostly in a sitting position. Bad posture and frequent headaches can result. Blockages in the energy flow can be produced by this tension. The following exercise releases tension and loosens the shoulders and neck.

As you inhale tilt your head slowly backward; as you exhale tuck your chin in toward your chest.

- Sit cross-legged and keep your back straight.
- As you inhale, let your head slowly tilt backward only as far as you can go without straining yourself. As you exhale, bring your chin down toward your chest. Repeat this movement very slowly seven times, almost as if in slow motion.
- Bring your head up and relax.
- Now move your head from side to side. First turn slowly to the left so that you can look over your left shoulder. Then slowly stretch your head to the right so that you can look over your right shoulder.
- Repeat this a few a times. Your spine should stay straight and your shoulders should not move. Your neck should remain slightly bent with your chin pointing downward just a little.

Don't try to push beyond your limits. Being overly ambitious is no virtue in the practice of yoga.

Keeping your spine straight move your head to the right and then to the left. Don't move your shoulders.

Exercise: Butterfly

This yoga exercise increases the flexibility in your legs and activates the root and sacral chakras.

This warm-up exercise is good for your legs and your lower chakras.

- Sit on the floor and pull your legs toward you so that the soles of your feet are touching each other. Grasp your feet with your hands. Now try to pull your heels as close as you can to your body.
- As soon as you have reached this position, begin to move your legs up and down slowly, like the fluttering of a butterfly's wings. Your knees should move up and down, but this should be done gently. Avoid abrupt movements or strain. Never push yourself past your limits.
- To loosen your legs, stretch them out and wiggle them. Then repeat the exercise.

Slowly flutter your legs up and down keeping your heels as close as you can to your body.

Exercise: Hip Circling

Loose, flexible hips are important to strengthen the kundalini power in your pelvic region. This will promote the upward flow of energy through all of the chakras.

The following yoga exercise helps dissolve energy blockages in the pelvic area and stimulates the root and sacral chakras.

- Stand straight and relax Look toward the horizon. Your feet should be shoulder-width apart pointing forward. Place your hands on your hip with your palms around the hip bones.
- Now slowly make a circular movement with your hips.
- First describe a very small circle, and then enlarge it with each rotation. Be sure the soles of your feet stay well connected to the floor. Move only your hips and your back. Your head and shoulders should stay still.
- Perform this exercise with clockwise and counterclockwise rotations. Keep your awareness directed toward your pelvic region.
- Return to the starting position, then lie on your back to give your hips a rest.

Begin with small rotations and let them increase in size. Head and shoulders remain still.

Correct Sitting Position

Many meditation and breathing exercises in chakra yoga are performed in the sitting position. Only in special cases—if, for example, you suffer from knee or hip problems—should you do these while sitting in a chair. Traditionally, yoga exercises are performed while sitting on the floor, since this makes it easier to absorb the power of the earth.

It is useful to have a firm pillow or, ideally, a special pillow for meditation. Only when you hips are raised high enough can you touch the floor with your knees without straining and at the same time remain balanced. Until you have developed sufficient flexibility in your hips and knees, perform the following exercises cross-legged rather than in the half-lotus position. Bear in mind the following:

A stable sitting position is essential for the practice of chakra yoga. It is best to sit on the floor, if possible, in the half-lotus position.

- Your spine should be as straight as possible.
- Your neck should be slightly stretched a little with your chin toward your chest.
- Your head should always be centered so that your navel and the tip of your nose are aligned.
- Your shoulders should be relaxed. Don't sit with your shoulders hunched up.
- The center of gravity in your body should lie just beneath your navel.

Exercise: Half-Lotus

Although you can execute chakra-yoga meditation while sitting in a chair or cross-legged, it is best to sit in the half-lotus position. It is very stable and can be assumed quite easily with some practice.

- To take the half-lotus position, bend your left leg, pulling your left foot as close as you can toward your body.
- Bend your right leg and lay your right foot on top of your left thigh. If it is more comfortable for you, you can reverse the position of your legs.
- Your hands should lie relaxed on your upper thighs or form one of the mudras we have described.

The half-lotus position is ideal for chakra yoga and with some practice can be easily learned.

Chakra-Yoga Program for the Root Chakra

Exercise 1: Warm-up and Relaxation

The yoga program for the root chakra begins with a five-minute period of deep relaxation and continues with the warm-up exercises.

Begin the exercises for the root chakra with a short warm-up and then a period of relaxation as described earlier.

Exercise 2: Lying Tree

- Lie on comfortably on your back with your legs slightly spread apart, your feet relaxed, and your palms facing upward. Relax in this position.
- Pull your right leg up; the left remains flat on the floor. Your right foot should glide smoothly up alongside your left leg until it reaches the knee.
- From this position, let your right knee fall slowly to the right. Your goal is to touch your knee to the floor, but don't force it. Over time you will become more flexible. Be aware of your limits. Let your knee drop only until you feel a slight tension in your leg. Stay in this position for thirty seconds, breathing deeply in and out.

In the lying tree pose bring your foot up to the knee of your other leg.

In then second stage of the lying tree pose, bend your leg toward the floor.

- Raise your right knee back up and then bring your leg down to the floor.
- Relax. Repeat this exercise with the left leg.

Exercise 3: Deep Squat

If you perform the deep squat correctly the soles of your feet will remain on the floor.

- Stand with your feet shoulder-width apart with your toes pointing slightly outward. Slowly squat, keeping your spine as straight as you can.
- Lay your upper arms relaxed upon your knees and try to keep the soles of your feet as much on the floor as possible. Don't push past your limits; just go as deep into your squat as you comfortably can. At first you may not be able to keep the soles of your feet fully on the floor. That doesn't matter. It will come in time.
- While in this deep squat, inhale and exhale seven times. As you inhale, pull your anal sphincter muscle slightly up. Relax it as you exhale.
- After seven breaths, stand up and shake your legs out.

Exercise 4: Wind-Relieving Pose

In these exercises you should concentrate on your root chakra and the bottom of your spine.

- Lie relaxed on your back. Pull both legs toward you, clasp your hands around your knees, and pull them as close as you can to your chest. At the same time, lift your head and bend your forehead toward your knees.
- Try to remain in this posture for seven inhales and exhales. At first you may find it difficult to stay in this position for long. If so, just breathe in and out a couple of times and then lay your head on the floor. After a short pause, repeat the exercise until you complete seven breathing cycles.
- While you are in the wind-relieving posture, concentrate on the root chakra at the bottom of your coccyx.

In the wind-relieving pose raise your head gently off the floor and try to get your forehead as close as you can to your knees.

Exercise 5: Chakra-Yoga Deep Breathing

- Sit comfortably cross-legged or in half-lotus. Relax.
- Close your eyes and let your thoughts and breathing quiet down.
- Focus your awareness on your root chakra and the lower region of your spine.
- Now inhale through your nose for eight seconds. While inhaling, first fill your stomach with air and then your chest.
- Hold your breath for four seconds and then exhale for eight seconds. (While you are holding your breath, strongly contract your anal sphincter and your pelvic floor muscles. As you exhale, let them relax.)

- Repeat this cycle seven times.
  "Breathe in for eight seconds —
  Hold the breath for four seconds and
  Tighten the anal sphincter —
  Breathe out for eight seconds."

Exercise 6: Root-Chakra Meditation

- Remain in a sitting position. Concentrate on your root chakra and be aware that this chakra connects you to the power of the earth and primal life force.
- Rest the backs of your hands on your knees and form a circle with the thumb and index fingers of each hand; extend the middle, ring, and little fingers loosely. This mudra will create a circle of energy that will stimulate the root chakra.
- Breathe deeply through the nose. As you exhale, intone the mantra LAM (pronounced LANG) seven times, quietly and calmly. The repetitions should be spaced evenly like the chimes of a clock so that the end of the repetition coincides with the end of the exhalation.
- Inhale again through your nose. Repeat this cycle seven times. Throughout the entire meditation period, your awareness should be directed to the root chakra.

In the meditation for the root chakra place the backs of your hands on your knees. Form a circle with the thumb and forefinger of each hand.

Exercise 7: Closing Relaxation

To practice deep breathing for the root chakra contract your anal sphincter and pelvic floor muscles.

- To end the root-chakra program with a period of deep relaxation, sit on the floor either in a lotus position or cross-legged. After you have loosened all your muscles by tightening and relaxing them (see page 226), give yourself some time to enjoy the pleasurable sense of relaxation of body and mind.

- At the end of this deep relaxation, use your powers of visualization to harmonize and stimulate the energy flow to your pelvic region.

- Imagine a small ball of red light lying in the area of your sphincter.

- Imagine that this ball of energy gets bigger with each breath until it fills the entire pelvic region with healing rays of red light. Let these red rays flow through your lower back, your digestive tract, and all your bones.

- End this period of deep relaxation slowly and carefully. Let go of your inner visualizations and become aware of the weight of your body. Gradually make your breathing deeper, and slowly reach upward with your arms. Stretch your entire body before finally opening your eyes to end this yoga program.

Give yourself plenty of time for the closing relaxation period and carefully end the exercise program.

Chakra-Yoga Program for the Sacral Chakra

Exercise 1: Warm-up and Relaxation

Begin the exercises for the sacral chakra with a short warm-up and then a period of relaxation as described earlier.

To begin the yoga program for the sacral chakra allow for a five minute period of deep relaxation.

Exercise 2: Crocodile

- Lie on your back, raise your knees, and keep your feet on the floor with your knees close together. Stretch your arms out to the side with your palms facing upward.
- Slowly turn your head to the left and at the same time move your legs to the right. When you first begin this practice, your knees don't have to touch the floor. Then reverse the movement, your head turning to the right and your knees to the left.
- Repeat this slow back-and-forth movement seven times. Let your breath flow freely.
- Raise your knees to the center and then lower your legs flat on the floor and relax.

In the crocodile pose you slowly move your head and legs in opposite directions.

Exercise 3: Head to Knee Pose

On no account should you try to surpass your physical limits. Regular practice will increase your flexibility. There is no need to strain yourself.

- Lie on your back, stretch your arms over your head, and let your spine stretch out. Bring your arms straight down until your hands rest on your thighs. ①
- Lift your head, then your upper back, and then your lower back off the floor. Tighten your stomach muscles. Continue this forward movement, stretching your hands along your legs toward your feet. Your legs should stay straight. Bring your head slowly toward your knees. The goal is for your chin to touch your knees and your hands to touch your toes. But don't push yourself beyond your limits or you can injure the vertebral disks. At the beginning, it is best not to have your knees straight but to bend them slightly. It's fine if your hands can reach only to your lower legs and your head doesn't reach your knees. ②
- Remain in this position for a few seconds and continue breathing easily. Concentrate on the sacral chakra. To come out of this position, just bring your back slowly to the floor. Lie flat and relax.

① ②

Slowly move head, back and arms as far forward as you can.

Exercise 4: Standing Tree

- Stand relaxed with your legs together and your back straight. Become aware of your contact with the floor and imagine that the soles of your feet are rooted to the ground. Breathe easily in and out. Your hands and arms should hang loosely at your sides.

Try to hold your balance in the tree pose for thirty seconds.

- Slowly shift your weight onto your right leg. Lift your left leg slightly with your toes still touching the ground. Find a point on the ground about six feet away to concentrate upon. This will help you maintain your balance.
- Concentrate on how your right foot anchors. Try to keep your balance on your right foot while you raise your left foot slowly until the sole of your left foot comes to rest on the inside of your right leg above or below but not directly on your knee.
- Make a ring with your thumbs and index fingers, turn your hands palms up, and lift your arms slightly.
- Try to stand upright in the tree posture. Breathe easily and feel the earth beneath your right foot. Don't arch your back.
- Remain for at least thirty seconds in this position, then let your left leg slowly drop.
- Repeat this exercise with the other leg.

While practicing the tree pose imagine yourself as firmly rooted in the ground. This will make it easier to stay balanced.

Exercise 5: Root Lock

As you practice the root-lock breath, send energy to your lower body and sacral chakra with every exhalation.

- Lie on your back and pull your upper thighs toward your chest. Open your knees and cross your feet so that the right ankle lies over the left. Stretch your arms through the opening between your legs. Grab your left foot with your right hand and your right foot with your left hand.

- Let your head rest relaxed on the floor. Lightly press your tongue against your upper palate directly behind your front teeth. This position creates two important circles of energy in your body.

- Relax your arms, face, legs, and stomach and allow your breath to come and go without interference. Now concentrate on your lower abdomen and your sexual organs. As you exhale, send energy to the sacral chakra.

- Now begins the most important part of the exercise. Take seven deep breaths. As you exhale, tighten your pelvic floor muscles. To do this, you must strongly contract the sphincter muscle in your anus. Hold your muscles tightly, as if you were trying not to urinate. Hold this tension through the entire exhalation. With each inhalation, relax all of these muscles. After seven breaths slowly return your legs and hands to the flat position. Relax and feel the effects of the exercise.

During the root-lock breath the tip of your tongue should rest on the gums directly behind your upper front teeth.

Exercise 6: Sacral-Chakra Meditation

- Sit in a stable position.
- Close your eyes and let your thoughts and breathing calm down. Concentrate on the sacral chakra and become aware that this is the center of your life energy, your joy in life, and your creativity.
- Place the back of your right hand on the palm of your left hand. The tips of your thumbs should touch. Your hands should rest below the navel with palms up forming a bowl. Through this mudra, a circle of energy will be formed that flows through the sacral chakra.
- Breathe deeply through the nose. As you exhale, intone the mantra VAM (pronounced VANG) seven times, quietly and calmly. The repetitions should be spaced evenly like the chimes of a clock so that the end of the repetition coincides with the end of the exhalation.
- Inhale through your nose. Repeat this cycle seven times. Throughout the entire meditation period, your awareness should be directed to the sacral chakra.

The concentration in meditation on the sacral chakra should be combined with the corresponding mudra and mantra.

Your hand should form a kind of shell, in which the right hand rests in the left and the tips of the thumbs touch.

Exercise 7: Closing Relaxation

- To end the sacral-chakra program with a period of deep relaxation, lie on your back. After you have loosened all your muscles by tightening and relaxing them (see page 226), give yourself some time to enjoy the pleasurable sense of relaxation of body and mind.
- At the end of this deep relaxation, use your powers of visualization to stimulate the energy flow to your pelvic region and sexual organs and harmonize them. Imagine a small ball of orange light lying three finger widths below your navel.
- Imagine that this ball of energy gets bigger with each breath until it fills the entire pelvic region with healing rays of orange light. Let the warm orange rays bathe your sacrum, the inner and outer sexual organs, and your kidneys and bladder.
- Enjoy this pleasant feeling as you nourish your organs with new energy. Your bodily fluids, especially your blood, will flow more freely.
- End this period of deep relaxation slowly and carefully. Let go of your inner visualizations and become aware of the weight of your body. Gradually make your breathing deeper, and slowly reach upward with your arms. Stretch your entire body before finally opening your eyes to end this yoga program.

These practices will provide energy to your pelvis, sexual organs, bladder, and kidneys.

Chakra-Yoga Program for the Navel Chakra

Exercise 1: Warm-up and Relaxation

Begin the exercises for the navel chakra with a short warm-up and then a period of relaxation as described earlier.

Begin the seven exercises of the navel-chakra yoga program with deep relaxation and warm-up exercises.

Exercise 2: Single Wind-Relieving Pose

- Lie flat on your back.
- As you exhale pull, your right leg toward your chest with both hands. Slowly and gently, pull your knee as close to your chest as you can.
- Your head remains relaxed on the floor.
- Breathe in and out seven times while remaining in this position. Then let go of your right knee and lay your leg back on the floor.
- After a short pause for relaxation, repeat this with your left leg.

In the single wind-relieving pose bring each knee (one at a time) as close as possible to your chest.

Exercise 3: Intensive Eastern Stretch

- Sit with your legs together stretched out straight in front of you on the floor.
- Put your hands backward with palms down next to your hips. As you inhale, push your hips up, tensing the muscles of your legs and press the soles of your feet into the floor. Your body should form a straight line.
- As you exhale, let your hips drop. Repeat this exercise three or four times.

Start in a sitting position
with your legs stretched out.
As you inhale push your hips up.

Exercise 4: Bow

Direct your attention to the navel chakra during these exercises. With the bow pose in particular be aware of your body's limits.

- Lie on your stomach with your forehead resting gently on the floor and your legs slightly apart. Bend your knees up with your feet pointing to your behind. Reach back and try to grab your ankles with your hands. Tense your stomach and pelvic muscles.
- With the next inhalation, lift your head and at the same time pull your legs slightly off the floor. Now you are in the bow posture. Concentrate on the navel chakra.
- Stay in this position for a couple of breathing cycles. Bend your spine only as far as you can without pain.

- Let go of your ankles and let your legs and head return to the floor and relax while lying on your stomach.

Try to hold the bow pose for a few breaths.

Exercise 5: Abdominal Lift

- Stand straight with your feet shoulder-width apart. Put your hands on your hips with your thumbs pointing toward your belly. Close your eyes and let your mind become calm.

With the abdominal lift pull your stomach in after exhaling and keep it tight for a few seconds.

- Breathe in and out a couple of times, fully relaxed. Exhale deeply. Holding your breath out, pull your stomach strongly inward. Imagine that the walls of your stomach are pulled upward and backward toward your spine. Hold this position for four seconds without breathing.
- Relax your stomach and inhale at the same time. Breathe in and out for a little while, then repeat this exercise two more times.

Exercise 6: Navel-Chakra Meditation

- While in a sitting position, concentrate on the navel chakra. Become aware that this chakra connects you to your emotions and is the power of your personality.
- Fold your hands in front of your chest. Place your palms against each other and lay your right thumb over your left thumb and enclose them within your hands. This mudra activates the navel chakra on an energetic level.
- Inhale deeply through the nose. As you exhale, intone the mantra RAM (pronounced RANG) seven times, quietly and calmly. The repetitions should be spaced evenly like the chimes of a clock so that the end of the repetition coincides with the end of the exhalation.
- Inhale through your nose. Repeat this cycle seven times. Throughout the entire meditation period, your awareness should be directed to the navel chakra.

In meditation direct your entire awareness to your navel chakra and see how this connects you with your emotions.

For the mudra that accompanies the meditation for the navel chakra the thumbs are crossed tucked in between folded hands.

Exercise 7: Closing Relaxation

- To end the program of exercises for the navel chakra with a period of deep relaxation, lie on your back.
- After you have loosened all your muscles by tightening and relaxing them (see page 226), give yourself some time to enjoy the pleasurable sense of relaxation of body and mind.
- At the end of this deep relaxation, use your powers of visualization to stimulate and balance the energy flow to your navel chakra.
- Imagine a small ball of yellow light lying three finger widths above your navel. Visualize that this ball grows larger with every breath until it fills up the entire region of your solar plexus and radiates through your internal organs and digestive tract and fills them with warm healing energy.
- Try to sense the feeling of well-being in your upper abdomen, as blockages and tensions are gradually released.
- End this period of deep relaxation slowly and carefully. Let go of your inner visualization and become aware of the weight of your body. Gradually make your breathing deeper, and slowly reach upward with your arms. Stretch your entire body before finally opening your eyes to end this yoga program.

End this yoga program with an extended period of deep relaxation. Feel your solar plexus being filled with radiant energy.

Chakra-Yoga Program for the Heart Chakra

Exercise 1: Warm-up and Relaxation

Begin the exercises for the heart chakra with a short warm-up and then a period of relaxation as described earlier.

Exercise 2: Variation on the Cobra Posture

A basic period of relaxation should precede the yoga program for the heart chakra.

- Lie flat on your stomach with your forehead touching the floor and your arms alongside your body. Your palms should face up. Breathe deeply in and out a couple of times. Bring your hands behind your back and interlace your fingers over your buttocks.
- With your next inhalation, lift your head and chest slightly off the floor and pull your shoulders back so that you open up your rib cage.
- Breathe in and out deeply two times while in this position. Direct your awareness to your heart chakra, and then lay your head and arms back on the floor and relax.
- Stay relaxed for another moment, and then repeat this exercise for a total of three times.

In this variation of the cobra pose pull your shoulders backward and stretch your rib cage.

Exercise 3: Triangle

- Stand straight and relax with your legs slightly apart. Turn your left foot so that it is pointing to the left and, keeping your shoulder relaxed, lift your right arm straight up so that the upper arm touches your right ear. The left hand lies on the outer side of your left thigh ①.
  - Slowly bend your body from the waist to the left side, lining your torso up with your leg. Your gaze should follow your right hand. ② Stretch your upper body until the fingers of your left hand can reach your left knee. Be careful not to press too hard on your knee. As you become more flexible, you may be able to reach your calf or even your ankle.
    - Stay in this position for a few seconds, breathing as deeply as possible. To return to the starting position, bring your right arm back so that it is straight up. Then slowly straighten your upper body, and when you are standing straight, move your left foot so that it is pointing forward.
    - Let your arms hang at your sides, relax for a moment, and then repeat the exercise in the other direction.

①

Start by lifting your arm so that your upper arm touches your ear.

②

Bend your upper body to the side and gaze at your outstretched hand.

Exercise 4: Fish

When you finish the fish pose lie on the floor for a little while to feel its full effect.

- Lie on your back with your legs stretched out and close together. Place your hands underneath your buttocks with your palms resting on the floor. ①
- Now stretch the rib cage. To do this, press your elbows to the ground to lift your neck and arch your back. ② Try to bring your elbows close together underneath your back. In the final position, the weight of your upper body should rest on your elbows and head. Breathe deeply into your chest a few times while in this position.
- To end this exercise, inhale, lift your head, and tuck your chin into your chest. Then exhale and lower your head to the floor. Loosen your arms alongside your body, and lie there for a short period of relaxation.

①

②

Arch your ribcage upward so that the full weight of your upper body rests on your elbows and head.

Exercise 5: Opening the Heart

- The breathing exercise for the heart chakra is done in conjunction with arm movements. In this exercise, breathe only through your nose.
- Stand straight with your legs wide apart and your feet turned slightly outward. After a few breaths, exhale deeply. With the next inhalation, lift both arms straight in front of you with your palms facing each other ①.

- While you are still inhaling, stretch your arms out to the side so that your body forms a letter T. At the same time, lift your head and look up. ②
- Hold your breath in this position for seven seconds. Slowly exhale. Let your arms fall to your sides, and bring your head back to an upright position.
- Repeat this cycle three or four times, combining the arm movements with smooth-flowing breath.

As you inhale stretch your hands out to both sides so that your chest feels wide open.

Exercise 6: Heart-Chakra Meditation

The heart-chakra meditation will help you connect with the power of love.

- Sit in a stable position (see page 234). Close your eyes and let your thoughts and breath quiet down. Concentrate on your heart chakra, becoming aware that this center connects you with the power of love and will foster openness and compassion.
- The mudra that is used to activate the heart chakra is different for men and women. Women should touch the thumb and the ring finger of the left hand and the thumb and the middle finger of the right hand. Men should take the opposite hand positions.

If you are a woman touch the thumb and ring fingers of the left hand and the thumb and middle fingers of the right hand. Men need to reverse the mudra. They touch the thumb and ring fingers of the right hand and the thumb and middle fingers of the left hand.

- Inhale deeply through the nose. As you exhale, intone the mantra YAM (pronounced YANG) seven times, quietly and calmly. The repetitions should be spaced evenly like the chimes of a clock so that the end of the repetition coincides with the end of the exhalation.
- Inhale slowly through your nose. Repeat this cycle seven times. Throughout the entire meditation period, your awareness should be directed to the heart chakra.

Exercise 7: Closing Relaxation

- To end the program of exercises for the heart chakra with a period of deep relaxation, lie on your back.
- After you have loosened all your muscles by tightening and relaxing them (see page 226), give yourself some time to enjoy the pleasurable sense of relaxation of body and mind.
- At the end of this deep relaxation, use your powers of visualization to stimulate and balance the energy flow to your heart chakra.
- Imagine a small ball of green light in the middle of your chest.
- Imagine that this ball grows a little larger with every breath until it fills up your rib cage with green healing rays. Imagine these green rays streaming into your heart, lungs, upper back, and arms and hands. Enjoy the liberating feeling that this produces.
- End this period of deep relaxation slowly and carefully. Let go of your inner visualization and become aware of the weight of your body. Gradually make your breathing deeper, and slowly reach upward with your arms. Stretch your entire body before finally opening your eyes to end this yoga program.

Through the power of visualization you can stimulate and harmonize your heart chakra.

Chakra-Yoga Program for the Throat Chakra

Exercise 1: Warm-up and Relaxation

Begin the exercises for the throat chakra with a short warm-up and then a period of relaxation as described earlier.

Exercise 2: Lion

Don't forget the relaxation techniques and the warm-up period before you practice the lion pose to purify the throat chakra.

The lion posture purifies your throat chakra while strengthening your throat and larynx.

● Sit in Japanese posture with your knees and shins on the floor and your buttocks resting on your heels. Place your palms on your knees and concentrate on the throat chakra.

The lion's pose is practiced in the kneeling posture with your buttocks on your heels.

- Inhale deeply through your nose. When you exhale, lean forward, stretch out your fingers, tighten your arm muscles, open your eyes and mouth as wide as you can, and stick out your tongue. At the same time, roar like a lion.
- After exhaling, close your mouth and relax the muscles in your face arms and hands. Breathe normally a few times and then repeat the lion pose two more times.

As you exhale let out a loud lion's roar. This pose will strengthen your larynx and throat.

Exercise 3: Crescent Moon

- Kneel on the floor. Bring your right leg forward so that it forms a ninety-degree angle.

In the first stage of the crescent moon pose your arms should hang relaxed at your sides.

In the crescent moon pose your arms hang down at your sides. Then you lift them straight up overhead.

- Place your weight on your right foot and at the same time straighten your left leg. Your arms hang loosely at your sides and your back is straight.
- Inhale and stretch your arms straight up; the palms of your hands should touch. Arch your back slightly by pressing your pelvis forward, with your gaze directed up. Feel the stretch in your legs. Take a few deep breaths.
- Slowly return to the starting position letting your arms slowly drop to your sides. Lie on your back for a moment to relax, then return to your knees and repeat the exercise with the other leg stretched forward.

In the second stage of the crescent moon pose lift your arms directly over your head and stretch your back and legs.

To perform the chin lock pose sit cross-legged or in a half-lotus position and close your eyes.

While in the chin lock pose hold your breath for only a few seconds while you tuck your chin into your chest.

Exercise 4: Chin Lock

- Sit in a cross-legged or half-lotus position. Close your eyes. Bring your hands together as if in prayer in front of your chest. Breathe in deeply.
- With the next exhalation, let your head slowly drop until your chin touches your chest. Don't breathe in for a few seconds, and press your chin lightly into your throat. Relax the pressure, raise your head, and slowly inhale again. Repeat this exercise three or four times. Breathe only through your nose.

Exercise 5: Humming Breath

- Remain in the sitting position. For this breathing technique, inhale through the mouth only. Press your tongue firmly behind your front teeth. Slowly inhale through your mouth, sucking in the air along the tongue to make a slight slurping sound. When you have finished inhaling, close your mouth and hold your breath for four seconds.
- Now exhale as slowly as possible through your nose. Your mouth stays closed. As you exhale, make a humming sound. Feel the loosening effect of the vibrations.
- Repeat the cycle of the humming breath—inhaling through the mouth, exhaling through the nose while humming—a total of seven times.

The humming breath is done differently than the other breathing exercises. Here you breathe in though your mouth and out through your nose.

In the meditation for the throat chakra perform the mudra as pictured to the right.

Exercise 6: Throat-Chakra Meditation

- In a sitting position, concentrate on the throat chakra. Become aware that this chakra forms a bridge between your thoughts and feelings and allows you to communicate with others.
- Clasp your hands in front of your chest with your fingers interlaced and your right index finger on top of your left index finger. Place your thumbs together; they should be straight and point up. Your upper arms should be folded and relaxed. This mudra creates a circle of energy that activates the throat chakra.
- Inhale deeply through the nose. As you exhale, intone the mantra HAM (pronounced HANG) seven times, quietly and calmly. The repetitions should be spaced evenly like the chimes of a clock so that the end of the repetition coincides with the end of the exhalation.
- Slowly inhale through your nose. Repeat this cycle seven times. Throughout the entire meditation period, your awareness should be directed to the throat chakra.

Try to become aware that your throat chakra makes it possible for you to communicate with other people.

Exercise 7: Closing Relaxation

- To end the program of exercises for the throat chakra with a period of deep relaxation, lie on your back.
- After you have loosened all your muscles by tightening and relaxing them (see page 226), give yourself some time to enjoy the pleasurable sense of relaxation of body and mind.
- When you feel deeply relaxed, use your powers of visualization to stimulate the throat chakra and at the same time harmonize the entire area of your throat.
- Imagine a small, light blue ball of light in the area of your larynx. Visualize this ball growing larger with every breath until it fills the entire region of your throat and neck with energy. Feel the soothing influence of the healing light blue rays on your throat, pharynx, windpipe, and esophagus and how it affects your breathing.
- Slowly end this period of deep relaxation. Let go of your inner visualization and become aware of the weight of your body. Gradually make your breathing deeper, and slowly reach upward with your arms. Stretch your entire body before finally opening your eyes to end this yoga program.

Chakra-Yoga Program for the Forehead Chakra

Exercise 1: Warm-up and Relaxation

After the preliminary relaxation and warm-up periods, stimulate your forehead chakra with eye exercises.

Begin the exercises for the forehead chakra with a short warm-up and then a period of relaxation as described earlier.

Exercise 2: Eye Exercises

- Sit cross-legged or in the lotus position with your hands resting on your thighs.
- Exercising your eyes will stimulate your forehead chakra. Move your eyes as described below—make sure to move your eyes only. Your head should stay still.
- First move your eyes up and down: look seven times with an alternating movement up to the ceiling and then down to the floor. Close your eyes and breathe in and out deeply.

Move your eyes up and down, then to the left and right, and then around in a circle.

①

②

- Now move your eyes laterally. Look to the left and then to the right as far as you can seven times without moving your head. ① Then close your eyes and breathe deeply in and out.
- Make a circular movement with your eyes. Roll your eyes 360 degrees in a clockwise motion seven times, then repeat counterclockwise. Try to make large circles. Move your eyes slowly and with awareness.
- Close your eyes one more time. Rub your palms together until they are warm, and then lay them gently on your closed eyes. ② Experience the warmth streaming from your hands into your eyes and concentrate on your forehead chakra.

After completing the eye exercises lay your hands on your closed eyes and feel their warmth.

Exercise 3: Half-locust

- Lie on your stomach with your forehead touching the floor. Your legs should be together, with the tops of your feet on the ground. Your arms should rest at your sides.
- Relax for a brief moment. Make fists with your hands. Push your fists next to your thighs with your thumbs downward against the floor.
- As you inhale, lift your left leg straight up from the floor. Breathe in and out deeply. Don't lift your leg forcefully; just tighten your leg muscles. Your hips should remain on the floor.
- Put your leg back on the floor and repeat with the other leg. Do this with each leg two or three times, then lay your hands under your forehead and relax for a short period. Feel the effects of this exercise.

In the half-locust pose use only muscular tension to lift your leg.

Exercise 4: Child Pose

Start the child's pose in the kneeling posture. If you need to, place a small pillow between your buttocks and heels.

- Kneel on the floor with your buttocks resting on your heels and your knees and big toes together. If you are uncomfortable in this position you can place a small pillow between your buttocks and your feet. Your back should be straight and your arms hanging loosely at your sides. Close your eyes and take a few deep breaths into your stomach.
- As you exhale, slowly bend your upper body forward until your forehead touches the floor. The backs of your hands and arms should lie on the floor. Breathe in a relaxed fashion and feel the gentle pressure of the movement of your breath against the tops of your thighs. Stay in this position for at least thirty seconds.
- Slowly sit up by unrolling first your lower back, then your chest, and finally your neck. This movement should be slow and gentle. Lie on your back for little while and relax.

Coming up, you should slowly unroll each vertebra.

Exercise 5: Alternate Nostril Breathing 1

- This exercise should be done while sitting. Close your eyes. Put your left hand on your left thigh.
- Bring your right hand up to your nose. Close your right nostril with your thumb and place your ring finger and little finger next to your left nostril. The index and middle fingers should be folded into your palms. Breathe in for eight seconds through your left nostril.

- Close your left nostril with your ring finger and little finger and at the same time open your right nostril and exhale for sixteen seconds.
- Then without pausing, breathe in through your right nostril for eight seconds and then close this nostril with your thumb. Then open your left nostril and exhale through it for sixteen seconds. Now you have completed one cycle of breathing.
- Repeat this exercise—left eight seconds in, right sixteen seconds out, right eight seconds in, left sixteen seconds out— seven times.
- All the while, concentrate on your third eye. Visualize it as a center of light from which rays stream throughout your entire body.

For alternate nostril breathing breathe in through one nostril and out through the other.

Exercise 6: Forehead-Chakra Meditation

While you perform the alternate nostril breathing direct your awareness to your forehead chakra and feel healing light enter your third eye.

- In a sitting position, concentrate on the forehead chakra. Become aware that this chakra connects you to your intuition, perceptions, and self-awareness.
- Assume the following hand position: Place your palms together and stretch your middle fingers up so that they point to the ceiling. The tips of your middle fingers and the tips of your thumbs should be touching. Your thumbs should point toward your chest. The rest of your fingers should be bent in, as illustrated. This mudra will stimulate the forehead chakra. Hold your hands slightly away from your chest.
- Inhale through the nose. As you exhale intone the mantra KSHAM (pronounced KSHANG) seven times, quietly and calmly. The repetitions should be spaced evenly like the chimes of a clock so that the end of the recitation coincides with the end of the exhalation.

To perform this mudra the tips of the thumbs and middle fingers of each hand should touch; the second joints of the other fingers should touch as well.

- Inhale through your nose. Repeat this cycle seven times.
  Throughout the entire meditation period, your awareness should
  be directed to the forehead chakra.

Exercise 7: Closing Relaxation

- To end the program of exercises for the forehead chakra with a
  period of deep relaxation, lie on your back.
- After you have loosened all your muscles by tightening and relaxing
  them (see page 226), give yourself some time to enjoy the
  pleasurable sense of relaxation of body and mind.
- At the end of this deep relaxation, use your powers of visualization
  to gently activate your forehead chakra and balance the flow of
  energy. Imagine a small ball of dark blue light in the center of your
  forehead.
- Visualize that this ball grows larger with every breath until it fills up
  the third eye and radiates through your entire forehead.
- Experience the lovely feeling of these healing rays of energy
  opening up blockages in your sinuses, eyes, and face.
- End this period of deep relaxation slowly and carefully. Let go
  of your inner visualization and become aware of the weight
  of your body. Gradually make your breathing deeper,
  and slowly reach upward with your arms. Stretch your
  entire body before finally opening your eyes to end
  this yoga program.

This meditation harmonizes and activates the forehead chakra the center for intuition and self-awareness.

Chakra-Yoga Program for the Crown Chakra

Exercise 1: Warm-up and Relaxation

Begin the exercises for the crown chakra with a short warm-up and then a period of relaxation as described earlier.

Exercise 2: Sitting Mountain

The yoga program for the crown chakra is gentle and safe. But be advised: don't overdo it.

- Sit cross-legged. Close your eyes and lift your arms over your head so that your palms are touching directly over your head. With your fingers pointing upward, lightly stretch your spine.
- Inhale and exhale deeply several times in this position. Come out of the position if you feel uncomfortable, but over time you should try to hold the sitting mountain posture for longer periods.

During the mountain pose your eyes should be closed and your back straight.

Exercise 3: Modified Head Stand

You should only do the head stand with the help of an experienced teacher, because you can strain the disks in your neck even if you do it correctly. Here is a modified version.

The modified head stand requires good physical control. At the beginning you only need to do the first stage of the exercise.

- Kneel with your buttocks resting on your heels. Place your palms shoulder-width apart on the floor. Touch your head to the floor so that your head and hands form a triangle. Bend your toes and stretch your legs back. The weight of your body should rest on your head and your hands. ①
- If at the first you cannot do the modified head stand, this position alone will suffice to activate the crown chakra. Remain in this position and breathe in and out seven times.
- To assume the modified head stand, take two small steps toward your head. Place your knees next to your elbows and slowly lift one foot at a time off the floor. Balance on your head and hands. ②

①

In the first stage of the modified head stand your weight should rest on your head and hands, supported by your feet.

- If you feel yourself falling backward, don't try to maintain your balance. Simply return to your original kneeling position.
- Remain in this position for seven breaths.
- To finish the exercise, first put your right and then your left leg down and resume your kneeling position.

Once you are able to perform the second stage of the modified head stand, stay in this position for the duration of seven breaths.

②

For the modified head stand you need to balance yourself on your head and hands.

Exercise 4: Dancer's Pose

Keeping your balance in the dancer's pose is not easy. Ideally one should hold the position for thirty seconds.

- Stand up straight with your legs together. Shift your weight to your right leg and bend your left leg up behind you.
- Grab your left ankle with your left hand. Keeping your right leg and spine straight, lightly pull your leg toward your buttocks. Don't bend your leg back too far.
- Now stretch your right arm straight out, pointing upward. Move your upper body slightly forward. While pulling your left leg up, push your foot into your hand. Try to keep your balance in the dancer's pose for at least thirty seconds.

- Let your right arm drop, let go of your left ankle, and stand on both feet.
- After a short pause, repeat the exercise standing on your other leg.

Exercise 5: Alternating Breath 2

- This exercise should be done while sitting. Close your eyes and relax your body and mind.
- Place your left hand on your left thigh. Close your nostrils using the hand positions described in Alternating Breath 1 (see page 266-267).
- Close your right nostril with your thumb. Breathe in for eight seconds through your left nostril.
- Close your left nostril with your ring finger and little finger and hold your breath for eight seconds.
- Remove your thumb, open your right nostril, and exhale for sixteen seconds.
- Without pausing, breathe in through your right nostril for eight seconds, then close this nostril with your thumb. Hold your breath for eight seconds Open your left nostril and exhale through it for sixteen seconds.
- Repeat this cycle of breathing: left eight seconds in, hold your breath eight seconds, right sixteen seconds out, right eight seconds in, hold your breath eight seconds, left sixteen seconds out. Repeat this cycle seven times.

In dancer's pose keep the leg you stand on straight.

Exercise 6: Crown-Chakra Meditation

During meditation concentrate on your crown chakra and how it connects you to the cosmos.

- In a sitting position, concentrate on the crown chakra. Become aware that this chakra connects you with the universe.
- The following mudra creates a circle of energy that activates the crown chakra. Touch the tips of your ring fingers together. Then interlace your other fingers with your right thumb on top of your left thumb. Hold your hands in front of your chest a couple of inches from your body.
- Inhale deeply through your nose. As you exhale, intone the mantra OM seven times, quietly and calmly. The repetitions should be spaced evenly like the chimes of a clock so that the end of the recitation coincides with the end of the exhalation.
- Slowly inhale through your nose. Repeat this cycle seven times. Throughout the entire meditation period, your awareness should be directed to the crown chakra.

To perform the mudra that accompanies the crown-chakra meditation interlace your fingers with your ring fingers pointing straight up.

Exercise 7: Closing Relaxation

- To end the program of exercises for the crown chakras with a period of deep relaxation, lie on your back.
- After you have loosened all your muscles by tightening and relaxing them (see page 226), give yourself some time to enjoy the pleasurable sense of relaxation of body and mind.
- When you feel deeply relaxed, you can use your powers of visualization to stimulate the crown chakra and at the same time harmonize the entire area of your head.
- Imagine a small ball of light resting on the highest point of your head.
- Visualize this ball of light as crystal clear or light violet in color. Imagine that it grows larger with every breath until it fills up the entire region of your head and radiates through your whole body.
- Concentrating on the crown chakra will provide healing energy to the entire organism.
- Try to feel how all the cells in your body absorb this energy.
- Slowly end this period of deep relaxation. Let go of your inner visualization and become aware of the weight of your body. Gradually make your breathing deeper, and slowly reach upward with your arms. Stretch your entire body before finally opening your eyes to end this yoga program.

During the closing relaxation period imagine that your body starting with your head is filled with healing energy.

11 Chakras and the Power of Love

Nothing affects people more deeply than love. Physical love is only a small part of it, a preliminary stage in the development of universal love, which has the power to permeate and transform everything. But even in its elementary stages, love can bring about remarkable changes and bind the material with the spiritual. How we expand the power that we call love depends on the development of the state of energy in our chakras. Conversely, the development of the chakras can also be hastened through the power of love.

In this chapter, we will consider the spiritual meaning of love, insofar as this is of interest for chakra practice. It is in this regard that the practical aspects of this universal energy will be addressed:

There is hardly a word that is as often misused, and hardly a theme about which there is so much to say, as love.

- How the power of love can bring about transformation
- How the development of the chakras has an effect on your choice of partner
- Which partner harmonizes best with you
- How cycles that exist in every partnership are related to the development of the chakras
- How blockages in the chakras can result in problems with conception, sterility, frigidity, or impotence
- How these blockages can be released
- How your life energy can be increased by uniting the heart and sacral chakras

The Power of Love

Love is the strongest human energy. Through its power, everyday activities acquire a spiritual dimension; the simplest tasks can become spiritual actions. The energy of love is clearly visible in the human aura. A person who is inspired by love is surrounded by an especially radiant aura.

The energy of love originates in two chakras, which flow from one into the other. The heart chakra is the actual well of love. All of the inspirational love energy goes out from the heart chakra and radiates to all of the other chakras. For this reason, the heart chakra is held to be our emotional center.

The sacral chakra is the second chakra that carries love energy. The sacral chakra is the center of sensuality and sexuality. It forms the foundation for the potential that lies dormant in the heart chakra. If the development of the sacral chakra is weak, the life energy that radiates from the heart chakra will always be somewhat impeded and not readily available. However, when the heart and sacral chakras are harmoniously developed, the power of love radiates into the world in which we live. Through the energy of the sacral chakra, love becomes a sensual experience that fuses masculine and feminine poles. In this respect, sexuality is an important aspect of the love between men and women.

As long as love is not based on sensual experience, it is difficult to cultivate higher forms of empathy. Ultimately, the spiritual path requires the transformation of physical love into a higher form of energy. It follows that in the case of physical love between people, we should not forget that this manifestation of love is only one of the forms of expression of the highest energy.

The heart chakra is the center of human feeling and the well of love. It radiates the energy of love to the other chakras.

Knowledge of chakra personality types can help in the search for an ideal partner.

The Influence of Love on the Chakras

The power of love influences the different chakras in different ways. When one works on love from the energy of the root chakra, one connects to the basic theme of this chakra. The connection to the earth can carry one beyond issues of individual survival and security. It can express itself in a deeper commitment to nature and one's family.

The energy of the sacral chakra is closely connected to the love energy of the heart chakra. When these two energies work harmoniously, love will be fully developed. Sexuality is filled with love rather than being dominated by impulses. The complete experience of love can penetrate every area of life. This contributes directly to creative development, which is the basic theme of the sacral chakra.

When love radiates out from the navel chakra, impulses toward control and influence, which strongly characterize the navel chakra, are channeled along the most favorable paths. The willpower of the navel chakra will be concentrated on changing the world for the better through compassion and by active, loving deeds.

Love energy is at home in the heart chakra, and therefore this center is not naturally transformed by the power of love. When the power of love is working, the heart chakra opens, and your energy can flow freely.

The power of love is especially transforming for the throat chakra. This chakra is an intermediary between the chakras that are above and below, and therefore also between the material and the spiritual realms. The energy of love working out of the throat chakra permeates not only feelings but also thoughts and communication. Through this, everyday encounters are intensified.

The forehead chakra prepares one to transcend the material world. The power of love is an absolute necessity for its highest development. The spiritual knowledge made possible by the forehead chakra must be pervaded by the power of love so that one can remain connected to the world of living beings. Love will transform the pursuit of knowledge into the possession of wisdom, the ideal to which the energies of the forehead chakra lead us.

The crown chakra is the well of energy that is free of duality. The power of love is the catalyst for the full development of the crown

All seven chakras are influenced in different ways by the power and energy of love.

chakra, in which the two poles of masculinity and femininity are unified. The power of love is the fertile soil that the energy of the crown chakra requires for growth.

Love can manifest itself in the smallest and largest things. Do not begin with the largest. Before we can love the whole world, the Divine, and the entirety of all that is, we should cultivate within ourselves a love for the smaller things, those we encounter every day—our friends, acquaintances, and family.

Love is closely connected to the positive development of the chakras and of human life.

Chakras and Partnership

It was stated in chapter 4 that every chakra, except the heart chakra, has a complement (see page 51). This complementary chakra is referred to as its mirror image. A chakra builds a unity with its complement in the same way that masculine and feminine poles support each other. These two chakras complement one another especially well. As it's said, "Opposites attract."

This does not mean, however, that a partnership between two people who have complementary dominant chakras will necessarily be harmonious. The relationship between two such people is based on a (mostly unconscious) feeling of deficiency. The partners are attracted to one another when one has what the other lacks.

Spiritually, these partners may be good for each other, and together they can advance their development. But in practice this is not always possible. Sometimes the tensions are too strong. This has to do in particular with the complementary chakras, the root chakra and the crown chakra. In theory, such a relationship is advantageous for both, but the reality is different. When one partner is completely rooted in the material world and the other lives completely in the spiritual realm, both feel mysteriously pulled apart, without enough common interests on which to build the basis for a healthy partnership.

An analogous circumstance is found with the complementary chakra types of the sacral chakra and the forehead chakra. Here as well, the differences are generally too great. On the other hand, the distance between the complementary chakras, the navel chakra and the throat chakra, is small enough to be bridged. At the same time, both chakras

The knowledge of
your dominant chakras
can make it easier to
understand your partner.

complete each other in an ideal manner. Relationships based upon the complementary dominance of these chakras have every chance of flourishing.

The aphorism "Birds of a feather flock together" is well known. People who belong to the same chakra type are on the same wavelength; their vibrations are harmonious. Only in the case of root-chakra and crown-chakra types is there a disadvantage in having a partner of the same chakra type. When these energies are reinforced, they can result in an unproductive standstill or stagnation.

It can be helpful to take into consideration the chakra activity in partnerships. When you know which chakra is dominant in your partner, you can develop a deeper understanding of him or her. Among the predominant chakras, there are different inclinations and interests, but there are also diffmerent perspectives. When you find out how your perspective differs from your partner's, it can be easier to solve problems. With the help of the chakra tests (see page 41), you and your partner can learn something about chakra activity.

It is not always clear who is better suited, partners whose dominant chakras are complementary, or partners for whom it is the same.

The root chakra person is a family person and needs a like-minded partner.

The Root-Chakra Partner

The best partner for a root-chakra person is with someone who has a dominant heart chakra.

Family is especially important to root-chakra people. They will not be very happy in relationships with someone who does not place a lot of value on family ties. In love, root-chakra people have problems in that, as a rule, they tend to think mainly about themselves. Therefore, a partnership between two root-chakra people is problematic, even though it seems as though they should be in harmony with each other. Their main tie is the family. As long as family life is running smoothly, this type of partnership can be harmonious, even when they do not allow much space for development.

Theoretically, a partnership between root-chakra and crown-chakra people is good for both. The most advantageous relationship for a root-chakra person would be with a crown-chakra person, who is harmonious with all the other types. Here the root-chakra person can develop without feeling overtaxed.

The relationship between forehead-chakra and root-chakra people is problematic. Such a partnership would be predominated by quarrels and misunderstandings.

The Sacral-Chakra Partner

Sexuality in a relationship is extremely important to sacral-chakra people. As might be expected, a partnership between two people with dominant sacral chakras is passionate and very fulfilling (at least in the beginning). More development can be expected in a partnership between sacral-chakra and heart-chakra types. The love aspects are optimally complemented in this relationship.

The sacral-chakra person has many possibilities for a happy relationship but should keep a distance from crown-chakra types.

Relationships with forehead-chakra people are seemingly ideal in every way. According to the chakra teachings, such a pair has the best possibility for development. The tone of such a relationship is often set by arguments and discussions. Constant squabbles lead them to relinquish their extreme positions and gradually come together as a result.

The least harmonious combination is between sacral-chakra and crown-chakra types. Their perspectives are so different that it is difficult for them to come together.

The Navel-Chakra Partner

Mutuality is the central theme in partnerships with navel-chakra types. Their greatest desire is to work in concert with their partner and to effect at least a small change in the world. Navel-chakra people harmonize especially well with their own type. In this case, their common foundation provides a fruitful basis for mutual ventures. Also favorable is a relationship with people with dominant heart chakras, who have a gentle and harmonious flow with navel-chakra types.

The most advantageous relationship is with a throat-chakra person. The throat chakra is complementary to the navel chakra. People of these chakra types are ideally suited to one another and bring out the best in each other. There are no types with whom a relationship with a navel chakra type would be problematic. Overall, the different requirements of navel-chakra people should be noticed and compensated for with those of sacral-chakra or crown-chakra types.

The ideal connection for a navel-chakra person is with the complementary throat-chakra type.

The Heart-Chakra Partner

Heart-chakra people are characterized by the power of their love. Therefore, in theory, there is no disharmony between them and people of any other chakra type. The love that they feel truly embraces all people and does not exclude anyone.

A relationship between two heart-chakra people is very harmonious, more so than any other combination. Such a pair has the best prospect for enjoying a fulfilling life that is permeated with love. These people positively influence their surroundings and build up a strong social network.

The heart-chakra type is the ideal partner, one who usually gives rather than takes.

The relationship between heart-chakra types and sacral-chakra types has the greatest possibility for development. In this case, both aspects of love meet and complement each other in an optimal way.

When heart-chakra people form a relationship with partners in whom both lower chakras are dominant, this can help them to reach a higher stage of development. Overall, heart-chakra types give much more in a relationship than they receive.

The love between two heart-chakra people can positively influence their surroundings.

The Throat-Chakra Partner

For some people with a dominant throat chakra, communication in relationships plays an especially important role. A relationship is probably most problematic for the throat-chakra type who meets a partner who is closely related to a root-chakra type. Root-chakra people are, as a rule, mainly too concerned with themselves to be able to engage in extensive, satisfying communication, which, for the throat-chakra person is precisely what gives meaning to life.

A harmonious relationship takes shape in a partnership between throat-chakra types and navel-chakra types. These two chakras complement each other in an ideal way.

A relationship with a heart-chakra person is also very good with a throat-chakra person. The positive balance that comes into being through the heart chakra in such a relationship protects the throat-chakra person above all from sometimes using his or her speaking and communication ability in order to manipulate others.

> Throat-chakra people will find in the heart-chakra type someone who can protect them from their negative tendencies.

The Forehead-Chakra Partner

The forehead-chakra person principally expects deep, reciprocal understanding within a partnership. Therefore, a partnership with another forehead-chakra person or a crown-chakra type functions the best.

In this kind of relationship, forehead-chakra types find enough spiritual nourishment to make them feel stimulated and fulfilled.

Two chakra types harmonize especially well with the forehead chakra type. These are the heart-chakra partner, whose love heals everyone, and the sacral-chakra type, which is the complement to the forehead-chakra person.

However, the latter relationship is often troubled by a lack of reciprocal understanding. The partners may be in tune on a sexual level, but the sacral-chakra person may not be able to fully participate in the life of the mind, which is so important to the forehead-chakra-dominated partner.

> Like goes well with like: forehead-chakra people feel spiritually fulfilled and happy together.

The Crown-Chakra Partner

Crown-chakra people do not enter easily into partnerships. The best match for them would be with a heart or a forehead-chakra type.

Partnership with crown-chakra people is often difficult. They live in a spiritual world that is not easily accessible to other people. Interestingly, it is not at all easy for crown-chakra people to form relationships with their own type. Often their interest in the spiritual world is so great that they prefer privacy and solitude to relationship. The most harmonious partnership for them to develop would be with a forehead-chakra or heart-chakra person. The most problematic relationship would be with a sacral- chakra person, who lives in the sensual world.

All of these combinations only describe fundamental tendencies. A pair whose chakra harmony is problematic can still enjoy a fulfilling partnership when both partners are aware.

Understanding Crises Through Insights Into the Chakras

Crises occur in every relationship. It seems that when a couple is not prepared to join together to work through a crisis and grow from it, separation and sorrow follow. In most cases, sorrow leads not to growth and maturity but only to flight, because separation is an impulse that is not based on insight.

It is easy to understand that participants in a relationship may want to flee when it becomes monotonous or unpleasant. The moment of separation seems to occur when there is nothing left to give. Your partner seems to have become someone else, or you yourself have changed. No one wants to persevere in a stagnant relationship.

From the background of connection and development of the chakra teachings, we can view things a bit differently. When we recall once again the phases of development of life (see page 83) it is clear that necessary changes must be made.

Each partner in a relationship goes through phases in which one chakra, and its specific theme, has a particular influence. The probability is great that the passage from one phase to another will bring the partnership into crisis. It is not a coincidence that one speaks of the seven-year itch; according to the chakra teachings, every seven years, all

The constant growth and development in nature, is evident in our relationships too.

the energy in all the chakras is changed. When you are aware of the connection, it will be easier to value the changes within your partner, or even within yourself, and to master the times of crisis. Then you will know not only the necessity of change but also see right away that crises are temporary. When the other partner also changes chakra phases, it is probable that original harmony will return to the partnership. When the crisis has been weathered together and both partners have grown spiritually, perhaps the harmony will be even greater than before.

Knowing the patterns behind the cycles governing human development makes one better able to master crises in a partnership.

Chakra Cycles and Partnership

The table on page 98 points out critical stages in a relationship. It may reveal that you have already gone through a crisis. A crisis in a relationship is very likely when one partner enters into a specific life phase governed by a chakra different from the other. Then you and your partner may feel out of sync.

An Example

The example of Maria and David allows us to take a good look at the ups and downs inside a relationship.

Maria and David meet when he is thirty-six years old and she is thirty-two. David has recently entered a phase in life when the forehead chakra and its theme of spiritual knowledge becomes important. Maria's stage in life is colored by the throat chakra. David and Maria get along very well. They can communicate with each other, and Maria is very sympathetic to David's increasing engagement with spiritual themes. After three years, the relationship suddenly begins to change. Maria becomes more inward-looking. She has entered a new chakra phase and is living through a personal crisis that David will cushion. The love between David and Maria grows. Through Maria's change into a new phase of life, the relationship has changed, and through it she has become more positive.

That is not so surprising when one considers that David and Maria are now in the same chakra phase and can much more easily come into harmony with each other. After seven years, a serious problem comes into their relationship. David, according to Maria, is less interested in her and is hung up in higher spheres. He often seems depressed. Maria is sad about this and thinks about leaving David. They have two children, and Maria remains committed to staying with David for the children's sake. She does not believe, however, that their love will come back to life. Three and a half years later, all of their conflicts have been resolved, and the pair feels almost like they are newly in love.

Which Chakra Goes with Which?

Chakra	Root	Sacral	Navel	Heart	Throat	Forehead	Crown
Root	+/−	O	O	+	−	− −	++/− −
Sacral	O	+	−	++	O	++/ −	− −
Navel	O	−	+	+	++	O	−
Heart	+	++	+	++	+	+	+
Throat	−	O	++	+	+	O	O
Forehead	− −	++/− −	O	+	O	+	+
Crown	+ +/− −	− −	−	+	O	+	+/−

++ ideal   + good   O average   − problematic   − − very problematic

Knowing the patterns that govern relationships can transform crisis into opportunity.

When he turns forty-three, David enters the crown-chakra life phase. This estranges him from Maria and almost leads to a separation. A few years later, Maria follows him into this life phase. The pair is once again on the same wavelength, and all their misunderstandings dissolve. It would have been easier for both had they taken a look at the mechanism of the crisis.

With the knowledge of the chakra teachings about human development, you are more easily able to understand your partner.

When both partners understand that a relationship depends on these patterns of change, fulfilling partnerships can endure periods of crisis and move toward mutual growth and deeper love.

Just having some insight into these stages of development makes it easier to understand your partner. It helps you to correctly characterize your own changes and to use them as an opportunity for mutual development rather than as grounds for separation.

When you and your partner work together on developing your chakras and harmonizing them, breaking down blockages and doing the same chakra exercises, you can mitigate potential crises from the start and transform them into positive energy for growth.

Overcoming Impotence and Infertility

Most couples want to have children at some point, but this is not always easy. In developed countries, women are commonly treated for fertility problems, and men for impotence or lack of potency. Impotence is generally defined as the inability to have an erection, or, in medical terms, erectile dysfunction. But this is not the same as a lack of potency. Erectile dysfunction is generally temporary, in contrast to a lack of potency, which has to do with blockages in the upper chakras, especially the throat and forehead chakras. These blockages can be loosened through exercises.

Blockages of the sacral chakra are the main causes of lack of potency in men and infertility in women.

In contrast, infertility in women is almost always due to a blocked sacral chakra. About half of all such couples can loosen their blockages. Then the strength of the energy in these chakras enables them to have a child. This also means, however, that the other half will not reach their goal.

If the failure persists, the chakra blockage has another quality. It is not that the couple's sacral chakra is blocked, but probably the harmony between their chakras is not aligned, and the energy for conceiving a child is not in a state of readiness.

Exercise: Svadhistana Adhara: An Exercise for Fertility

This exercise helps to attune the sacral and heart chakras of both partners. Through it, a lack of potency and infertility can be overcome. Before you do this exercise, the blockages in your partner's sacral chakra should be loosened through chakra yoga or chakra healing. Otherwise, this exercise not only will be insufficient but can transfer the blockage to the other partner. This exercise is simple yet effective for harmonizing a couple's sacral chakras. It offers a childless couple the possibility of conceiving. In any event, it is enriching for any couple; bringing a man's and a woman's sacral chakras into harmony introduces more sensuality, understanding, and love into the relationship.

Many couples wish to have children, but their wish cannot always be fulfilled without complications.

- The man and woman sit facing each other, if possible in the lotus position, and if not, with crossed legs. The hands rest on the lower part of the belly. The man places his left hand over the right, and the woman, the right over the left. Both should now concentrate for a while on the energy of their sacral chakras.
- The man lifts his left hand and extends it with the palm facing the woman. She now lifts her right hand and lays her palm against the man's palm. As she exhales, the woman gently pushes her hand forward. The man returns the motion and inhales. Then the man exhales and gently pushes his hand forward. The woman returns the motion and inhales.
- This results in the feeling that each partner releases the inhalation of the other. Each time one inhales, support and energy are given to the other. Performing this action results in the flow of a current of energy through the hand chakras and the aura, which, at the same time, transplants the vibration of the energy flow into the partner's sacral chakra.
- Over the course of a month, this exercise should be performed for at least ten minutes every day. Done in this way, it should contribute to overcoming infertility and lack of potency.

Exercises for fertility harmonize a couple's sacral chakras.

Strengthening Life Energy Through Chakra Work

According to the chakra teachings, the energy form that we call life energy originates in two chakras: sensuous love in the sacral chakra and spiritual, universal love in the heart chakra. The union of both chakras expands the entire potential for human love.

The power of love changes the world through emotional understanding, through the capacity for insight, empathy, practical help, and loving thoughts. Love brings about a multitude of positive changes. Love brings more happiness in the world. Those who do the small, everyday things with love take more joy in doing them. This diminishes sorrow in the world. The power of love overcomes the power of hatred and violence. It brings more knowledge into the world. We only truly know what we see through the eyes of the heart.

The power of love touches everything. You can increase your success in the material world when you do what you do with love. When your deeds are permeated with the power of love, you will be more successful at everything you do.

With the power of love, you can heal emotional wounds and release blockages. When you call to mind old emotional wounds and cover them with a mental image of love, you will find that they disappear and that new powers are built up within yourself.

You can use the power of selfless love to form a closer bond with your fellow human beings and through it gain happiness in life. Visualize the people with whom you have problems and try to let the power of love flow through your image of them. You will notice that you feel more relaxed and happier about them. You can brighten the world when you meditate on the power of love and radiate love to the world. You will not lose energy as a result but gain it instead. Because the power of love is so important, it is good for us to let this power awaken and grow within us. When you work on your chakras, you do this anyway. By releasing blockages in your sacral and heart chakras, you increase the power of love. Through this you can once again attain a state in which your heart and sacral chakras harmonize with each other. Here are some exercises to help you.

According to the chakra teachings, love originates in the heart and sacral chakras.

When we're in love, we come to realize how much positive energy love releases in us.

Exercise: Harmonizing your Heart and Sacral Chakras

For this exercise, it is best to sit in a half-lotus position, but the most important thing is that you feel comfortable. The more you use this technique, the more effective it will be. You can also do it when you are sitting on a chair or on the subway, when you are lying in bed, and even when you are taking a walk.

In order for this exercise to be effective, it is important that neither your heart chakra nor your sacral chakra is strongly blocked. If that should be the case, work on loosening chakra blockages as described in previous chapters.

Bringing the heart and sacral chakras into harmony can have the greatest effect on expanding the power of love.

- Sit down, in the lotus position if possible. Relax and breathe in and out a few times.
- Put your right hand (if male) or your left hand (if female) on your chest above your heart chakra, and the other hand on your lower abdomen, underneath your navel, over the sacral chakra.

- Gently close your eyes. As you inhale, imagine that energy is flowing from your sacral chakra to your heart chakra and that as you exhale, the energy current reverses and goes from your heart chakra to your sacral chakra.
- Perform this exercise for a duration of seven inhalations and exhalations.
- Now change the position of your hands, without touching your body with your palms. Move your hands in a semicircle from one chakra to another. The lower hand now circles over your heart chakra, and the upper hand below in the region of your sacral chakra.
- Inhale and visualize a current of energy from your heart chakra to your sacral chakra and, when you exhale, a current of energy from your sacral chakra to your heart chakra. Do this for a duration of seven breaths.

Repeat this exercise as often as you like. After you do this exercise for the first time, you will notice a pleasant change in your body, mind, and spirit. Peacefully continue. There are no boundaries to the positive changes from chakra work.

Exercises for harmonizing your heart and sacral chakras enable the power of love to increase.

The Path of the Heart

In order to cultivate the power of love, you should free both chakras, the sacral chakra and especially the heart chakra, from blockages and raise the level of the energy in them.

Systematic exercises in the form of chakra work or chakra yoga are not the only possibilities for achieving this. The most natural way is to cultivate qualities in your life that are associated with the power of love, empathy, patience, and insight. The power of love is manifested in these special qualities, and cultivating them (or, better, putting them into practice) will elevate the power of love.

It is not by chance that the opposite qualities of craving, hatred, and ignorance are called by the Buddha the three hindrances to enlightenment.

Empathy

Empathy is the power that makes people really become human. To empathize with those around you, to make their pain your pain and their joy your joy, is an important aspect of the way of love. True empathy is the result of the work we do to develop ourselves, the efforts through which we grow and develop our potential. The first step is to be attentive. We can only be empathetic toward people when we are attentive to them and as part of loving them truly perceive them and know them.

It is only too easy for empathy to be an illusion. For example, we see a homeless person and imagine what it would be like if we were without means. In order to rid ourselves of a rising unpleasant feeling, we quickly throw a coin to him. That is much more like blatant selfishness than empathy. We feel uneasy and redeem ourselves for the cheapest possible price. Above all, empathy means that we are so attentive to the other person that we respect him or her as much as we do ourselves. Only then are we on the road to really empathizing with others.

Attend to the qualities that are bound together with the power of love, above all, empathy, forbearance, and understanding.

Only by being attentive and sympathetic to all living beings can you realize the true power of love.

The power of love can grow when we understand that we are not the center of the universe.

Consideration of Others

Love also means being able to forgive, not thinking of ourselves as too important, and being able to see the beauty and good in all things. When we are considerate of other people, we increase our potential for the power of love.

Tolerance is not indifference. Only when we can accept the other person without reservations, can we practice tolerance.

Tolerance is often confused with indifference. We may be opposed to situations, actions, and other people, but as long as we are not indifferent to them we can be open-minded and considerate.

When, for example, we are indifferent to the religion a friend practices, it is impossible for us to be open-minded in this relationship. Being tolerant and patient means that we love another despite their different outlook or their faults.

Forgiveness and patience go together. When we can imagine and understand that our personal point of view is not the central point or the measure of all things, we can be open-minded and patient. Only then can we forgive and allow the power of love to grow.

Insight

Insight seems to be more rational and intellectual and less emotional and feeling. But in practice, true insight into another person, into his or her thoughts, feelings, and deeds, always comes about sooner when we meet the person with love. This makes it easier to forgive faults and bad deeds. When we take the trouble to be insightful and try to recognize the good that is innate in all people, our love toward the people around us will grow, and the world will be a little bit better.

Exercise: A Meditation about Love

Through meditating about the power of love, it is possible to bind your upper chakras intensively to the energy of your heart chakra.

- Close your eyes and, for a while, fully concentrate on your heart chakra. Imagine that your heart fills with a warm, radiant light. Let this light, which has the intensity of love inside it, grow.
- Next, let that light grow within your body and then into your aura. Let the light expand ever farther and flow to people who play an important role in your life. Embrace them in your thoughts, and open your heart to them. Let the light radiate into an even wider circle that encompasses even more people.
- By working on these exercises and increasing the energy in your heart chakra, you will succeed in radiating the light of love out ever farther, not only toward your partner and your best friends, but also to acquaintances and finally into the cosmos.

Many people world-wide meditate on love. This helps the power of love to radiate through the whole world.

The power of love passes through many people, from one to another, and mutually strengthens them. There is a form of meditation that strengthens this same kind of power. In meditation, many people connect with each other in a "circle of love." A special mandala is used for the circle of love that makes it easier for people to attune to the same vibration.

Tables

The following tables will provide an overview of the different significations of the chakras, including their most important symbols and their correspondences to planets, vowel sounds, and sensory functions.

Sensory Function, Position on the Body, Central Theme

Chakra	Sensory Function	Position on the Body	Central Theme
7. Chakra	cosmic consciousness	top of the head	spirituality, enlightenment, self-realization
6. Chakra	reason, intuition	middle of the forehead	intuition, perception, fantasy
5. Chakra	hearing	larynx	communication, truth, inspiration
4. Chakra	touch	center of the chest at the level of the heart	love, empathy, humanity
3. Chakra	sight	above the navel	will power, personality, self-control
2. Chakra	taste	below the navel	sexuality, sensuality, fertility, creativity
1. Chakra	smell	between the anus and sexual organs	will to live, security, trust, self-preservation

Colors, Deities, Planets

Chakra	Colors	Deities	Planets
7. Chakra	white, violet, gold	Shiva	Neptune
6. Chakra	dark blue, indigo	Paramshiva, Shakti-Hakini	Uranus
5. Chakra	light blue, sky blue	Sakina, Sadashiva, Indra	Saturn
4. Chakra	green	Isa, Kakini	Jupiter
3. Chakra	yellow	Agni, Lakini, Rudra	Mars
2. Chakra	orange	Vishnu, Rakini	Venus
1. Chakra	red	Brahma, Dakini	Mercury

Bodily Function, Glandular Function, Mental Level

Chakra	Bodily function	Glandular function	Mental level
7. Chakra	Brain, the entire organism	pineal gland (serotonin, melatonin)	self-realization
6. Chakra	cerebellum, nervous system, hormonal system, eyes, ears, nose, sinuses	pituitary gland (vasopressin)	fantasy
5. Chakra	throat, neck, esophagus and windpipe, shoulders, jaw	thyroid and parathyroid (thyroxin)	communication
4. Chakra	heart, lungs, blood, arms and hands	thymus (immune system)	empathy
3. Chakra	digestion, small intestine, liver, autonomic nervous system	pancreas (insulin, digestive enzymes)	emotion
2. Chakra	sexual organs, kidneys, bladder, blood circulation	testicles and ovaries (estrogen, testosterone)	awareness of one's own body
1. Chakra	pelvis, bones, large intestine, nails, teeth	suprarenal glands (cortisone, adrenalin, noradrenalin)	will to live

Spiritual Level, Correspondences in Nature, Elements

Chakra	Spiritual Level	Correspondences in Nature	Elements
7. Chakra	enlightenment	mountain peaks	—
6. Chakra	wisdom	night sky, stars	—
5. Chakra	truth	blue sky, calm sea, still water	ether
4. Chakra	love	forests, fields, wilderness	air
3. Chakra	sense of self	sunlight, fire, yellow flowers	fire
2. Chakra	creativity	moonlight, flowing water	water
1. Chakra	basic trust	dawn and sunset, red earth	earth

Mantras, Rhythms, Tonalities

Chakra	Mantras	Rhythms	Tonalities
7. Chakra	om	stillness	silence
6. Chakra	ksham	varied	major or minor
5. Chakra	ham	gliding	major or minor
4. Chakra	yam	calm	minor
3. Chakra	ram	fiery	major
2. Chakra	vam	dance	pentatonic
1. Chakra	lam	pulsating	overtone

Developmental Stages

Chakra	Developmental Stages	Strengths	Weaknesses
7. Chakra	Completion of first cycle (43–49)	Spirituality, connection with the Divine	Superstition, apathy, illusion
6. Chakra	Awareness (36–42)	Healing energy, self-confidence, intuition, imagination	Lust for power, over-confidence, irresponsibility
5. Chakra	Unfolding (29–35)	Discrimination, multi-faceted interests, musicality	Need for admiration, intolerance
4. Chakra	Maturity (22–28)	Love, empathy, humanity	Narcissism, bitterness, arrogance
3. Chakra	Early adulthood (15–21)	Sensitivity, spontaneity, emotionality	Sentimentality, self-pity, jealousy
2. Chakra	Youth (8–14)	Vitality, creativity, joy in living	Uncontrolled drives, compulsiveness, guilt feelings
1. Chakra	Childhood (1–7)	Life energy, endurance, rhythm, connection to nature	Egoism, lack of self-control

Physical and mental disorders

Chakra	Physical Disorders	Mental Disorders
7. Chakra	Cancer, immune system disorders, chronic illness	Depression, confusion, flight from reality
6. Chakra	Headaches, sinusitis	Poor concentration and learning disabilities, anxiety
5. Chakra	Thyroid ailments, neck pain, speech defects	Shyness, inability to express oneself
4. Chakra	High or low blood pressure, coronary and respiratory disease	Lack of feeling, problems with relationships, poor boundaries
3. Chakra	Digestive problems, stomach ailments, diabetes, obesity	Aggression, insecurity, nightmares, sleep disorders
2. Chakra	Impotence, prostate disease, problems in the female reproductive system, kidney disease	Addiction, lack of sexual drive, mental weakness
1. Chakra	Constipation, back pain, diseases of the bones	Basic fear, lack of trust, disorientation

Vowels, Musical Instruments, Affirmations

Chakra	Vowels	Musical Instrument	Affirmations
7. Chakra	Silence	Gong	"I am aware in every moment."
6. Chakra	I	Woodwinds	"I open myself to my inner light."
5. Chakra	E	Voice	"I open myself to the power of truth."
4. Chakra	A (as in father)	Bowed instruments	"I send myself and others love and compassion."
3. Chakra	A (as in made)	Stringed instruments	"I trust my own feelings and spontaneity."
2. Chakra	O	Percussion	"I take pleasure in life with all of my senses."
1. Chakra	U	Drums	"I trust the power of the earth and feel my own body."

Essential Oils, Precious Stones, Metals

Chakra	Essential Oil	Precious stones	Metal
7. Chakra	Incense, rosewood	Diamond, rock crystal, amethyst	Gold
6. Chakra	Cajeput, lemongrass, violet	Blue sapphire, opal, blue tourmaline	Platinum
5. Chakra	Eucalyptus, camphor, peppermint	Aquamarine, topaz, lapis lazuli	Silver
4. Chakra	Rose, jasmine, tarragon	Emerald, chrysoprase, jade, rose quartz	Copper
3. Chakra	Lavender, chamomile, lemon, anise	Chrysoberyl, amber, tiger's eye, citrine, yellow jasper	Quicksilver
2. Chakra	Bitter orange, pepper, myrrh, sandalwood	Hyacinth, gold topaz, aventurine, coral, fire opal	Iron
1. Chakra	Cloves, rosemary, cypress, cedar, vanilla	Ruby, hematite, garnet	Lead

Spices, Herbs, Bach Flowers, Phases of the Moon

Chakra	Spices	Herbs	Bach Flowers	Phases of Moon
7. Chakra	—	—	Wild Rose, Wild Chestnut	New moon
6. Chakra	Bay leaf	St. John's wort, spruce, eyebright	Crab Apple, Vine, Walnut	Waning moon
5. Chakra	Star anise, clove	Peppermint, sage, coldsfoot	Agrimony, Cerato, Mimulus	Waning moon
4. Chakra	Saffron	Whitethorn, thyme, melissa	Red Chestnut, Willow, Chicory	New moon, full moon
3. Chakra	Cardamom, anise	Fennel, chamomile, juniper	Impatiens, Scleranthus, Hornbeam	Waxing moon
2. Chakra	Vanilla, pepper	Yarrow, parsley, nettle	Oak, Olive, Pine	Waxing moon
1. Chakra	Ginger	Valerian, lime blossom, elderberry	Clematis, Sweet Chestnut, Rock Rose	Full moon

Name, Meaning of Name, Symbol

Chakra	Name	Meaning of Name	Symbol
7. Chakra	Sahasrara— crown chakra	Sahasrara = thousandfold	Lotus blossom (lotus with a thousand petals)
6. Chakra	Ajna—forehead chakra or third eye	Ajna = awareness	Winged circle (lotus with two petals)
5. Chakra	Vishuddha— throat chakra	Vishuddha = purity	Circle (lotus with sixteen petals)
4. Chakra	Anahata— heart chakra	Anahata = flawless	Hexagon (lotus with twelve petals)
3. Chakra	Manipura—navel or solar plexus chakra	Manipura = sparkling jewel	Triangle (lotus with ten petals)
2. Chakra	Svadhisthana— sacral chakra	Svadhisthana = sweetness	Crescent moon (lotus with six petals)
1. Chakra	Muladhara— root chakra	Mula = root dhara = support	Square (lotus with four petals)

Konecky & Konecky
72 Ayers Point Rd.
Old Saybrook, CT 06475

Copyright © 2002 Ullstein Heyne List GmbH & Co.

Translated by Sean Konecky

English translation copyright © 2004 Konecky & Konecky

All rights reserved.

ISBN: 1–56852–472–2

NOTE FROM THE PUBLISHER

Any information given in this book is not intended to be taken as a replacement for medical advice. Any person with a condition requiring medical attention should consult a qualified physician or practitioner.

The translator wishes to thank Sibylle Dausien, Janet Foster, and Laura Munro for their able assistance with the translation.

Printed in China

Photo Credits

All photos provided by Ingolf Hatz, Munich (Visagist: Sacha Schulte; Stylist Sybille Oberschelp; Model:Arisha), except as follows:

Bilderberg, Hamburg: 73 (E. Grames), 90 (N. Baumgartl); IFA-Bilderteam, Munchen: 15 (Digul); Image Bank, Munchen: 59, 295 (David de Lossy), 60 (Elyse Lewin), 65 (Regine M.), 89 (Baker Jack), 112 (PaoloCurto), 116 (Pete Pacifica), 118 (R. Lockyer), 142 (M. Romanelli), 154 (Color Day), 160 (Zao Audebert), 278 (S. Messens), 283, 286 (Chronoscope), 293 (Britt Erlanson), 298 (H. Carmichael) Jump, Hamburg 4L–10, 122 (A. Falck), 55, 222 (M. Sandkuhler), 57, 195 (K. Vey); Kerth Ulrich, Munich 225; Mendell Institut, Bruchsal: 180; PPW Max Kohr, Berlin: 68 (Gaul); Schwarz Anja, Munich Titel/Einklinker, 202; Sudwest Verlag, Munich 71 jump/K. Vey), 93 (A. Eckert), 127 (S. Sperl), 129, 219 (M. Nagy), 12, 177, 204 (S. Lauf), 206 (S. Kracke), 297 (J. Heller); Tony Stone, Munchen: 76 (Dugald Bremner), 120 (D. Steward), 210 (P. & K. Smith), 226 (Ernst Haas), 289 (Walter Hodges), Transglobe, Hamburg: 110 (Stock Photography), Zefa Dusseldorf. 16 (M. Thomsen), 18 (Jaemsen), 20 (Masterfile), 42 (Lukasseck), 62 (Glanzmann), 74 (Wood), 86 (Allofs), 93, 97 (G. Baden), 106 (A. Inden), 108 (Westrich), 114 (Gulliver), 148 (Kehrer), 172 (Photex), 182 (RGN), 185 (Masterfile), 186 (Weiler), 280 (Pinto), 284 (A. Inden), 291 (Benelux)